WRITING TO INSPIRE

Writing to Inspire

Edited by William Gentz

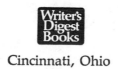

Writer's
Digest
Books

Cincinnati, Ohio

Library of Congress Cataloging in Publication Data
Gentz, William H., 1918-
    Writing to inspire.
    Bibliography: p.
    Includes index.
    1. Christian literature—Authorship—Addresses, essays, lectures. 2. Christian literature—Publication and distribution—Addresses, essays, lectures. I. Roddy, Lee, 1921-   . II. Title.
BR117.G46   808'.0662021   82-1928
ISBN 0-89879-064-6   AACR2

Book design by Charleen Catt.

*To the scribes of past and present
who help spread the good news*

ACKNOWLEDGMENTS

I would like to acknowledge the work of the many people who made this book possible:

The many Christian writers and editors who took precious time from their busy schedules to respond thoughtfully to our questions, and my twenty-eight coauthors, who gave more than full measure to their appointed tasks.

In addition I am grateful for the conscientious work of the Writer's Digest Books editorial staff—Carol Cartaino and her able team of project editors, copyeditors, assistants, and designers, all of whom were essential to the making of this volume.

W.H.G.

CONTENTS

❦ Part Two

CHAPTER FOUR: *HOW TO GET STARTED*
by Cecil Murphey

38 Even before you sit down at your typewriter, there are some things you should know about Christian writing. Personal preparation is very important in this field. Then there are the basic skills involved in getting words on paper. This chapter tells you how to get started, how to keep going, how to keep your courage up when rejections come, how to avoid the pitfalls—everything you need to set you squarely on the road to successful religious writing.

CHAPTER FIVE: *WHO ARE THE READERS?*
by William Gentz

54 Religious writing covers a multitude of different subjects and reaches into the lives of many different kinds of people. To be successful, you need to know the audience for which you are writing. Readers of religious material come not only in different sexes, races, age groups, and from different parts of the country, but they also represent differences in belief, denomination, and degree of commitment. This chapter will help you get firmly in mind the very specific audience for which you are writing.

CHAPTER SIX: *WRITING TO INSPIRE*
by Dina Donohue

64 The main objective in all religious writing is to inspire—to reach into the readers' lives and move them to action in the right direction. Here the author, from a background of long experience in inspirational writing, offers insights on what makes writing inspire the reader. What subjects lend themselves to inspirational treatment? What qualities must come through? What are the essential ingredients of this kind of writing? These are the questions answered here.

CHAPTER SEVEN: *HOW TO GET INTO PRINT* by Sally Stuart

80 Writing is one thing—getting into print is quite another. Many writers handicap themselves by not putting their work in the proper format. Here is complete and precise instruction from an expert freelancer on the mechanics of preparing your manuscript in a professional way. The author also explains the special requirements of preparing religious material for publication.

CHAPTER EIGHT: *SOME GOOD PLACES TO START*

❧ *Part Three*

CHAPTER NINE: *WRITING THE INSPIRATIONAL ARTICLE* by Georgiana Walker

CHAPTER TEN: *WRITING INSPIRATIONAL FICTION* by Lee Roddy

CHAPTER ELEVEN: *WRITING THE INSPIRATIONAL BOOK* by Lee Roddy

CHAPTER TWELVE: *WRITING INSPIRATIONAL POETRY*
by *Viola Jacobson Berg*

❧ *Part Four*

CHAPTER THIRTEEN: *WRITING FOR CHILDREN AND YOUTH*
by *Patricia McKissack*

CHAPTER FOURTEEN: *WRITING FOR OTHER SPECIAL AUDIENCES*

CHAPTER FIFTEEN: *WRITING CHRISTIAN CURRICULUM*
by Herb Montgomery

Curriculum publishing is based on well-researched and carefully made plans of publishers and their religious sponsors. Yet most of the material written for these markets is done by freelancers who are assigned based on their understanding of the need, their training and their ability to produce the material that will lead readers to the desired educational goals. This chapter will teach you how to become a part of this "team" of curriculum writers. **228**

CHAPTER SIXTEEN: *WRITING IN OTHER SPECIAL FORMATS*

Some of the writing being done by Christian authors is quite specialized. Special talents and formats are sometimes needed, but it is also a matter of learning what the market wants and discovering new ways to provide it. Here the authors show what is involved in writing a column, religious news, inspirational greeting cards, games, puzzles, songs and hymns. **240**

CHAPTER SEVENTEEN: *WRITING FOR CHRISTIAN TELEVISION AND FILM*
by Donald Davenport

In this electronic age, a lot of writing does not end up on paper, but as sounds and images on a screen. This area of the religious communication business is growing rapidly, but it requires special interests and skills. In this chapter a successful writer of prize-winning films explains the essentials of success in the visual arts. **258**

❧ Part Five

CHAPTER EIGHTEEN: GETTING HELP AND TRAINING by Norman Rohrer

270 The serious writer in the religious field is going to want more information than can be provided between the covers of this book. In this chapter the most knowledgeable person in this field today lists the many ways a writer can improve, and eventually perfect, his craft—through workshops and conferences, correspondence courses, community education classes, books, periodicals, newsletters, cassettes, and local critique groups. There is no lack of help available, and this chapter will show you where to find it.

CHAPTER NINETEEN: CAREERS IN CHRISTIAN WRITING
by Roland Wolseley

286 Have you wondered if religious writing could become a full-time career? Here a university professor who has trained hundreds who are today in such careers tells what the possibilities are, and how to go about getting ready for them.

CHAPTER TWENTY: THE REWARDS OF CHRISTIAN WRITING
by Charlie Shedd

294 When all is said and done, are the rewards of religious writing what they have been cracked up to be? "Yes," says this best-selling author and teacher of writers. The glory may in fact be an amazing mixture of ego trip and humility factor, but there are many personal satisfactions that come from honing our skills, knowing we are of influence, the money that comes as a result of our work, and—most important—the knowledge that we are pleasing the Lord and extending his kingdom.

305 *BIBLIOGRAPHY*

315 *INDEX*

WRITING TO INSPIRE

PUBLISHER'S NOTE

WHY THIS BOOK? The field of Christian writing is growing, burgeoning, exploding. Each year there are more publications looking for religious material and ever more potential writers. Christian writers' conferences are springing up all over the country—more than thirty of them are conducted on a national scale and there are others of a more regional nature. New correspondence courses aimed specifically at Christian writers are being introduced. Local writers' groups are being formed in unprecedented numbers. One denominational publishing house has organized forty of them in the past year.

The need for Christian writing has always been great and there was a day when less skilled writers were nurtured along by dedicated religious press editors. That day is long gone! Competition is keen. The best of writing is needed in the inspirational field and the best of inspirational writing will cross over into other fields. A very good reason for Writer's Digest Books to create this book to reach a wide variety of writers.

Early in the process, the Writer's Digest Books staff queried Christian writers, editors, workshop leaders, and teachers of religious writing, asking essentially three questions: Is a new book for religious writers needed? What subjects should be covered? and Who should do the writing? Responses were quick and enthusiastic about the need for such a book and literally hundreds of suggestions of both subjects and writers were made. The multitude of ideas was both encouraging and frustrating. It was good to know that there is much to write about, but how does one begin to boil down suggestions to a manageable size?

This information led Writer's Digest Books to believe that no single writer could deal authoritatively with the many subjects to be covered. And an editor well experienced in the field should be engaged to plan the book, choose the writers, and mold the various contributions into a unified book. A quarter-century spent as a book and magazine editor for religious and secular publishers as well as long experience as an author helped to prepare me for the editing of this volume.

As we looked at the need as well as the existing literature in the field, one point came through rather clearly. What was needed was a book that covered the essential "how-to" of writing and marketing but one that did so consistently from the religious writer's point of view. There are scores of books on writing per se (many of which are excellent), but they aren't written from the specific perspective of the religious writer. And the majority of the books that *are* published specifically for the religious writer—perhaps unconsciously—have tables of contents, treatments, and emphases that are little different from most secular books on writing. Others are confusingly organized for the beginner, or cover some topics well and omit others. As we prepared the guidelines for authors, and every step along the way, we kept these pitfalls in mind. And above all, we wanted a book that would speak to the needs of the religious market of *today*.

A decision was made early to concentrate on *Christian* writing. Writers in other religious traditions will receive much help from this book, but the principles involved in the writing, and the desired end product are so different that it seemed wise not to approach this subject from an inter-faith point of view.

Once we had established these guiding principles, it was primarily a matter of boiling down to the essentials, the topics that we and our advisers felt *must* be covered. In view of the broad character of the Christian market and the varied points of view of Christian writers, the book needed to be both comprehensive and specific. We are confident that as you use this book you will find the information you need most to improve your skills and extend your effectiveness in your writing ministry.

We chose the authors of this book for three qualities: 1) experience in actual writing or editing in the field; 2) ability to communicate their knowledge in writing; and 3) their reputation as teachers or workshop leaders at Christian writers' conferences. You should recognize many of these names. We think we have the best available and we are pleased that these friends were willing to take on their assignments with enthusiasm.

As we put this book together, we had three large groups of people in mind. First, the committed Christians who want to express their faith in writing, who have a message or story to tell but need help putting words on paper and guidance in finding an appropriate publisher. For the more experienced Christian writer we wanted to provide a comprehensive and up-to-the-moment guidebook. We have sincerely intended, too, to speak to accomplished writers in other fields who have just begun to put these skills to work in the Christian field.

Wherever you are on the scale of commitment to the Christian cause or ability to express your most profound thoughts on paper, *Writing to Inspire* is for you. Use it!

—William H. Gentz

❧ Part One

❧ CHAPTER ONE

THE CHALLENGE
OF CHRISTIAN
WRITING
by Lee Roddy

Lee Roddy of Penn Valley, California, has spent all of his adult life in commu-nications—working for newspapers, ad agencies, radio stations, and TV and motion picture producers. He has also had broad experience working with beginning writers at conferences and workshops across the country. As a freelance writer and teacher, he is well qualified to see the challenge that lies ahead for writers of Christian material.

A LONG DISTANCE phone call from a Chris-

tian leader I'd never met: "I need writers. Can you help me out?"

"I'm really snowed under. But maybe I might be able to recommend a few. How many do you need?"

"A hundred."

"A hundred writers?"

"Yes, and I need them right now. They're not all for me, but for organizations and ministries associated with us."

I gave the caller the names of some writers who might be able to help. But 80 percent of his request went unfilled. And that's typical of what happens to the vast opportunities in this growing field.

Exciting trends are developing in the religious and inspirational writing market, especially in the evangelical area. New and growing challenges exist in all media—print, electronic, and film—and more are on the horizon. You want to know how to successfully write for the hungry (but specialized) religious and inspirational market. (Reported sales of religious publications exceed $600 million each year.) This book will help prepare you to fill the need seen by such leaders as Billy Graham: "Everywhere I travel, I hear a cry for more Christian literature. The field is wide open."

Dr. Sherwood Eliot Wirt, now editor emeritus of *Decision* magazine, was president of the Evangelical Press Association (EPA) when he declared: "Millions of young Christians may be found in the land, but how many know there is a promising career waiting for them in religious journalism?"

At an EPA convention, Stan Mooneyham, president of World Vision International, spoke directly to Christian writers. "We, your readers, need you. Stretch our minds. Sensitize our consciences. Stimulate our courage. We want to care. We want to do something to help our hurting world."

Perhaps you can help meet this vital need. But to do so takes more than just learning the *writing* craft. I've known veteran secular writers who failed when they tried to write in the religious field. What they didn't understand was that in order to write literature for the Christian market you have to understand the Christian message embodied in the person of Jesus Christ as presented in the Bible.

It isn't enough to attend church, or to have faith. According to a recent Gallup poll, six of ten unchurched Americans agree that "most churches (and synagogues) have lost the real spiritual part of religion." It won't do to add writers to that problem if they do not have an understanding of what publishers and readers expect.

Today's writer will be read by an amazing number of fellow citizens who are keenly interested in religious matters. Consider some more Gallup facts:

Of 220 million Americans, nearly 40 million say they had a specific conversion experience, asking Christ to be their personal savior.

Nearly half of all Protestant teenagers claim a "born again" experience. Seventy percent of those have tried to encourage someone else to believe in Jesus Christ or accept him as savior. Some 8 million of these teenagers (27 percent) report they're involved in Bible studies.

Twenty percent of all Americans aged eighteen or more consider themselves evangelicals. The same percentage of Americans prefer their children to have some kind of religious training.

The polls showed 80 percent of Americans believe that Jesus Christ is God or the son of God. That includes the 60 percent who do not attend church.

Can you write for this vast potential audience? You can if you understand the message and are willing to learn your craft.

I believe that people are born with the gift to write—the desire to communicate and the ability to use words on paper to express ideas. If you have these qualities, and the willingness to put time and effort into training, you can develop your skills, because technique can be learned.

It's something like a diamond in the rough. It can be polished and faceted to great beauty and price, but it must have been created a diamond in the beginning.

VAST OPPORTUNITIES FOR WRITERS

If you are willing to discipline yourself, there are vast opportunities open to you. There are many rewards in this field, too, including ones beyond the usual measurable ones like money.

Writers are indispensable. Without writers, there'd be no Bible. There'd be no books, magazines, newspapers, newsletters, television programs, or motion pictures; no appeal letters and few radio programs, for many of the latter are scripted.

Furthermore, since all good writing has the same basic elements, you may become a "crossover" writer. I did. The person who can write successfully in the religious field can cross over to writing in the secular field, too. Many of the needs are the same.

WHO NEEDS CHRISTIAN WRITING?

There are several major areas of publishing where Christian writers are needed. We'll examine here a few top possibilities, some of which aren't all that obvious.

Readers, viewers, and listeners need Christian writers. They're needed in every media: print, film, and electronic. They'll be needed in new forms of media that may be developed, such as video discs. A veteran writing friend who's spent his life in motion pictures and television recently told me, "The changes that are coming in media writing will be as dramatic as it would have been to switch from using a mallet and chisel on stone to Gutenberg's movable type press." My own interviews with many new video producers convinces me that great changes are coming here, too. These include what one company representative called "video publishing." Several book houses are already into this field. And the infant electronic publishing industry plans to put computerized information in your home over telephone lines.

People need writers to entertain, inform, and help. Writers are needed to heal the hurts of those who struggle to cope with a world of pain and doubt and fear. People need writers to give them the spiritual or biblical principles they need to deal with today's problems.

Publishers Need Christian Writers

Most aspiring writers in the Christian field begin with Sunday school take-home papers and related items. From there they may move on to writing for the major Christian magazines or the publishers of hardback, quality trade paperback, and mass market paperback books.

The field is wide open. For example, recently a Christian publisher's representative flew to my area to discuss the need for a series of books. Yesterday, another publisher called to ask if I'd be interested in helping with half a dozen books his house is going to bring out.

It isn't that I'm such a great writer; I'm not. I've yet to write something which completely satisfied me. Yet I've learned to produce a usable product in an allotted time, and publishers have found it met their needs.

You can do the same if you have the basic natural talent and willingness to meet the requirements of this field.

You can learn to write for the hundreds of Christian publishers listed in *Writer's Market* and *The Religious Writers Marketplace*. The print media are never closed to Christian writers.

All along the way, you'll find friendly editors who'll help and encourage you. Why? Because they need you! Without you, they're out of business. They have no product and no ministry. So publishers of everything from take-home papers to magazines and books need Christian writers who will meet their needs.

Children Need Christian Writing

Whether they read the take-home Sunday school papers or books, children need Christian writers. The seed must be planted in our youth if they are to grow up to be spiritually strong. You will find more information on writing for children and youth in Chapter 13 of this book.

Dr. Albert F. Harper, retired professor at the Nazarene Theological Seminary in Kansas City, Missouri, declared, "The years of youth are the most spiritually fruitful period of human life. More than 70 percent of all conversions occur before fifteen years of age; 86 percent of all Christians are saved before they are twenty-one."

But there are some alarming statistics among the young people, too: "Seventy percent of young people leave Sunday school between the ages of twelve and eighteen, and most of them never return," writes Dr. Harper. "Two out of every three boys and girls who enter the junior department of the Sunday school are lost to Christ and the church by the time they are eighteen."

One way to influence the youth of today, in or out of Sunday school, is through writing for that age group. If you can write for children, you influence lives both now and for eternity.

For those growing-up years are years of decision; decisions which stretch into adult life and beyond. As Dr. Harper noted, "We know that if we fail to win a pupil to Christ before he is eighteen, there are four chances to one that we shall never win him at all."

Write to influence that decision!

Write to help make spiritual career decisions, too. In a study of men in the ministry, according to Dr. Harper, it was learned that 65 percent of them made their decision "to answer God's call to preach before they were seventeen years of age, and most of them had not wavered from that decision."

When you write for youth, you may influence a whole life. I distinctly remember reading material in my formative years that has had a lasting impression on my life. I suspect you can, too.

That's one reason most religious publishers want character-building, religious values incorporated into stories and articles they buy for young readers.

Women Need Christian Writers

Women especially need writers. Seventy-five percent of all books, Christian and secular, are bought by women. The Christian woman buys an impressive number of books.

A recent survey shows that there were 1,461 religious books published in one year, an increase of 10 percent over the previous year.

During the same period, secular book titles decreased by 10 percent Yet, in another recent year, 530 million secular mass-market paperbacks were sold. Between 60 and 80 percent of those were bought by women aged eighteen to thirty-four.

The Christian paperback field is just beginning to open up, with entertaining novels written to satisfy the needs of readers who want a rousing good story that emphasizes spiritual values more than secular ones.

Man the Nonreader

The challenge of Christian writing includes the special challenge of reaching out to the average American man. Often men are not as avid readers as women, but that doesn't mean they can't be reached by writers. There are opportunities to influence this nonreader by writing for television, motion pictures, audiovisuals, radio, and other nonprint media. Not only will the nonreader be reached, but many readers will be influenced as well.

One nationally known Christian leader for whom I've done some writing recently urged me to consider writing fewer books and more films. He quoted figures showing that the average person spends almost forty-eight hours a week watching television but only twelve minutes reading a book.

Writers are needed everywhere, whether for print, film, or audio. My first religious stories and articles were for the print media. My initial assignment as a full-time professional freelance writer was for a famous Christian radio program. I later wrote film scripts for Christian organizations including some for audiovisuals and television.

Producers Need Christian Writers

Although I've taught screenwriting and teleplay writing at Christian writers' conferences, I've found most attendees are afraid of this most popular of the media. But if believers don't write for this film market, those who don't understand the Christian message will. Too often, secular film writers and other strictly profit-oriented film professionals do not present the Christian message as spiritual minded viewers expect it should be. To many believers, secular films about the Bible or other spiritual subjects often are not faithful to the original concepts as Christians understand them.

If you can write in the dramatic rather than the narrative form, there's a possible opportunity for you in Christian film production companies or other organizations with religious affiliations. (Dramatic refers to re-creating scenes as a playwright would. *Narrative* is the descriptive or telling form of writing.) However, you must learn your craft and particularly the difference in the disciplines. The techniques of the print form are not applicable to the visual form. The number of Christian film producers is still small. But it will increase as the demand grows for wholesome family and Christian entertainment.

One nationally known Christian film producer wrote me, "We are always desperately looking for good freelance material. We can't pay top Hollywood rates, but we are certainly willing to pay decent rates for good material." He added, "But most of the stuff sent us is hopeless."

That's because the aspiring Christian film writer tends to start at the wrong place. He or she begins with the writer's needs instead of the producer's. Remember, to succeed as a Christian writer you must find the other person's need and fill it. That includes understanding the totally different form in which dramatic material must be presented. That also includes studying Christian producers' specified requirements, and submitting according to those needs.

Christian film producers need writers who understand the medium and submit material within the confines of that discipline. You'll find helpful suggestions on the visual media in Chapter 17 of this book.

Christian Leaders Need Writers

When I began writing full time in 1974, I had no idea of writing for the Christian market. I didn't know a single major Christian leader. I had little knowledge of their organizations, or ministries as they're usually called. But this field was so much in need of writers that I began easing into it and soon had written or edited for some of the world's top Christian leaders.

Sometimes through direct contact and sometimes through representatives, I met many respected Christian leaders, for whom I provided a writing or editing service. For example, one time, Corrie ten Boom, the well-known author and personality, needed a film edited. She also needed articles for her newsletter. I was privileged to provide some of those services and to write up some personal anecdotes from this remarkable woman.

Similar opportunities came from Dr. Bill Bright, president of Campus Crusade; Brother Andrew ("God's Smuggler"); Dr. Ralph Winter, director of the U.S. Center for World Mission; and more than two dozen more.

The number of Christian leaders both at home and abroad is increasing, and so are the opportunities to write and edit for them. Are you willing to meet the challenge and match your God-given writing ability to these national and international leaders? Through them you will reach and influence thousands of others!

Christian Ministries Need Writers

There are staff positions available for writers in many religious organizations or ministries. These include writing and editing magazines, books, booklets, radio and television programs, and films. These same organizations frequently need outside or freelance writers to do these jobs, as well as write appeal letters, newsletters, and other special projects.

You may be assigned to travel as a Christian freelance writer (as I have) to foreign countries such as Korea, Japan, Baja, Scotland, and England. In each case, all expenses were paid in addition to the payment for my editorial services.

A couple of years ago I obtained a list of writing opportunities with Christian ministries through a clearinghouse specializing in this field. There were so many "writers wanted" I couldn't begin to count them.

True, some ministries didn't pay well. Some even require that writers provide their own support. But many of these same organizations will engage qualified nonstaff writers and pay them well.

TRENDS IN CHRISTIAN WRITING

No matter what type of writing you prefer, from curriculum to motion pictures, there's an opportunity for you if you have the gift, understanding of the Christian message, and the willingness to learn your craft.

Some types of writing will continue to grow, such as fund raising and direct mail appeals. Again, this is a highly specialized field of writing. A knowledge of what motivates people to donate to a ministry is required. The psychology of ink color, stock (paper), and many other factors enter in. It's much more complex than simply writing a letter. Most ministries need the services of a good fund letter writer, and this opportunity should grow. Yet the number of writers who can successfully do it is limited.

It has been said that no ministry can exist without a good "house organ," commonly called a newsletter. This can also be a magazine mailed to supporters and constitutents. Unfortunately, many newsletters (including those from Christian organizations) are not well written. Yet these publications, whether from an organization or an individual, no matter how exalted their purpose, must compete with all the other colorful periodicals and publications. Unless these newsletters are well written, they'll never achieve their goal.

UPCOMING FORMS OF COMMUNICATIONS

Technology is opening up some exciting possibilities for the writer in the religious and inspirational field. For example, video disc will augment (and perhaps even supplant) such relatively recent innovations as video cassettes for home playback units. Someday viewers may be able to see every great Bible story come to life through video discs played with laser beams, or the standard cassettes. But unless writers who are committed to the Christian cause adapt those great narratives to the visual form with their spiritual message intact, secular, profit-oriented producers will fill the void.

Children's nursery classics have been packaged with cassettes or records to sell in grocery and toy stores, but so far as I know, there are no Bible stories or spiritual stories done that way.

Many more new television channels are being considered by the Federal Communications Commission to fill local or limited-power frequencies. They'll need writers. Today's unscripted Christian channels will ultimately have to become more professional to compete with secular programs. And that means writers!

The Christian Broadcasting Network, for example, is working on spiritual programs utilizing professionals at all levels, including writers. As this example catches on, more writers will be needed across the country.

The growing trend toward more private schools means more writers will be needed to provide Christian textbooks and extracurricular reading.

Foreign book markets will expand and new domestic ones will open. My first Christian young people's novel was translated into Norwegian and Finnish. My second such novel went to an unlikely country: the government of the People's Republic of China selected my Christian adventure novel as one of a limited number by American authors for exhibiting in six Mainland China cities. Until recently, that vast potential market had been totally closed to Gospel writing.

As time passes, more book racks may be filled with Christian literature, as books move out of bookstores to airports, bus terminals, supermarkets, and other places now offering only secular materials.

These are only a glimmering of what may come as publishers move to meet the demands of a spiritually hungry reading public. Undoubtedly, there will be other ways for writers to reach the world, ways now unknown to us.

But you must prepare to write well for these existing and potential forms which can communicate the Gospel. "Piety is no substitute for competence."

NEW AND GROWING CHALLENGES

These preceding pages have spelled out one writer's view of the opportunities in the religious and inspirational field. Those opportunities are endless, and growing. But without writers there can be no religious publishing or media production.

Give the average person a sheet of blank paper and little will come of it. Give that same sheet to a writer, and he will fill it with words that not only provide information and entertainment, but may change the world.

What an opportunity! What a challenge! Will you accept the challenge of being a religious/inspirational writer?

Dr. Mooneyham, in his remarks to the Evangelical Press Association, summed up with these words: "You have burning hearts, keen minds, and a way with words. Use them all! Use them with abandon. Use them fiercely. Use them as rapiers to make me bleed. Use them tenderly to bring forth empathetic tears. Use them thunderously to wake my soul. Use them passionately to make my nerves tingle. Use them as a trumpet blast to send my blood racing until my heart literally throbs!"

The challenge of Christian writing is before you. This book will tell you how to get started. It will keep you going when you feel the need of encouragement or fresh inspiration.

Use your God-given writing ability to help the world's hungry, hurting people. Write to heal, to offer the spiritual dimensions missing in so much on the market today. Write professionally. Prayerfully submit the finished product to carefully studied markets—and leave the rest to God.

CHAPTER TWO

WHY WRITE?
by Sherwood E. Wirt

Sherwood Eliot Wirt is known throughout the world as an instructor and counselor of Christian writers. The founding editor of Decision magazine, Dr. Wirt is the author of fifteen books and editor of several others. He also has helped establish numerous writing schools and has taught at workshops for Christian writers in fifteen countries. Countless writers consider "Woody" the person who led them into the field of Christian writing.

WHY WRITE? WHY BOTHER to spend

interminable hours wriggling fingers at the typewriter, inserting sheet after sheet, filling the wastebasket? What are we trying to prove? And who in heaven or on earth cares what emerges from all our frowning cerebration?

It's one thing to have an assignment, a deadline, an eager editor stroking us with lovely words of expectation and encouragement. But most religious writers have to hack it without such amenities. We manage, while groping along the twisting corridors of our thinking, to stumble on an idea, and assume that it is not only worthy, it is original, unique, and magnificent. It must be "written up."

Motive? It's hard to say what our motive is. Let's leave for the moment our lofty goals, our personal spiritual commitment, and our far-ranging life purposes. Let's just make it clear that we're not in it simply for fame or money. C. S. Lewis told me that writing is a lust; it is "scratching where you itch." Perhaps he got that from Robert Browning's "Epistle of Karshish, the Arab Physician":

> I half resolve to tell thee, yet I blush,
> What set me off a-writing first of all.
> An itch I had, a sting to write, a tang!

And I guess that many of us would confess that we write simply because we have to. We're "word people," and if we cannot preach like Peter or pray like Paul, at least we can write like the devil.

Many excellent justifications can be found for Christian literature, once we stop to think. We shall look at them, for they are important. They form the framework not only of our writing but also of our very being, our raison d'etre, our total outlook on life. For the truth is, we are on the battlefield for our Lord. We are the Red Cross knights of justice and truth, tilting our Spenserian lances at Sansfoy, Sansloy, and Sansjoy. We'd like to be literary salt and light, permeating the culture as many inspirational writers have done in the past. But if the culture will not accept us, we still intend to uphold truth along with beauty and aesthetics. We are for the Good.

And right now we're trying to beat down the objections of an assistant editor who feels that what we're trying to say is not quite what his magazine is trying to say. We're willing to concede that black is speckled gray, but we aren't quite willing to sell our souls for a check. So we're caught in the give-and-take of the commercial market, and our motives are interpreted in a most peculiar way by the Internal Revenue Service.

Therefore, it might be well if we pushed away from our typewriters with their unclear sentences and from our desks with their annoying stacks of returned manuscripts and just thought about our motives. Not about what the psychologists call our "perseveration"—that compulsion that makes us keep on knocking out copy even after the thought has evaporated. But rather, about what in our highest moments we would say to justify our calling as scribes in the temple.

PERSONAL COMMITMENT

We begin by returning to our personal spiritual commitment. This is the sine qua non, for without it we're back in the world with its commissions, advances, and rejections—and its scrambling, ghosting, plagiarizing, and compromising. Freelancing without commitment soon becomes a struggle for survival with not much to say and a simulated style in which to say it.

Christian writers believe that Jesus Christ, who gives meaning to everything to life, gives meaning and purpose to their writing. From him they receive more than they do from the seven muses; they receive the Spirit of the Lord. Without that Spirit, they believe, it's easy to confuse "full-serve"—writing that's intended to serve God and man—with "self-serve"—writing that seeks only to aggrandize the writer one way or another.

Having said that, we need to admit that religious and inspirational writing is not in the mainstream of today's literature. We would like it to be. John Bunyan and John Milton made it in their time; but if you read a volume such as Parrington's *Main Currents in American Thought*, or the even more ambitious *Literary History of the United States*, you will soon discover that in the literary world of the twentieth century, religious and inspirational writers are pretty much "out of it."

How I wish it were not so! How I'd love to write something that would not only "justify God's ways to man," but would also achieve a standard of literary excellence that would win its way on sheer merit. After half a century I realize that if it is to happen, my inspiration must take a "great leap forward"; and meanwhile my motivation must adjust itself accordingly.

As a writer I'm not excused from turning out the best of which I am capable. A paucity of gifts can be partly compensated for by much rewriting and polishing. Spiritual writers are not called to grind out second-rate copy. Our standards are as high as anybody's. If the reviewers do not class us with Salinger, Mailer, Bellow, and Nabokov, literarily speaking, we're going to keep trying; nothing else will justify our divine vocation.

Assuming our limitations, then, let's examine carefully our commitment. What is our real purpose in writing for the religious and inspirational market?

Speaking for the evangelically oriented Christian (using that term in its broadest sense), I have to say that our motive is to spread the blessings of the Christian message. Rather than proclaim the Gospel from the house-tops, which seems a singularly unproductive medium in our day, we prefer the printed page. We believe that in the teachings of Jesus Christ, and even more in his life, death, and resurrection, our Creator was unfolding to the human race the mystery of our existence and the key to our survival.

THE POWER OF THE PRINTED PAGE

So we are bearers in the nuclear age of a life-and-death message. We couch this message in different literary forms, but it remains essentially the same: Jesus Christ died to save sinners. And while the same message may be channeled through many other media, we writers remain stubbornly committed to the written word. Marshall McLuhan to the contrary, we remain unconvinced that the age of Gutenberg is past. McLuhan's own books are solid evidence that he was wrong; the linear expression of type will last as long as human technology lasts. And when paper gives out, we will go back to chiseling the Gospel on rocks.

A basic reason for our choosing the written word is that we're convinced of its power. Many major movements in the recorded history of the world have been brought about through literature. Let me mention just a few writings that have exercised influence in the shaping of human destiny far beyond the clashing of arms: the Ten Commandments; the writings of Confucius; the New Testament; the Koran; *The Imitation of Christ; Pilgrim's Progress*; the Declaration of Independence; *Uncle Tom's Cabin; Origin of Species; The Communist Manifesto; Mein Kampf.* To these could be added any number of less significant writings that have helped shape their time.

The very existence of the Christian church is dependent on the writings that were first penned, then preserved in a way that no other has been kept. We Christian writers are aware not only of the extensive power of the printed page, but also of its permanence. Today in our local libraries, we can (just by asking) communicate with all the great thinkers of the ancient world whose words have come down to us.

EFFECTIVE WRITING

What a challenge to us today to join that noble group who has transmitted to humanity its legacy of thought. What a thrill it would be to us to pass along something in published form for such posterity as may follow us. Instead of "footprints in the sands of time," we would leave something infinitely better: a word "fitly spoken" and committed to writing that might influence a life or even save a generation.

In the immediate sense, then, Christian writing seeks to be not only cognitive but also causal; not only enlightening but also efficacious. It wants to make things happen, to sway opinion, to change people's lives by turning them around. At its best, Christian literature is action literature, designed to rouse people from their stupor so that by precept, admonition, example, parable, poem, and every known literary device, men and women may be informed of their opportunities, inspired by their Lord, and warned of their peril.

Those acquainted with the history of literature ancient and modern will recognize that such a motive differs radically from the impulses that lie behind much of the world's great writing. We stand in awe of the creative and artistic genius that fills the world's great books. Our stuff seems so meager and moralistic by comparison. We are looked upon as enthusiasts, partisans, time-servers, and mere protagonists who invade the literary forms simply to impress and dragoon, to serve our own religious ends, to drive home a point, just as the Marxists do. And there is some truth in it.

But what we lack in genius, we make up for in earnestness of purpose. We care. We want to help. We are concerned about other people, living out their lives of "quiet desperation." There are writers, excellent writers, who care nothing about reform, who scorn reformers as meddlers and hypocrites. But we do not classify ourselves as reformers so much as healers and teachers, following Jesus of Nazareth. We find it hard to "live and let live" when every day we encounter the ravages of sin and suffering.

Other writers whose interests are not religious are also concerned with human need, and we don't presume to preempt the field. We simply wish to make clear our motive: to take hold of one small corner of the human burden and lift, together with anyone else who will join us. If we had to choose between swabbing the dirty kitchen of a nursing home and writing a brilliant essay that won international acclaim but helped nobody, we would swab the kitchen.

THE QUESTION OF MORALITY

Part of the reason we are in dead earnest about our motivation is that so much poor copy is being turned out. If words can save, words can also corrupt. The pornography market is mushrooming and has reached the status of a major industry. It's been estimated that 90 million copies of porn literature are published and circulated every month.

This is a world about which many people know little, but it holds a fascination for the inquisitive mind of youth, and it can soil the imagination for life. Such pornography isn't confined to the underworld; it has invaded all the major bookstores. What used to be passed furtively from hand to hand is now advertised and reviewed in the most "respectable" publications. Religious bookstore owners tell of people with no religious interest coming into their stores and asking, "In God's name, have you anything decent to read?" These are people who are tired of buying filth passed off as exciting literature.

Christians are motivated to write, then, partly because they recognize that a taste gap exists in American literature. Some of us wish we were better qualified to fill it; but fill it we shall, for we are determined that Main Street shall not be turned into an open sewer. Some elitists will scorn us for our efforts, but we shall strive to please God first and then people.

The question of morality is not restricted to the pornographic output. What we face is a cultural trend, a disintegration of values, a gradual abandonment of the taboos Western society erected for its own protection on the basis of the Old and New Testaments and Roman law. To illustrate this well-known and well-documented phenomenon, let me quote a description of the climate in American fiction in the early years of the present century: "The public that adored Pollyanna and her sisters would have nothing to do with novels that denied its belief that virtue was rewarded in this world as well as the next."

How distant it all seems! Contrast the foregoing statement with Lolita, the twelve-year-old "heroine" of a Nabokov novel of the fifties, whose name has become a synonym for sexual precocity. Nabokov is a respected author in literary circles and it's not my purpose, or indeed my business, to judge him. All I'm seeking to do is illustrate the stunning reversal that has taken place in the literature of our century.

Did the moral scene affect writers, did writers affect the moral scene, or was it a case of interaction? I don't know. What I do know is that from the Christian perspective, American writing is on a moral toboggan and it has not yet hit the bottom of the slide. And each of the distinguished authors of our century, including such names as Henry James, Jack London, Edith Wharton, James Branch Cabell, Sinclair Lewis, Willa Cather, William Faulkner, J. D. Salinger, John Dos Passos, Ernest Hemingway, John Steinbeck, Saul Bellow, Norman Mailer, William Burroughs, and others has his or her own place and platform somewhere along that slide.

What I'm attempting to depict isn't simply a literary phenomenon but—as I said earlier—a radical shift in the behavior patterns of Western culture. I call attention to it only to make vivid the background against which the Christian writer sits down to compose an inspirational paragraph. He finds himself swimming not against a stream but against a massive flood. Desperately he looks around for words of principle such as *virtue, modesty, honor, reverence*, and even *integrity*, only to find they have been torn to shreds by people who weren't even aware of what they were doing.

If he dares to pick up such concepts and use them in his writing, he exposes himself to ridicule as an anachronism, a throwback, a fossil, a quaint and curious relic of an antiquated past. Why then does he bother?

I'll tell you why: He doesn't care. Such epithets mean nothing to him. He calibrates his compass not by the B. Dalton bookstores but by the north star. He draws his own inspiration from a clear rivulet that has come down through the centuries quite apart from the muddy floods: from Paul, Augustine, Francis, Lady Julian, Thomas à Kempis, Luther, Bunyan, Oswald Chambers, and Amy Carmichael.

18 The Christian writer takes to his typewriter because God in his sovereign grace has stooped down and lighted his candle. No longer is he his own man or she her own woman. Their lives have been claimed; they are now the occupied territory of the Holy Spirit. The prophet Habakkuk's orders were: "Write the vision and make it plain, that he may run who reads." And Paul wrote to Timothy, "Bring the books and the parchments!"

So writing becomes our ministry. We are commissioned not just to write evil down, but to write God up. We are instructed to teach, to train, to interpret, to inform, to edify, to kindle the imagination, to narrate stories as Jesus did, and even to entertain. We are to provide milk for children, solid foods for full-grown men and women, and the elixir of poetry to express our love for our Creator. We are to write about good and evil, frustration and victory, justice and mercy, sin and redemption, joy and adversity, and always grace and glory. We are to cover the waterfront of human experience, to run the gamut of life, and so give people a handle to grasp as they seek to attain a worthwhile and productive existence under Christ.

THE RELIGIOUS MARKET

Now here is the beautiful part of it. The Christian writer of inspirational material finds that he has a built-in market. Out there in the reading public, he discovers, are hundreds of thousands of people who are looking for something to read that will make them better than they are. They want something that will uplift them, give them a new hope, a fresh horizon, a glimpse of what they were made for. They are found in every walk of life and are of every kind of persuasion, Christian and non-Christian. They have not yet been jaded by the tastes of the prurient or disillusioned by the promotions of the exploiters. They are waiting for us to produce. If we can meet their demand for quality, we will be bought and read.

So now our challenge is clear. We draw our motivation not only from divine mandate but also from human yearning. If God commands it, people also want it. And we come face to face with the question: How do we prepare for this task? Most of the people who read these lines know it's too late to start at the beginning. They're already in midstream. If they are to become writers, they must begin where they are.

MOTIVATION

Elsewhere in this volume there is plenty of how-to advice for the aspiring writer, and I do not intend to comment extensively on that topic. I find, however, that my own motivation is conditioned and strengthened by a number of factors that may be worth mentioning.

The first is *contacts*. The writer lives by encouragement. He is essentially a lonely person, and when the rejections pile up and the interest wears off, he soon slides into a "downer". To a writer who's wondering whether either God or man wants his stuff, I have a suggestion to make: Cover your typewriter and walk out the door. Pay a call on a fellow writer or better yet, an editor. Talk over your writing with someone who can and will take a professional interest in what you are doing.

A telephone call to or from an editor-friend is likely to send me back to my typewriter with an entirely different attitude. I'm filled with energy, eager to work. I feel encouraged. I seem to be on the right track. The fact that I have to throw away fifty pages of hard-wrought creativity doesn't matter, for now I know where I'm going. No, I don't have a contract or even a solid assurance of acceptance. But I have hope! And hope is the New Testament's greatest motivator.

The Gospel teaches us that when we get to heaven it's not what we know that matters, but whom we know. In the marts of trade on earth the word is the same. Everything is done by contacts. For every successful writer today, there are ten people who are their equals or betters when it comes to talent but who lacked one thing: a contact with the right person at the right time who happened to have the right need.

The second factor is *tools*. Man has been called a tool-making animal. Give an artisan a set of dull tools and he will soon lose interest in his work. Give him sharp tools and they will motivate him; he will find satisfaction and even joy in his work.

Some authors have turned out masterpieces in prison; others in rooms filled with relatives, including crying babies; others have written books in longhand, lost them, and written them again. I admire such writers, but have no desire to imitate them. My output comes hard enough without making it difficult. At some pains I have collected what I consider the proper tools and equipment for a Christian writer. To come into my study, to sit down, to insert paper in the machine, to begin to write, are distinct pleasures.

Elsewhere I've written, "Give me food and sleep and exercise, and put me in a room by myself with an electric typewriter, a Bible, some dictionaries, a synonym finder, and an idea, and for three hours I wouldn't trade places with anyone on earth." Let me expand on that. I'd also like a good light over my shoulder. I'd like a reliable Bible commentary, a book of quotations, an atlas, a concordance, and a good encyclopedia. I'd want some good bond paper, a multidrawer filing cabinet, a book of markets, an address file, a copying machine, a manual of style—the list goes on and on. The freelance writer needs sharp tools to turn out good work.

Tools will not substitute for ideas. Tools will not inspire. C. S. Lewis wrote better with a nib pen than I ever will on an electric typewriter. But I can do better on such a typewriter than I could with a nib pen, and I'd feel more like doing it. If you wish to be a craftsman, you would do well to equip yourself for the craft.

A third factor is *discipline*. Logically, discipline should be the natural outflow of motivation. If we want something badly enough, we expend the energy and pay the price. But the truth is that discipline is itself a powerful motivator. For example, if a writer swings into the habit of writing something every day, he finds that his output increases markedly. The clock becomes part of the motive.

Disciplined habits mean overcoming our natural laziness, and writers are notoriously lazy. Huck Finn's epic closes with the words, "There ain't nothing more to write about, and I am rotten glad of it, because if I'd a knowed what a trouble it was to make a book I couldn't a tackled it, and ain't a-going to no more." A friend of mine, a freelance writer, tells me that when he's composing on the typewriter he sometimes paces around the house, and invariably he finds himself standing either in front of the refrigerator or the bed.

But books are not written, as a rule, in beds or around iceboxes. Suppose we are working on a piece and need to look up a word or check a date. It means making the effort to pull a book off the shelf. Ah, but we decide we can get by without going to such trouble! Shortcuts in research mean absence of discipline and nearly always result in a drop in quality.

We might ask, Why did Paul tell Timothy to "endure hardship . . . like a good soldier of Christ Jesus"? What specifically did hardship have to do with the work of an evangelist? Obviously Paul felt that training in discipline was vital to the success of his ministry. The medium was the message. No discomfort, no kerygma. But discipline entails more than discomfort; it involves accuracy and dependability and follow-through. A soldier may think he can win a war without saluting. A mechanic may think his aircraft will lift off without his checking a valve. The opposite of discipline is shoddiness and carelessness, and it is the same in writing. The reading public soon ascertains whether a writer's statements can be trusted, and an editor learns even more quickly.

Some authors discipline themselves by rising early to write; others prefer the evening. Feodor Dostoevsky's custom was to write through the night, beginning about midnight. It's up to the individual writer to establish the discipline that suits him best. Set times are not important. What is important is to plunk oneself down in the chair and get rolling.

I come back to the original question: Why write? If we need the money we might better look elsewhere. Christian publications do remunerate, but not in large enough amounts to take care of mortgage payments. If we crave an outlet for our ego, we can save ourselves the effort; bragging draws a poor market in Christian circles. If we're looking for something more aesthetic, such as self-fulfillment through creativity, we would do better in a secular field where such motives are more apt to be understood.

The selection of a worthy and challenging topic can provide excellent motivation for the writer. Grapple with a big issue: the acculturation of the church, or God's image in man versus the self-image, or evangelism versus revival. Many topics need a fresh airing in our decade, from a fresh viewpoint.

The receipt of a letter from a reader saying that he has made his peace with God or has been filled with the Spirit as a result of reading something I wrote is enough to send me straight to my typewriter. It is the highest possible kind of motivation.

Apostle John tells us that one day during his prison discipline on the island of Patmos, he was in the Spirit on the Lord's day "and I heard behind me a loud voice like a trumpet, which said: 'Write. . . .' " Here is the original Christian Motivator. The command comes through in unedited form, pure and authentic. Certainly when the Holy Spirit calls the writer to his desk, he comes with no quibbles, no reservations, no second thoughts about postponing the task until a more convenient season. Nor does he need to explain to anyone what he is doing or why he is doing it.

But motivation alone, no matter how strong, will not make the writer successful. He needs many things, as will become clear when you read on. Christian writing may look easy to the outsider (it can be done at home during one's spare time at no expense). All one requires, it would seem, is a reasonable grasp of the language. . . .

No way! It's a good deal more complicated than that.

My guess is that under normal conditions, a beginner needs five to ten years to become a successful, professional freelance writer, assuming that the aspirant works at it, seeks help, surmounts discouragement, and learns the rules and nuances of the game. That takes a strong motive, for a Christian or for anyone.

Of course, you may make it sooner than that. It took me longer. But in any case, welcome to the craft. Very soon, we hope, we'll be seeing your name in print and be giving glory to God.

CHAPTER THREE

WHERE ARE THE MARKETS?

by Elaine Wright Colvin

Elaine Wright Colvin of Helena, Montana, is a freelance writer, poet, and Christian writer's consultant with extensive publishing credits. A market specialist, she is the coauthor of The Religious Writers Marketplace, *a writer's market guide to more than 1,500 publishers and publications in the religious field. She has served as the associate director of the Mount Hermon Christian Writers' Conference in California since 1978. She has been a leader at other writers' conferences across the country and is the organizer of the Idaho Fellowship of Christian Writers and the Montana Christian Writers' Fellowship.*

THE WIDE-REACHING religious market is

open to the serious freelancer who is willing to study, work, and pursue his craft with diligence. In limited areas of the religious market, an increasing amount of staff-written or assignment material is being used. But every editor is looking for that freelancer who has something to say and can communicate it in a lively manner to his eager audience.

Knowing and studying the markets are vital for the writer who wants to be successfully published. Here are some steps for keeping in touch:

1. Obtain a thorough religious market book. The first comprehensive book in this field, *The Religious Writers Marketplace*, by William Gentz and me, was released early in 1981 by Running Press. One longtime friend of writers is the annual *Writer's Market* published by Writer's Digest Books. It contains many religious listings classified both by subject and age/interest divisions.

2. Obtain or consult the library's reference books. Check carefully the listings of books mentioned throughout this chapter.

3. Read or scan every religious publication you come across. You can find these magazines and periodicals at church libraries, Christian colleges and seminary libraries, friends' homes, doctors' offices, Sunday school, religious education directors' or pastors' offices and libraries, newsstands, Christian bookstores—even grocery stores and drug counters—and of course, your own subscriptions.

Study the markets and know them before you try to reach them has been the plea of editors for years. Material that meets the needs of the reading audience is in demand by every editor.

4. Skim general writers' magazines for guidance on finding your markets. Religious-market information can be found in the December issue of *The Writer* magazine and occasional items are listed in the monthly *Writer's Digest*. *Publishers Weekly* features special religious issues semiannually.

5. Study several other publications that are geared toward the needs of religious writers and that regularly contain information on current markets. Here are a few: *Charismatic Writers Association (CWA) Bulletin*, 237 N. Michigan, South Bend, IN 46601; *Christian Author Newsletter*, 396 E. St. Charles Rd., Wheaton, IL 60187; *Christian Writers' Newsletter*, 300 E. 34th St.,

(9C), New York, NY 10016; *Cross & Quill*, P.O. Box 1708, Brooksville, FL 33512; *Currents*, 1604 East Taylor Ave., Harlingen, TX 78550; *Penkraft*, 3840 Fifth Ave., San Diego CA 92103; *Quill-o'-the-Wisp Quarterly*, Box 707, La Canada, CA 91011.

The many types of religious publications make a lengthy list: magazines, periodicals, take-home papers, newspapers, journals, trade publications, regional publications, house organs for all interests and ages, curriculum, music, scripts for radio, TV, movies, and stage. Determine your specialty and study the field that you will endeavor to reach. It's impossible to provide an exhaustive description of all market areas in one short chapter; we will deal only with the major ones.

Read carefully the other chapters of this book in which you will find some very specific suggestions about the markets for the particular kind of materal that they discuss.

A key word in marketing vocabulary is "current." If the market lists you're using are even a few years old, you can be sure that some of the editors will have changed houses, some of the publications will have changed their name or will have ceased publication. Addresses and locations need to be updated frequently. Manuscript needs of publishing houses change almost annually (if not more quickly). When using an older reference book for your market lists, always send for an updated "Guidelines for Writers" to the house to which you are considering sending your manuscript.

Aiming incorrectly and flooding editors' desks with unwanted and irrelevant manuscripts is not the way to be published.

Denominational Magazines

The easiest periodicals to be "on target" with are the denominational markets of your church. Needs, slants, and theological viewpoints are as diverse as the lengthy list of national church bodies. And even within one broad group (Baptists, for example) there is a wide expanse of varying doctrines and practical differences. Many churches have extensive lists of publications—e.g., Broadman Press (Southern Baptist Sunday School Board) and Board of Discipleship/Graded Press (United Methodist Church), to name just two. The familiar adage "You must know them to write for them" is even more important when writing for the large denominational market.

General Magazines

The writer of religious nonfiction will find abundant markets if his article is well written, thoroughly researched, and addressed to a "felt need" of the readers of the magazine to which the manuscript is submitted.

The major evangelical general magazines include: *Moody Monthly*, circulation 325,000; *Christian Herald*, circulation 270,000; *These Times*, circulation 215,000; *Christianity Today*, circulation 185,000; and *Eternity*, circulation 50,000.

Magazines for Women, Men or Families

The women's magazines are a fairly recent commodity on the religious market. There are more than a dozen non-church-affiliated ones available, and most denominations have at least one. Circulation ranges from 35,000 to 100,000. These magazines are looking for articles about the role of women in our changing society; how they are exerting power, achieving equality, and succeeding with their families and careers, as well as articles stressing biblical principles for women. Two of the women's "slicks" to make it big in the past couple of years are *Today's Christian Woman* and *Virtue* magazine. Two new magazines in this field are *The Reborn Woman* and *Equity*.

Magazines for the family have found an increasing place of importance. These seek to enrich Christian marriage and family life. There are at least fourteen religious family magazines, one newsletter for men entitled *Dads Only*, and three magazines specifically for senior citizens (*Mature Catholic*, *Mature Living*, and *Mature Years*).

Magazines with a family emphasis include *Christian Home*, *Family Life Today*, *Home Life*, *Is There a Family in the House?*, *Marriage and Family Living*, and *Today's Christian Parent*.

Magazines for Children and Youth

The juvenile religious market encompasses both magazines and various other denominational publications for the graded age groupings of young children through teenagers. Multiple submissions are a popular way to get maximum mileage for your manuscript in this field, since the circulation and reading audiences do not overlap. Diligent religious freelancers have often sold the same story more than a dozen times by offering reprint rights to different publishing houses.

We've heard it said that the market for fiction is decreasing. This is not necessarily true for the religious writer. Short stories will always be needed by youth/young adult magazines and by Sunday school take-home papers for all ages. Real marketability will depend on making characters come alive, and facing the readers with realistic, challenging situations and depths of feeling young people can relate to.

Curriculum Materials

A steady market for freelancers has been and always will be that of curriculum materials for the Sunday school and the vacation Bible school. Curriculum is strictly defined as that of student books and teachers' guides. But within this field are myriad other teacher resources and supplies.

Other curriculum items to watch and write for in the 1980s include church-time materials, children's choir curriculum, teaching children to read music, family study guides stressing family participation and strengthening the family, videotapes, teacher training aids, teaching aids, books, games, crafts, banners, supplies, charts, duplicating masters, Pict-o-graphs, bookmarks, memory cards, coloring books, Dot-to-Dot activities, puzzles and quiz books, posters, plaques, bulletin covers, puppets, bulletin board ideas, and more. The editor in charge of product development is usually the one to query for the house's needs and projections into the future.

A useful resource tool for digging up specific information about this market is the annual *Suppliers Directory* published by Christian Booksellers Association, Inc., 2620 Venetucci Blvd., P.O. Box 200, Colorado Springs, CO 80901, (303)576-7880. Your local Christian bookstore usually has a copy and will probably let you browse through it. Of value and interest is the detailed alphabetical listing of every supplier—and the classification of merchandise lists which break down for easy reference, and the type of merchandise provided by each religious publishing house.

Theological Journals

Journals range widely in their focus and theological persuasion. Most are aimed at the clergy and the academic community. They use highly specialized articles that reflect scholarly research in various theological and related disciplines. Few journals offer cash payment—the usual practice is to compensate in offprints, tearsheets, or complete issues. Reference books that specialize in market information for this field include:

- *Directory of Publishing Opportunities in Journals and Periodicals,* Fourth Edition (Marquis Academic Media, Marquis Who's Who, Inc., 200 E. Ohio St., Chicago, IL 60611). This directory contains detailed marketing information for eighty-eight entries under the subject of "Religions and Theology." Included are theological journals whose "specs" (specifications) are often difficult to obtain in other market lists. The information in most entries includes name, address, phone, subscription data, sponsoring organization, editorial descriptions of magazine content, audience, manuscript information, subject field(s), manuscript requirements, author information and reprints, disposition of manuscript, whom to submit to, and any special stipulations.

- *Scholar's Market: An International Directory of Periodicals Publishing Literary Scholarship,* by Gary L. Harmon and Susanna M. Harmon (Publications Committee, The Ohio State University Libraries, a Division of Educational Services, Columbus, Ohio, 1974). *Scholar's Market* is the first comprehensive reference work on periodicals of all types that publish literary criticism, history, or bibliography. Their section entitled "Interdisciplinary: Literature and Psychology, Religion, Politics, Philosophy, Science, or the Arts" contains titles of such scholarly journals as *Christianity and Literature, Interpretation: A Journal of Bible Theology,* and *Journal of Biblical Literature,* with specific information pertaining to the marketing of manuscripts to these publications.

Poetry

A recent survey of markets for the Christian poet has turned up several specialty magazines for the religious writer. Information about these periodicals is available in *The Religious Writers Marketplace.* You should send for each publication's guidelines to determine submission details. Many pay only in copies of their magazine. Poetry magazines include *Arkenstone, Wellspring, Beyond the Rapture, For the Time Being, A Time for Singing,* and *Channels.*

Many general and denominational magazines publish poems in each issue. In nearly every issue, children's Sunday school take-home papers publish poems suitable to the publication's audience and theme.

The Religious Book Market

There is a burgeoning market for religious books as is evidenced by the more than 5,000 new religious titles that appear annually in member stores of the Christian Booksellers Association.

A recent article in the *West Coast Review of Books* claimed that from a secular viewpoint "The religious market is now considered 'hot.' "

A major factor in this growth appears to be the "crossover books" that publishers are finding may add volume to their sales. When a book can cross over and make its way in both the religious and the secular markets, it often climbs to the top of bestseller lists. Books that became solid examples of this principle include Jimmy Carter's biography, *Why Not the Best?; Angels,* by Billy Graham, and *The Total Woman,* by Marabel Morgan.

What subjects comprise the book market? It could be a long list with infinite variety; here are a few: Christian living, contemporary concerns, marriage and family, Bible prophecy, personal experience, school textbooks, theological, devotional, inspirational, celebrity conversion, missions, pastors' helps, Bible studies, Bible commentaries, counseling, biographies, evangelism, church growth, church history. Academic: history, philosophy and religion, psychology, language and literature, reference, sociology. Christian education: youth, handcraft, communication resources, teaching enrichment resources.

A trade journal valuable to freelancers wanting to keep abreast of what is happening in the Christian booksellers' world is *The Bookstore Journal*. It recently carried an article by Jarrell McCracken of Word Books that reported, "Since the mid-60's when Word and Tyndale announced their first lists, innumerable new Christian publishers have sprung up and flourished." The number of new titles and publishing houses represented on the shelves of our religious bookstores would certainly attest to this fact.

Nonfiction

So you want to write the next great bestseller? Your chances for acceptance are ten times greater for a nonfiction book than a novel. This is true of the overall book market, and it is especially true of the religious market. There are some 160 publishers of religious books—it's a wide market.

Let's look at the needs of some of these book publishers a little more in depth. These would fall into several categories: self-help, topical (covering important issues of the day), personal experience, family life, psychology, Christian living with a how-to approach. Today's religious nonfiction book must relate to people where they hurt; offer tangible solutions to problems faced by individuals, and address current issues as the Bible relates to them. God should be proclaimed as the true stability in our time of uncertainties and shortages. Fresh approaches to Bible studies, devotionals, theology, and pastoral helps are needed.

Biographies and Personal Experience

Publishers are becoming more selective in the biographies and personal experience stories they publish. "They must be unusual and highly inspirational," according to one publisher. "Christian celebrity" or "crisis of the moment" books are often lacking in solid intellectual content but generally sell well. The human-interest story that shows God at work in individuals and true stories of how Christ changes and enriches lives are still in demand.

Books for Men

An important new market for the author of the '80s is for books "designed to be bought and read by men." For years it has been true that women between the ages of 25 and 65 purchase and read the bulk of the evangelical books published. Exceptions to this are, of course, reference books, textbooks, and study aids. Now a conscious effort is being made to attract male readers. Some publishers are even looking at the possibilities of action/adventure thrillers. Books by and about Christian athletes are also widely read by men. Chuck Colson's *Born Again* and *Life Sentence* have been successful in reaching the male market. A new release by Chosen Books will be popular for this market: *Strong at the Broken Places* by Max Cleland.

Men are also becoming more involved in reading some of the newer bestsellers relating to family-life problems, such as the books of James Dobson. One publisher reports, "We are going to see an increase in the number of male readers very quickly."

Books for Senior Adults

Have you considered that by the mid-1980s there will be about 20 million more adults and the average age of the U.S. population will have increased considerably? There are now 24.5 million persons past the age of sixty-five in the United States. As churches and communities become more aware of the needs of this significant group of citizens, so do publishers. "Senior adults want to learn, and we must produce more material for the elderly," reports one publisher.

Books for Single Adults

You may want to try writing for the single adult. There are 56 million people who are now in this largest minority in America. This group of the never-married, widowed, divorced, and single parents represents a growing market, if you discover their interests and needs and reach out to them.

Books for Youth

Many publishing companies are also looking for books that will appeal to young people. Most books for teenagers are bought by women—mothers and grandmothers—to give to young people. These books must have a catchy title and topic to induce the teens to read them. They must meet teens where they live today. Contemporary settings are generally required for this market. Publishers are looking for books that deal with the difficult problems facing today's teen: drugs, sex, alcohol and alcoholism, racial discrimination, theft, vandalism, abuse, and more. The problems the characters confront in today's books should be realistic and complex—as is life.

Books for Children

The children's-book market has always been strong with certain religious publishing companies. Books designed for children just learning to read, books with substance, value, and enduring qualities, books that impart life-related, biblical truths that children can relate to everyday living are popular with religious publishers. As one editor said, "I believe the future of children's books lies in publishing books that teach—so that parents want them in their children's hands—and that are entertaining, so that children enjoy learning." Another publisher has designed a series to satisfy children's hunger for "nature, mystery, and adventure." Children's-book publishing is costly because of the rising prices of paper, printing, artwork, etc. Still there remains an impressive number of publishers committed to providing quality children's literature that will help children grow spiritually.

Textbooks

Some publishing houses are recognizing the need of providing quality textbooks for the growing number of Christian schools. According to Jim Braley, education director for the Association of Christian Schools International, three Christian schools are being founded per day. Some of the religious houses interested in publishing textbooks include Fleming H. Revell Company, Moody Press, Scripture Press, Mott Media, and David C. Cook.

Self-help Books

There is a market for the self-help book because of our nation's personality. People have the time and the inclination to delve into self-improvement and analysis. Learning to cope is a popular theme. Other topics include how to eat better for less; coping with retirement concerns; personal adjustment; money management, family life, interpersonal relationships, healthful living; preventive health; coping with and adjusting to illness and handicaps.

Self-help books should be original, thoroughly researched manuscripts with practical information that readers will be motivated to adopt. Manuscripts written in an informal, interesting, easy-to-read style will have the best chance. Most publishers prefer a human-interest angle to a strictly clinical/professional one. Books must, of course, represent the latest fndings on a certain subject and if scientific in nature should be properly documented.

Bible-related Books

There appears to still be a market for new Bibles, translations, paraphrases, study-Bibles, Bible studies, and basic reference materials. Christian discipline and commitment to biblical principles are stressed by some publishers. Other publishers are also becoming involved in a new wave of eschatological, end-time books, especially those written imaginatively rather than as in-depth scripture text studies.

Some editors are looking for books for Christians about the quality of life in the free world. Should we be striving for a better lifestyle or standard of living while people in the Third World are starving? When the rug of materialism is pulled out from under us, does the Christian's lifestyle have enough quality to say something to searching Americans?

Fiction

There is a market for the *good* religious novel, of course, and many publishers are looking for that exceptional one that will meet their needs. But the market for fiction remains more limited than that for nonfiction. If you are writing that great Christian novel, it must maintain literary excellence, as well as be intriguing. Biblically based fiction is coming into its own in popularity as evidenced by recent major releases of several religious publishers: *Joseph* and *I Came to Love You Late* by Joyce Landorf (Revell); *Abigail, Hagar, Ruth,* and *Lydia,* all by Lois Henderson (Christian Herald); Roberta Dorr's recently published *Bathsheba* (Chosen Books); and *Song of Abraham* and *John, Son of Thunder,* by Ellen Gunderson Traylor (Tyndale). Biblical fiction is successful, according to one publisher, when the author "has genuine talent, does meticulous research, and gives significant new insights into Biblical times, feelings, and developments." You will see the occasional hardback novel suitable for book clubs and the like, but the majority today are being published as entertaining mass-market paperback.

Works of general fiction have been successfully published by Zondervan in both their Sebastian Thriller series of absorbing adventures and their Hearth Romance series which encompasses a broad range of genres. The recent Chime Books imprint of David C. Cook is another example of new areas opening in Christian fiction. To reach this market you must present a dynamic, fast-paced manuscript that will focus on realistic problems and pressures of a Christian in today's world. Reader identification is a definite plus in securing acceptance.

Poetry Books

The market for books of poetry is limited. The religious poet who is determined to publish a book of poems will most likely be able to do so only through a self-publishing venture. Many gifted poets publish their work privately. The exceptions are well-known poets with outstanding reputations. A poetry manuscript is more likely to receive favorable consideration if some of the poems have appeared in magazines. It's also helpful to develop your manuscript around one unifying theme that meets a "felt need" in today's society. Recent popular books of poetry include works by Luci Shaw (Harold Shaw Publishers) and Ulrich Schaffer (Harper & Row), and an anthology of Christian poetry, *The Country of the Risen King* (Baker Book House). Books of prayer-conversations have also found a waiting audience and been successful for Judith Mattison (Augsburg), Harold Myra (Tyndale), and Virginia Thompson (Harvest House).

Self-publishing endeavors usually mean the writer will be responsible for editing, layout, and for paying the printer. After this comes the chore of marketing the book.

Audiovisual Markets

More than 125 producers of religious audiovisual software are listed in *Audiovisual Market Place (AVMP)*. This multimedia guide, published by R. R. Bowker Co., 1180 Avenue of the Americas, New York, NY 10036, contains individual listings with names of industry and related sources, addresses, telephone numbers, key personnel, product lines, services, activities, and other particulars. The needs of producers of religious audiovisual materials usually include 16mm and 8mm films, sound and silent filmstrips, slides—singles and sets—audio cassettes, overhead transparency sets, musical and nonmusical records, videocassettes and tapes, and multimedia kits. This is a booming field with lots of potential for the enterprising freelancer. Queries to each company are necessary to determine the particular needs and submission guidelines.

Music Markets

Many possibilities exist in the religious and gospel music field. Publishers advise writers to study what's on the radio to learn what to write for the market. They say they receive so much archaic material and it is not only time-consuming to return it but difficult to give encouragement to the writer, which they like to do even if a song is not for them. More than forty religious music publishers are mentioned in *Songwriter's Market*, published by Writer's Digest Books. More than a dozen other markets are described in a special section of "Writing for Music Publishers" in *The Religious Writers Marketplace*. Stated needs of music publishers include children's (choruses for young age groups for Sunday school); choral (sacred); solo/choral for all ages; instrumental for handbells, organ, recorder, and orchestra; Gospel; religious country and western; easy listening; traditional; contemporary, and more. One music publisher has said that "a great song touches something, illuminates some kind of truth, has an originality—something that's never been said that way before." All music publishers are looking for songs that have been "worked, checked, rewritten, edited, and improved until they are good." So go after it—submit your lead sheet and the best demo that you can afford.

The growth of specialized musical ministries has been prompted by the industry's concern in reaching the needs of individual groups, such as children, within the Christian listening audience. Also represented in the Christian community is Gospel music, which has become a major seller in the nation's record outlets.

Other Market Reference Books

Here are some other reference books which may be found at your local library:

- *Ayer Directory of Publications,* published annually by Ayer Press, 1 Bala Ave., Bala Cynwyd, PA 19004, (215)664-5205, William J. Luedke, publisher. As a "basic, authoritative reference tool for professionals," this volume is quite workable. There are more than 900 classifications listed alphabetically, including five pages of listings of religious publications. It is a unique book because the entries appear first by states in alphabetical order and then by the towns and cities in which they are published. Information in each listing includes date established, frequency of publication, type of publication, circulation, advertising, editor, publisher.
- *Guide to Social Science and Religion in Periodical Literature,* published by National Library of Religious Periodicals, Box 47, Flint, MI 48501, contains listings of articles by subject, title, periodical, date of periodical, page number, author, and number of words in the article for 106 religious periodicals.
- *International Directory of Little Magazines and Small Presses,* Len Fulton, editor/publisher. Dustbooks, P.O. Box 1056, Paradise, CA 95969. Contains approximately fifty religious-market listings not found in other sources.
- *Literary Market Place* is the directory of American book publishing, published by R. R. Bowker Company, New York. The subject lists of book publishing and magazine and newspaper publishing often contain information valuable to the freelancer

trying to obtain addresses, phone numbers, names of specific in-house employees, subjects, and number of titles published, etc.

- *Magazines for Libraries* by Bill Katz and Berry G. Richards, published by R. R. Bowker Company, contains annotated listings of some 141 magazines of interest to the religious writer. Its religion listings are categorized by the following audiences: general, alternatives, denominations, secular, and teenage. Included in a listing are "Title, Date Founded, Frequency, Price, Editor, Publisher and Address, Illustrations, Index, Advertising, Circulation, Sample, Date Volume Ends, Refereed, Microfilm, Indexed, Book Reviews, Audience."

- *The Successful Writers and Editors Guidebook,* Robert Walker, editor, was published in 1977 by Creation House, Carol Stream, Illinois. It contains "more than 300 religious markets for books, articles, photos, short stories, and poetry" divided by category. It's a handy reference segregation when you are specializing in one particular field.

- *Ulrich's International Periodicals Directory,* a Bowker serials bibliography of R. R. Bowker Company. Entries are arranged by subject. Therefore, periodicals of interest to religious writers are found under several headings; the largest of these, "Religions and Theology," contains twenty-four pages of listings of the religious periodicals in some forty countries. Other lists of religious periodicals in this directory are found under the headings Religious Education, Religious Societies and Missions, Children and Youth, Music, Publishing and Book Trade, and Women's Interests.

- *The Writer's Handbook,* edited by A. S. Burack, The Writer, Inc., Boston, contains market lists of more than 2,500 magazine and book publishers who are looking for manuscripts. Because there is not a separate index or listing for religious publishers alone, it takes a little more time to use this source.

- *Writer's Market,* edited by P.J. Schemenaur and John Brady, Writer's Digest Books, Cincinnati, Ohio, has religious periodicals and magazines scattered throughout in several categories: Religious, Church Administration and Ministry, Music, Juvenile, Teen and Young Adult. This is an extensive but by no means complete listing of religious markets; however, there is some information here not found in the other reference books.

- *Writing Award-Winning Articles,* by Glenn Arnold, Thomas Nelson Publishers, Nashville, Tennessee, includes the Evangelical Press Association Market Guide list of eighty-seven religious periodicals. Name, address, phone, circulation, frequency, readership, purpose, manuscript needs, and whether or not a query is required are contained in the listings.

Yes, the markets for your writing are all around you. Start where you are by exploring the needs of your church bulletin, your club and/or church newsletter. Become a church or a club reporter for the local newspaper. Then widen your circle and look to your denominational papers and magazines. These may be diocesan, district, regional, or state as well as national. You will also find listings of these newspapers and magazines in *Associated Church Press Yearbook, Catholic Press Directory, Evangelical Press Association Directory*, and the *Canadian Church Press Directory*.

Don't let your market research become so much fun that you steal valuable time from your writing. But remember that this is an important part of every freelancer's business. When you have selected the markets that are right for you, you can produce that article or story that is just right for the publication, or that book that is perfect for the publishing house. It is the little successes that put you well on your way to becoming a professional freelancer for the booming religious market.

Part Two

♣ *CHAPTER FOUR*

HOW TO
GET STARTED
by Cecil Murphey

Cecil B. Murphey of Riverdale, Georgia, is a prolific writer and teacher of writers. His published works include some 150 articles, and ten nonfiction and four fiction books. He has taught writing courses in a junior college, at church-sponsored institutions, and at several workshops in Georgia, Michigan, and Illinois. He has organized and led three self-help writers' groups in the Atlanta area. He is the pastor of a Presbyterian church.

"I AM EMBARKING on the road of Christian

writing," the letter began. The writer went on to say that a mutual friend had given her my name and concluded with the request "Can you help me?"

This letter is only one of many such personal appeals that have come my way in the past few years. Some ask how to contact other writers. "What can I write about?" asks another person. All have this in common: They want to get started writing for the religious market.

If they're serious, I say, "Here are three principles to remember before we get into specifics."

THREE PRINCIPLES

1. *Read.* Don't limit yourself to religious publications. Dabble in everything from fine print on cereal boxes to skimming through scholarly magazines. Learn about physical fitness, psychology, and natural science. Know a little about a wide variety of subjects. The more widely you read, the broader your interests and the more you stretch yourself. Too many Christians confine their article submissions to rehashing a Sunday school lesson or recycling a sermon based on an obscure text in the King James Version of the Bible.

2. *Write.* Many writers would rather express themselves on paper than pick up a phone or meet a stranger in person. They've learned that they communicate most fluently and concisely in written form.

Send letters to editors. Correspond with friends. Complain to or praise businesses and charitable organizations by mail.

The late José Bento Monteiro Lobato, a prominent South American writer, began his career with a protest letter to a Brazilian newspaper. He produced such an original letter that the editor featured it on the first page, thus launching Lobato's career.

The simple act of writing letters while I served six years as a missionary to Africa taught me the basics about communicating through the printed word. Coworkers mailed mimeographed letters. I have an aversion to off-the-reel news, so each month I typed seventy personalized letters to friends in America.

Although it was a tedious task, I disciplined myself to sit in front of the portable typewriter and peck out those letters. As I typed each letter, using the previous one as a guide, I edited. I changed an adjective, deleted a clause, or added a new paragraph. I felt the seventieth letter read the most smoothly.

3. *Rewrite.* Christian writers may need this exhortation more than others do. Because we believe in a Holy Spirit who guides, we sometimes confuse guidance with divine inspiration.

For instance, my wife, Shirley, receives unsolicited manuscripts for *These Days*, a devotional magazine. Occasionally a would-be writer sends in a series with an attached letter that says, "Since the Lord inspired these, they will not need editing and you can print them as they are." Shirley says she has never yet found any devotionals that didn't need some editing.

At a writers' conference, a woman charged through a group of students after a class, waving a sheaf of papers. "Here! Read these!" As she thrust them into my hands, she added, "I know you'll like them." She must have seen the hesitancy on my face because she immediately said, "I pray fervently before I write. Then the Spirit directs every word I put down."

In her case, the inspirational guide spelled poorly and would have flunked a sixth-grade grammar course.

GETTING MOTIVATED

Some wit said, "Most people don't want to write, only to have written." For many that may be true. But if you feel an inner, often undefinable, tugging that commands you to express yourself on paper, you know you can't escape. You *have* to write.

Because of that inner compulsion, you have to be a self-starter. You can depend on no one to push you, especially when you first begin. You need to find your own motivation. Epictetus said, "If you wish to write, write." However, it may not be that simple. Many Christians who speak about putting pen to paper usually say, "I want to write, *but . . .* " Don't allow yourself anything but a period after the word *write.*

During my first TV interview, the host asked: "Why do you write?" While I tried to think of an appropriate answer, he said, "Aren't we already overloaded with books and magazines? What makes you different so that you feel you have to write?"

I don't remember my answer (and I never saw the showing of the tape). As I reflect in the quiet of my office, I can give reasons why I write. These reasons motivate me and keep me productive.

Because you're reading this chapter, I assume you have at least a desire to write. I'm offering you several reasons why you can write—all reasons that motivate me.

1. *Because you're a Christian, you have something to say that enriches lives.*

The first article I ever wrote came about because I heard people remark, "Pastor Howell preached a great message yesterday." But when they were asked what he said, the answer came out, "I can't remember, but it was a fine sermon."

So I wrote an article called "Are You Listening, Brother John?" on how to listen actively to sermons (and sold it, too, by the way).

The second article I wrote came out of my own situation. I am a busy pastor. Sometimes members see my rushing figure and hesitate to call, even when they have a genuine need. My second sale, "Call for Help," dealt with when to call your minister.

My friend Marion Bond West has written four books and dozens of articles for religious magazines. All of her material comes out of her own experiences as she strives for Christian maturity. She's the mother of four and has that uncanny ability to grasp spiritual lessons in every problem. That's why she writes on subjects such as rearing twins, learning how to enjoy the game with her football-fan husband, and letting go when her first daughter married. Her articles enrich the lives of her readers.

In his autobiography, *On Being Different*, Merle Miller said, "I have always thought that one of the obligations of a writer is to expose as much of himself as possible, to be as open and honest as he can manage—among other reasons so that his readers can see in what he writes a reflection of themselves, weaknesses and strengths, courage and cowardice, good and evil. Isn't that one of the reasons writing is perhaps the most painful of the arts?"

Even though Miller did not write from a Christian perspective, his philosophy holds true for us as well.

2. *You write as a catharsis.* You struggle with the same problems others do. As you relive them on paper, you not only help others, but you also find a better understanding of yourself.

My book *Comforting Those Who Grieve* (John Knox Press) grew out of my own life. During a four-week period in 1977 I lost four significant people in death. I wrote out of my own pain but also to tell how people had helped or hindered me. The book aimed at those who want to minister to the bereaved. Sharing those insights provided a personal catharsis, and from the responses I've had to the book, I know that other people benefited as well.

Part of that catharsis involves sharing your failures. However, if failure tells the end of your story, don't send it to *Guideposts* or *Power for Living*. They want the story after you've struggled, failed, struggled again, and finally overcome. Overcoming may be as simple as learning how to cope with a rude coworker, facing your own proneness to criticize others, or learning to live with the loss of a parent or a mate. Lessons learned in your own struggle, and the help you received from God and other believers make the writing inspirational.

3. *You write because it's a ministry.* Through a single article, you have the potential to reach thousands of people. A single sentence in your writing might revolutionize someone's life.

My Christian experience changed through the reading of one article. Like a yo-yo, I went from believing to doubting, from wondering to wishing. My faith level depended on my mood. Someone handed me a religious magazine, and one article spoke to me. I've long forgotten the title and the author, but not the content; it was on faith. The author warned against going on our feelings and said, "The Bible tells of one man who went by his feelings—and he got fooled." He referred to the story of Isaac, who, as an old man and nearly blind, thought he was laying his hands on the head of his firstborn son, Esau. Jacob, however, had killed a goat and covered his hairless arms with its skin. The father felt his younger son and not discovering the deception, blessed him.

That simple illustration, and actually a kind of play on words, hit me. I decided my emotional state would no longer determine my spiritual commitment.

4. *You write because you have to write.* We in the religious field write because we have something within us that yearns to be said. We have a sense that no one else can say it in quite the way we can.

5. *You write primarily for emotional rather than financial rewards.* That doesn't mean religious markets don't pay. It means they often pay less than the general trade.

I can rattle off the names of a dozen people I know who live totally from their income from writing (which also includes personal appearances and speaking engagements). But they're a minority.

6. *You write because it's a gift.* The New Testament speaks of God's gifts to his people "for the common good" (I Corinthians 12:6 [RSV]). Lists of gifts appear in passages such as Romans 12:6-8, I Corinthians 12:4-11, I Peter 4:10-11. Although God does not specifically speak of writing, I believe it is one of the gifts. I write for a variety of reasons, one of which is that God has given me the ability to communicate by the printed word.

At first I didn't recognize this as a gift. I started because writing appealed to me. Afterward I recognized that it's God's gift and when I write, I exercise that gift.

My friend Tom Are started writing because he developed a concept of stewardship beyond campaigning for money. "Stewardship involves every aspect of the Christian life, so why reduce it just to an annual plea for increased giving?"

He wrote a book, *Lifestyle Stewardship*, which sold well, then he turned out articles on a variety of subjects. Recently his second book hit the market. Tom's exercising his gift.

In the beginning Phil Barnhart felt he had only one story to tell, the story of his work as a white pastor in a black community. He published his autobiographical account, and then the writing bug bit and he published a second book (on sermon starters), started editing a quarterly magazine, and recently signed a contract for another book. He acknowledges his talent as the Lord's gift.

COMMITTING YOURSELF

As you move toward a decision to write for the religious market, I offer three suggestions before you actually put the words on paper.

1. *Assess your strengths.* What excites you about the religious field? Can you zero in on personal experiences that caused you to change? Do you have a gift for teaching the Bible? Perhaps you want to bridge the gap between science and religion. Do the lives of great Christians of the past and present cry out to you to tell their story? It's a wide-open market; assess your areas of interest. While I encourage writers to try a wide range of articles, most of us specialize in one or two forms.

My friend Suzanne Stewart has written two excellent books, and they come out of her own experience. Yet she has difficulty in writing about ideas and would probably never attempt to write Sunday school curriculum.

Charlie Shedd (who wrote the last chapter of this book) has given readers valuable insight into human relationships, offering sage advice on the family and marriage. That's his forte. He knows his strengths.

What are your strengths? Think about the ideas that excite you. What do you enjoy reading? This is an excellent clue to evaluating your strengths.

2. *Survey the field.* Know the religious magazines and book publishers. When I first started writing, I studied the ads from various publishers in the magazines. I saw that John Knox Press emphasized the scholarly, Fleming H. Revell aimed at the conservative evangelical, Christian Herald marketed primarily for women buyers. That doesn't mean these publishers won't go beyond those limits, but it shows their general approach.

The same holds true for magazines such as *Christianity Today*, *Christian Century*, *Sojourner*, and *Eternity*. Reading a few issues helps you recognize the audience they want to attract. If you enjoy reading any of them, that also gives you a hint as to the market you might wish to write for.

Visit a Christian bookstore. Become familiar with what's on the shelves. Is your specialty marriage? Find out what's in print on that topic. Ask yourself, What have I got to say that hasn't been said already, and perhaps said better?

I've published two books on prayer—probably the most overworked subject in the field of religion. Why did I nevertheless write on prayer? Prayer had become increasingly significant in my own life, and much of what I read on prayer sounded mechanical and dull. I didn't attempt to reveal great secrets, hidden from the time of the apostles. I asked myself how to get past all the encrusted formulas, flowery phrases, and stereotyped images. I had to find my own angle—one that differed from the 13,597 books already written on the topic.

When you visit a book dealer, ask questions such as, "What kind of books would you like to see on the subject of family and marriage? On practical Christian living?" Or whatever topic you have in mind. Good book dealers know their buyers; they know what their customers want to read.

3. *Contact an established author whose work you enjoy reading.* Write to him or her and ask for help. Although that writer might not respond, most of the ones I know in the inspirational field remember the help they received in getting started, and they like to return it.

I began writing for publication because I took a course taught by Charlie Shedd. As busy as he is, whenever I wrote to him, even long after the course, he always took time to respond to my questions.

A number of writers I'm in contact with tell me of letters they receive from beginners and how much they enjoy responding to them. If a seasoned writer senses your commitment to writing, you may be amazed at the help he can offer. Established writers know editors and publishers. They also know the market. Most of all, they care about people.

My first book came into being because a publisher asked my friend Charlotte Allen to write a book for him. She was overcommitted at the time and said, "I have this friend who's only been writing a year or so, but . . . " The publisher contacted me, we talked, and I produced four chapters that he liked—he offered me a contract.

Why not attend a writers' conference? I don't think they teach you everything about writing—they may not even teach a great deal about it—but they do inspire. They challenge. They put you in contact with other fledgling authors, as well as established writers and editors. You develop a sense of camaraderie. You may even start saying, "I am a writer" at a conference.

FORMING GOOD HABITS

You're committed to writing. You want to write for the religious and inspirational market. You have experiences to share and insights to offer. Then write.

Only it doesn't work that way.

"I want to write," I hear frequently, "but I can't find the time . . ."

I never take that statement too seriously. We all have the same number of hours in a day and we all determine how we'll use them. A more truthful statement says, "Writing does not hold that high a priority in my life."

If you're going to write, you'll never *find* time, but you can *steal* it from other activities. You may have to give up singing in the choir or forgo watching six hours of television a week. You make choices, and your commitment to writing shows in the choices you make.

I'm tired of people who talk about how they'll write when they retire. Or they could produce if they could just lock themselves up in a motel room for three weeks. Maybe. But why not write now?

In my first five years of freelancing, I could count on only one hour a day. I now steal two hours every day, and if I'm very clever with handling my time, I add a few extra by the end of the week.

In those years of writing one hour a day I published six books and fifty articles.

That's one side of my career. By profession, I'm an ordained minister and pastor. Each week my church responsibilities receive a minimum of fifty hours. I don't anticipate a golden era when I'll regularly have ten hours every day to write. Nor do I particularly want them! But I use the time I have.

How do I produce so much in a small amount of time? I make every minute count. I do my writing on the typewriter. I type sixty-five words a minute and think at least twice that fast. It makes for poor typing but keeps the thoughts flowing.

Another advantage is that my wife, an assistant editor, offers valuable criticism before any article heads for a final draft. Also, a woman in our church who enjoys doing finished typing saves me valuable time.

However, that doesn't explain it all.

Here are a few of the things I've learned to make that hour count.

1. *I allow no interruptions.* In my case, I reach my office shortly after seven in the morning, lock the door behind me, and disengage the phones. My secretary has strict orders not to interrupt me until nine.

2. *When it's time to write, I write.* I don't sit and stare at my typewriter for an hour. Not even for ten minutes. Writing goes on in my head throughout the day. When I shave, I think about my lead sentence. An outline forms as I drive across town to visit a hospital. When I drop off to sleep at night, my mind is constructing the closing paragraphs.

3. *I discovered my own rhythm.* I discovered two things about myself after the writing virus attacked. I'm a morning person. You can get me pecking away at 7 in the morning, but please don't demand mental activity from me after 9:30 at night.

I've also recognized that I work best in fifty-minute segments. Perhaps that comes from having been a student and then a teacher for the first half of my life. When I have a two-hour period, I take a quick breather after fifty minutes—a few calisthenics, a cup of coffee, or even a short phone call to clear my head. But no more than ten minutes. Then I'm ready to work again.

On the other hand, Charlotte Allen began her writing career working after midnight while her husband and her son slept.

I have a friend who has published four articles in the past year. He did all his writing on a lined pad while commuting to work.

We all have a different rhythm. Think about yours. When are you freshest? That's the time to write. When you reach a low energy level, stop forcing yourself. We need to write at the time best for our individual personalities. Forming habits that work along with your own body rhythms makes the writing task that much easier.

4. *I allow material to simmer.* An idea jumps into my head and I want to develop the article immediately. However, the article may not be ready to write. So I go on to something else, while this current idea develops in my subconscious mind.

This lesson came home to me a few years ago when my turn came to cook the evening meal. Carefully following directions for brown rice, I brought the mixture to a boil, put a lid on it, and placed the pan on the back burner to simmer for thirty-five minutes. Sautéing onions on the front burner for a curried gravy then occupied my attention. While I stirred the onions over high heat, the rice simmered away on the back burner. When I finished cooking the gravy, I reached to the back burner and tended once again to the rice.

That's how my writing gets on. Some of it cooks at high heat while other ideas simmer on the back burner. One article demands all my conscious efforts, and another slowly matures in the subconscious part of my mind.

I usually have two or three projects going at the same time. If I get stuck on one article at only twenty-three minutes into my hour, I push it to the back burner, by placing it in a file on my desk. Out comes a second file that I've been mentally editing for the past three days.

5. *Discipline.* That's the real secret. Because I manage the rest of my time well, it gives me more opportunity to write. Yet discipline extends beyond time management. I've also learned a few other things that have helped me form the writing habit and hold to it. Here's an important one: *Write in the same place and at the same time every day.*

I do my writing at my office in the morning. Occasionally I squeeze in an evening at home when I'm free to write. Even with a desk, typewriter, and a quiet room I have trouble getting started. I used to wonder why. The other day someone said to me, in a different context, "We form habits and then habits form us."

We write better in the place where we've accustomed ourselves to write. When we sit down, habit takes over. Our minds are already moving in an established pattern.

Write every day, regardless of how you feel. This establishes the habit and trains your mind to work even when you're running a slight fever or have the blahs. For me, this was the hardest habit to acquire. I helped myself by making a chart with three columns. The first contained the date; the second, the amount of time I actually wrote; the third, comments on what I wrote. At the end of the first month, I had six blank spaces. The next month there were only two missed days. By the third month I knew I had formed the habit of writing daily.

The habit has become so ingrained that on a day when I don't write, I feel guilty. Then I give myself permission to *not* write. Quite a reverse of my early days.

Set goals for yourself. Determine to finish a full article by Friday. Have it outlined by Wednesday. Decide how much you intend to accomplish during each day's session. Check up on yourself regularly. Ask yourself, "Did I make it?" "Am I setting too high a goal for myself?" "Not enough of a challenge?"

Because I'm highly self-competitive, I impose a deadline for every article or book. Then I work toward beating my own deadline.

Discipline also means learning to accept rejections. Don't let these discourage your attempts at writing. Like most writers, I have a file of rejection slips. One article, "I Thought You Ought to Know," which has since been published and reprinted by two different magazines, received eight Thank-you-for-submitting-to-our-magazine—but . . . letters.

It might help to remind yourself of St. Paul's words to Timothy, "Take your share of suffering as a good soldier of Christ Jesus." (2 Timothy 2:3, RSV) Christian writers receive as many rejections as non-Christians. We grow by learning to accept disappointments in all areas.

Nothing hurts more than a cold, printed rejection form. Ignore them, because they tell you nothing. However, when you receive an added note, or occasionally an actual letter with the return of your manuscript, read it carefully. That editor who took time to make personal comments may offer insight as to why that particular magazine didn't want your manuscript. The comments may help you in revising, or offer a suggestion for another market.

When your manuscript comes back, ask God to help you write better and to guide you in knowing where to send your material. Remind yourself also that the editor did not reject *you*, only a piece of your writing. *Then forget the rejection.* Concentrate on finding the right home for your baby.

LEARNING THE BASICS

Good writing doesn't happen—it's something you work at. And keep working at. I like to say about any finished product of mine, "This is the best writing I can do at this stage of my development." I'm always learning to construct better sentences.

The other day a woman said, "I like your latest book much better than anything else you've done." She flushed and said, "I don't mean to hurt your feelings, but this one flows better."

I thanked her, "That's a compliment." I hope people will always like my newest book better than the previous one. And if I continue growing as a person and as a writer, why not?

Make it a goal not only to learn the basics but also to keep learning all through your writing career.

Good writing is always good writing, whether done by a beginner or an old hand. Read other writers; see how they do it. Buy books on the craft. If religious writing has the power of the Spirit behind it, it ought to be as good as, or even superior to, secular writing. Unfortunately, much so-called Christian writing comes across as poorly constructed, preachy, and disjointed.

As a Christian writer, why settle for being less than the best? I made a commitment to God when I published my first book and recognized that he had given me a gift to develop: "Lord, with your help, I'm going to be the best writer I'm capable of becoming."

That means a willingness to rewrite a dozen times. It means allowing an editor, a mate, or a friend to make suggestions, and learning to listen nondefensively. It means always knowing that you did your best but that next time you'll know how to do better.

The best way to move toward superior writing is to begin with the basics. Here are a few basic rules for Christian writers:

1. *Rid yourself of stained-glass vocabulary.* We write not only for lifetime church members but also for new converts and for those outside the faith. After completing an article, look for the religious terms and phrases that may convey meaning to you personally but leave the uninitiated in confusion. That includes theological terms such as *redemption, justification, grace.* It also means phrases such as *saved at the altar*, or *born again*, or *total surrender*.

2. *Demonstrate, don't narrate.* That's another way of saying, "Show me, don't tell me." Paint pictures. Help your readers understand by the way you construct your sentences or make your points.

In "Grace Builders," a chapter of my book *Somebody Knows I'm Alive* (John Knox Press, 1978), I recounted an experience with a woman I called Florence. I could have written it this way:

> Florence, a wealthy woman, invited me to visit. She served me tea, and all the time she let me know what she did not like about the way I had changed things at the church since becoming pastor.

Instead, I wrote it like this:

"Since you came, Mr. Murphey, our church has lost some of its dignity," Florence said as she served me tea from an ornate silver pot resting on a silver tray. And with the next breath she asked, "Milk or sugar, Mr. Murphey?"

"One lump of sugar, please," and I reached for the cup.

"We had such—such quiet dignity before you came. Now, I don't want to hurt your feelings telling you all of this. But you call those children to the front for a children's sermon. And they're so—so noisy. It absolutely disturbs the sanctity of the whole worship hour."

Which one paints a picture and enables you to visualize Florence?

3. *Build bridges from one thought to the next.* Write good transitions.

As a writer, I may understand how I leaped from altar calls in New York to baptism in Nigeria. But the reader may be stranded on the other side of the ocean, not knowing how to cross. Transitions form the vehicles that transport readers from one thought to the next.

When your mind flits along at 200 words a minute it may be painful to move from one thought to the next with transition words: *such as, for example, on the other hand, next, therefore, as a result, however, by contrast.* But the reader needs those little street signs.

Recently I realized how we make mental transitions but don't always take our readers along. As I walked to the post office with a friend, we talked about Jim, a church member who was in the hospital. I lapsed into silence, remembering the patient in bed, his gaunt features expressing his pain. That reminded me of his doctor, who had a thin, emaciated look about him. And thinking of emaciated people, I said aloud, "We're so unconcerned about starving people in the world."

My friend threw me a puzzled look. My mind had clicked along, quite logically, but silently. My friend knew only the two things I'd said: Jim lying in the hospital, followed by a statement on starving people. Fortunately my friend knows some of my quirks.

But in writing we don't have the opportunity to explain our in-between steps of thinking. We owe it to our readers to take their hands and lead them each step.

4. *Use active verbs to forge ahead.* Static verbs (forms of *to be*) impede action. Verbs pace; they express feeling.

Compare these two sentences: Jesus was sad. Jesus wept.

Here's a device I used to train myself to use active verbs. After completing a manuscript (and before the final typing), I took a page at random, and circled in red ink every time I used a form of the verb *to be*. My page often looked as though measles had infected it. But the exercise made me more careful about action verbs.

5. *Keep the voice active; avoid the passive.* When you write in the active voice, the subject performs the action. In the passive voice, the subject is acted upon.

Compare these sentences: Helen broke the jar. The jar was broken by Helen. The active voice energizes sentences; the passive slows them down. Active verbs make writing stronger, easier to understand, and more emphatic.

I suspect many beginning writers favor the passive voice because it sounds more literary. It also sounds dull.

The passive voice not only lacks vitality, it also requires more words. Compare the above two sentences with four words for the active voice and six for the passive. Multiply that by thirty uses in a single article and it helps you understand why I put this high on my list.

6. *Vary sentence length, but strive toward shorter ones.* Since Rudolph Flesch changed the style of newspaper writing after World War II, sentences in print are shorter. Flesch suggests that sentences average twenty-three words. Charlie Shedd limits his to fifteen. One writing teacher suggests an average of ten words to a sentence. Shorter sentences read faster. They squeeze out excess verbiage, saying what needs to be said without unnecessary embellishment. Try this: Take one page of your writing and count the words in every sentence. If you find several long sentences, break them up. Cut words. Divide those rambling statements into two sentences.

Flaubert said, "Whenever you can shorten a sentence, do." And one always can. The best sentence? The shortest.

I had difficulty learning to follow Flaubert's advice. I was trained in the academic world where professors lauded lengthy statements and the passive voice. I also discovered that few professors buy books in the inspirational market!

7. *Avoid sesquipedalians.* That is, words a foot and a half long. Your extensive vocabulary may impress your parents and even your three best friends, but *Reader's Digest* aims at people who read on a sixth-grade level. That's about the average level in the United States. Nothing communicates better than simple, direct words. I recognize a hirsute man, but I'd describe him as hairy—everyone understands that.

Polysyllabic words often work against a writer. I have a pastor-friend with a high-caliber vocabulary, which he uses profusely. Although he impresses people, he also intimidates them, making them feel stupid or inferior for not understanding him.

A member of my friend's congregation received a mimeographed letter from the church. The next day she went to his office and said, "I don't understand what you're saying."

The opening sentence read: "At the present point in time, we are undoubtedly aware that our congregation has been experiencing very considerable, potentially explosive expressions of irreconcilable attrition."

"He means," the pastor's secretary said, "that we're losing members and we might lose a lot more." In two simple sentences she explained the rest of the letter.

If you feel compelled to impress people with your vast vocabulary, write letters to the editor. Fill the mails with your erudite syntax as an excellent device to lose contact with old friends. But if you want to communicate, say it in simple, easy-to-understand words.

8. *Keep paragraphs short.* Give your reader plenty of white space on the page. Today's reader already has an information overflow, so make your point quickly. Then move on.

To understand how our paragraphs have shortened pick up a contemporary novel along with one written in a previous century. Compare the white space in each book.

I'll never forget a scene in *Les Miserables* where Valjean climbs over a convent wall. Victor Hugo stops the action by going into a parenthesis, two pages long, describing the wall. No popular writer would get away with that today.

9. *Hoard adjectives.* Limit your use to one per noun. Dole out adverbs sparingly. Descriptive words slow the action down. Use only necessary words.

In the uncorrected proof of a recent novel I found this passage:

> Phinehas shaded his eyes with his arm and stole a *quick* squinting *glance* at the sun. It was only midmorning and already the sun was a glazing white fire, beating down upon the tortured earth and bouncing back into the air in shimmering waves of heat. Only an occasional breeze stirred the barley fields and touched his hot sweaty face with a cool but fleeting caress. Insects hummed and buzzed in the still air. Clusters of tiny gnats hovered around his head; he swatted at them and blew through his mouth in a futile attempt to chase them away. The path was powder-dry, and every step he took sent little clouds of dust swirling up beneath his tunic to cling to his legs and irritate his skin until his sweat turned into rivulets of mud. Birds wheeled and called overhead, sounding cacophony of complaint against the heat and grating on Phinehas' ears. *Little burrowing rodents* scur-

ried across the path, annoying Phinehas with their *smallness* and ability to hide among the sheaves from the relentless glare of the sun.

Phinehas was *hot* and *cross* and *sweaty* and *dirty* . . .
(Mary LaCroix, *The Remnant*, Avon, 1981)

52

I've italicized unnecessary adjectives and relevant nouns. A glance *is* quick. *Little* and *small* mean the same thing. *Rodents* generally refer to small animals such as mice or rats, which we glean from the context. The writer didn't need to say that the rodents burrowed because the sentence tells us that they hide among the sheaves.

The author displays four adjectives about the man: *hot, cross, sweaty,* and *dirty.* We've already picked that up in the previous paragraph.

10. *Hook your reader with the opening sentence.* Start at the highest point of drama in your story. If you're writing about your recovery from a heart attack and what you learned from it, don't begin with a medical history. Start with the action. You can always flash backward as well as move forward. But with a ho-hum beginning, the reader may never give you the chance to tell the exciting part.

How's this for a beginning:

> "You're a dirty nigger-loving Communist." There was a click and the gruff voice was gone. My hands shook and I felt sick at my stomach.
>
> It was just an isolated incident, I thought. I tackled the work piled on my desk and soon felt better. The phone rang again.
>
> "We don't want you around here, Whitey. Get the hell out!"
>
> I went home that night a man without a country. The whites didn't want me and the blacks didn't need me.
> (*Don't Call Me Preacher* by Phil Barnhart, Eerdmans, 1972)

11. *Cut out flabby words.* Good inspirational writing conjures up a lithe figure sprinting across the fields. Flabby writing trudges along, perspiring with each step, burdened by extra poundage. Both reach their destination; the difference lies in the journey.

In flabby writing, words that actually have little value weigh sentences down. (Such as the word *actually* I just used.) Here are others: *so, very, such, a few, just, that, some, at all.*

12. *Limit your use of absolutes.* Because we Christians believe in ultimate answers to life, we tend to hand people ultimate statements. Watch words such as *never, always,* or *totally.* One exception to your statement invalidates what you've said. Here's an example. "Christians have always believed in the trinity." Always? If you make that statment, you've revealed your ignorance of church history. The early theologians debated the issue of the godhead for nearly four centuries!

13. *Don't heap on the guilt.* Inspirational writing means just that: uplifting material that encourages readers. Avoid using *must, ought, should.* When you use those terms, you impose guilt or speak as divine authority. I avoid saying "Everyone ought to read the Bible." I prefer an approach like this: "Daily Bible reading enriches my life. Maybe you would find it enriching, too."

One final tip. Before concluding an article or a chapter, I ask myself one question: *So what?*

Because I am a Christian and because I write for the inspirational market, I want my writing to make a difference in people's lives. Asking "So what?" forces me to rethink my material. Has my writing done more than merely report facts or convey information? Have I given the reader help in facing life? Provoked thinking? Does my chapter enrich or challenge?

CHAPTER FIVE

WHO ARE THE READERS?

by William Gentz

William H. Gentz of New York City, the editor of this book, has been involved in religious publishing for the past quarter-century in several capacities. He has been a book editor for major religious and secular presses. He has worked as a magazine editor, public relations director, and as a parish pastor of Lutheran churches in Wisconsin, California, Oregon, and New York. He is the author or editor of five books including The Religious Writers Marketplace. *He does freelance writing and editing for several publishers and is the editor and publisher of the* Christian Writers Newsletter. *He has been an instructor at writers' conferences in Oregon, California, Kansas, and New Jersey. He also serves as publications director of the Church and Synagogue Library Association.*

ONE OF THE MISTAKES made most often by beginning writers of religious material is to underestimate the great variety of the readers they are writing for. Even the seasoned religious writer is often unaware of the vast audience waiting out there. This is true of writers in all fields, but perhaps because the religious market is more fragmented and specialized, writers are apt to get into the rut of aiming for one special audience and missing the manifold opportunities that are as near as their typewriters.

Thus, when this book was planned, I insisted on this chapter being near the front of the book. I'm convinced that no one can reliably write marketable material unless he has a definite reader in mind. Each of the chapters of this book and especially chapters 8, 14, and 16 will detail for you special audiences for which you are writing: this chapter is an overview of the great variety of people who read religious material in one form or another.

Let's look, then, at the audience, or more correctly, audiences, for which religious materials are being produced. The one key word is variety.

VARIETY OF AGES

One of the ways readers of religious material can be classified is by age. From the moment that a child can look at a picture or a page of words and make sense of it, that child is a "reader" of religious material. As is pointed out in Chapter 13, many publishers are producing materials for a very young age— "lap books" as they are sometimes called. These are usually purchased by parents or grandparents to read to the youngest children on the age scale. To write for this age group, for example, one must have the interests, needs, and capabilities of small children clearly in mind. This is so obvious, it hardly seems necessary to say it here, but my years spent as an editor who received piles of unsolicited material in the mail every day taught me that a good many writers do not understand this principle at all or seem to forget it when they sit down at their typewriters. If you're writing for very young children and don't happen to have any preschoolers around the house to try things out on, or haven't had experience with this group, you can get some firsthand knowledge fast by volunteering to teach this age group in your Sunday school or vacation Bible school. Or perhaps there are other places in your community where you can "get inside the heads" of your potential audience.

What I've just said about very young children applies to each age group. The concepts, ideas, and religious truths in your writing must be appropriate for the age you're aiming for. These gradations have been worked out well by the specialists in religious education and are based on sound psychological knowledge of each age group. So if you're writing for a particular age group—say juniors, ages nine to eleven, grades four to six—learn all you can about this group; get acquainted with some children of this age. Test your ideas with them, talk to their teachers, get some opinions from people who know (if you don't) and then write your material to fit this group. Choose words that are within their grasp. If you are unsure about this, graded vocabulary lists are available. Also make sure to deal with religious concepts that this age group can understand. For example, juniors need concrete ideas and images instead of abstract words. The word "sin" may mean little to juniors, but if you talk about stealing, or cheating, or lying, they will understand. Be sure to give examples of what you are talking about.

Don't overlook the fact that adults, too, come in varieties of ages. They range from sixteen (high schoolers do read adult books and magazines) to 100 or thereabouts. The religious market publishes material for people all along this age scale. A college-age person's reading will be quite different from that of a person in middle age or a senior citizen. This top age group, by the way, is fast becoming the largest group in our population, and much reading material is being produced for them.

So when writing religious material, be very conscious of the age for which you are writing—even among adults. Publishers and editors in the religious field are very specific about this. If you follow their example they will bless you for it and, more important, they will buy what you offer.

SEX DIFFERENCES

Religious readers are both men and women, boys and girls. A perfectly obvious division, often neglected by writers. As you will discover in your study of the markets, many publications are designed specifically for these different sex groups. Chapter 14 deals with this in detail. In all cases keep the sex of your readers clearly in mind if you are writing for publications that cater to one group or the other. If this is not clear from the title of the magazine or journal, the author's guidelines will spell it out for you.

Equally important to remember when you are writing for a publication that includes both men and women among its readers is to think of both sexes as you write. Many reader surveys, including those of the religious market, will tell you that women read more than men, but this does not mean that everything should be written from the point of view of women. Address both sexes in the material you write. Consider their interests, points of view, and needs. One of the reasons that men have not read religious material as avidly as women is that they are left out in the minds of the writers and it shows in the material produced. The sex of the reader is vitally important to the writer of religious material.

It is equally dangerous to leave out women when you write. Sometimes this is done unintentionally. The feminist movement has brought to everyone's attention the fact that our language is often sexist—referring only to the male when we mean both sexes, for example. It's extremely important in the religious market to remember this. Most English translations of the Bible were done when sexist language wasn't questioned, and the hymns of the church and much of Christian literature have picked up these biblical images. The writer of religious material today can be of great help in broadening the appeal to both sexes by being careful to use pronouns and other words that are nonsexist in nature. A number of publishers have made studies of this issue and have suggested word lists and ways of solving the problem. Ask for help on this from your editor or find it in your library. Many of your readers, and thus your editors, will be very sensitive to sexist language. It is more important than ever that the writer reflects *his or her* knowledge of this fact.

VARIETIES OF FAITH

Unless you have lived a very isolated life, it should be quite obvious also that religious beliefs come in an infinite variety. If you are writing for the religious market, you must study carefully and investigate in detail the particular set of beliefs of the readers for whom your material is being written.

When first entering the religious field, writers are tempted to think of the "Christian market" as one homogeneous group. Not at all! Although there is a core of Christian teaching that is common to all members of the body of believers, and therefore all its publications, Christians have many different shades of belief, different ways of worshipping, different ways of expressing their faith, and they are known by different names and labels. They also have differing vocabularies—an essential item for the writer to be aware of. There are at least three factors that we should be concerned with under this heading of "faith": denominations to which people belong, emphases within and across those denominations, and the commitment on the part of each individual. Let's look at these carefully.

Denominations. In some ways this is the most obvious way to tell the difference between Christians and therefore identify the particular person for whom you're writing. It may seem like an impossible task if you look at a list such as that contained in the *Yearbook of American and Canadian Churches* which shows that there are 232 separate national church organizations in the United States alone! This is not quite as discouraging as it would appear, however, since most of these national bodies can be classified into about a dozen "families" of churches—such as Baptist, Methodist, Lutheran, Presbyterian, Churches of God, etc. But even this shorter list presents a problem for the writer. Though he need not have intimate knowledge of a denominational group in order to write for a particular church publication, an understanding of some of the basic differences between denominations is a high priority.

A good encyclopedia of religious knowledge or perhaps several should be on every inspirational writer's bookshelf. Before you write even a query letter to a publication that is affiliated with a denomination or sponsored by that group, look it up in the encyclopedia. Know at least some of the basic doctrines of the church; know something of its history; know its general theological position on the scale of liberal-moderate-conservative-fundamentalist. Most important, familiarize yourself with the terminology of the group. This will prevent, for example, your calling a local church a "parish" if you are writing for a Baptist or Methodist publication, although this is the common word among Catholics, Lutherans, and Episcopalians. Some knowledge of doctrine also will prevent your assuming something like Infant Baptism with a group that insists on "Believer's Baptism" by immersion. This kind of background will help you know what not to say as much as what to say, which is essential for the Christian writer.

Do learn the fundamental doctrinal emphasis of a church before you try to write for its publications. At the very least, look up information on the denominational background of the publication or publisher for whom you're writing. Find out if it's sponsored or has a commitment to any one group. Let the editor know both in your letters and your copy that you understand this and that you're writing with this point of view in mind.

Emphasis. Growing out of differing denominational positions on basic Christian beliefs and yet superseding them in many ways is the larger question of the theological or spiritual emphasis of a publication. By this I mean, where does it stand on questions of the inspiration of the Bible, the person of Jesus Christ, the process by which one becomes a Christian, and so forth? There are many differences among Christians, who take either conservative or liberal stands on all of these points. These emphases cut across denominational lines. Both "evangelicals" and "liberals" can be found in almost any of the denominations and their constituent churches. Therefore, you need to know a publication's emphasis as well as its denomination to know who its readers are. What you write may be intended to move them from that position, one way or the other, but know first of all where they are so that you can intelligently reach them. Here again, the words you use are important and can help or hinder your attempt to address them and to be understood and accepted.

A Christian writer today should, as far as possible, also be aware of the current movements within religion. For example, you can hardly write for the religious market today without some knowledge of the charismatic movement. This movement, which stresses the action of the Holy Spirit among Christians, is a part of every denomination today, Protestant and Catholic. The gifts of healing, speaking in tongues, and other "glossalalia" (one word you should know) associated in the past only with the pentecostal denominations now have a place in every major group. Charismatics hold large conferences annually and in some cities there are weekly meetings as well. In addition, there are some publications and publishing operations that cater exclusively to the charismatic movement.

A broader and more inclusive emphasis is variously known as the "evangelical" or "born again" movement. National secular magazines such as *Time* and *Newsweek* have analyzed this movement and its effect on all of our population. Any Christian writer, whether or not he or she wants to be considered a part of this movement, needs to know the basics of the evangelical point of view. There are many books and magazines that can give you the background and current trends of this historical movement and keep you abreast of what is happening. Reading this literature will also help you learn the language peculiar to those influenced by this emphasis. Here, too, you must learn what not to say as well as what to say, what words to use if you want to reach readers in this group.

Two words of caution in this connection. You can't assume that because a magazine and its readers are in the evangelical camp they will all believe exactly the same on all points of doctrine. There are wide differences between evangelicals, too. Secondly, just as there are readers who are looking for materials written from the evangelical point of view, there are many others, and therefore some publications, who are completely turned off by this point of view and this kind of language which is foreign to them. It is essential, again, that you have the religious emphasis of the reader very clearly in mind as you write.

Commitment. Knowing where your readers are on the scale of individual commitment to the Christian faith is probably the most important and difficult readership question of all. Sometimes it is easy to determine this by the subject you are writing on or by the nature of the publication the material is intended for. But when writing for the larger and more general publications it is often much more difficult. Nevertheless this is an important characteristic of the reader of which you must be aware.

Analyzing the commitment of readers is much like knowing what age your readers are—in this case we are talking about "spiritual" age—the religious commitment of the readers you are addressing. At the top of the scale we find those people whose life is completely dedicated to the Christian cause—the clergy and other religious career persons. Some publications are intended specifically for these people and when you are writing for these, you can assume intense commitment.

To write for this group you often need to have sufficient background and training but on the other hand, the clergy and religious are also anxious to read the point of view of the laity. If you're planning to write for them, get to know something of their life and interests. Study their publications. Ask questions of the people that you know in this group. Test your knowledge and point of view before you submit your writing. Learn their vocabulary. But remember, too, that this vocabulary is not static. It changes from year to year with the trends in religious thinking. Therefore you need to keep abreast of theological developments through your own reading of books and magazines in this field.

Next on this scale is the vast audience of deeply committed Christians who are not professionals but volunteers in the work of spreading the Gospel, either within or outside of the Christian church—such as Sunday school teachers, choir members, church officers, church librarians, and so on down the list of the hundreds of ways in which Christians express their faith in action.

If you're writing for this group, it should be quite easy to get to know them. They are visible in every congregation. You may be a member of this group yourself. If not, seek them out in your church. Find out their ideas, their problems, their needs so that you can address them in your writing. Read the publications written for them before you attempt to write for this group. Know what has been written, what needs to be written. Here again, study the trends you see emerging among these volunteers in the work of the church. Know their concerns. As you sit at your typewriter, have a very definite person in mind, such as a Sunday school teacher, a deacon, trustee, or other church officer, or perhaps the president of the church's women's group. Picture that person before you as you write to that person's interests and needs.

Another group of readers are those whose lives are committed to the cause but who feel the need of regular inspiration or instruction. They need to find within their own experience and daily tasks new places where they can apply their faith. The majority of Christian publications you find listed in the market guides are attempting to reach this large group of religious readers. We are describing here the readership of the more general religious publications. Included among them, of course, are the two groups described above—the career Christians and the active volunteers—who need their faith bolstered just as much as anyone. As a writer you probably find yourself in this category, too, and will find it easy to sit down at your typewriter and "talk" on paper to your fellow-Christians who have interests and needs very similar to your own.

Among the readers of Christian literature there is another group who might be classed as "doubters" or to use an old-fashioned word, "backsliders." These are the people who were schooled in the faith but who somehow have neglected their Christianity for some time or have turned off for one reason or another and are no longer as committed as they once were. Every Christian magazine to a certain extent considers these people a part of their potential readership. Some magazines and publishers lay a heavier emphasis on this group of readers than others. But to all, such people are important and you as a writer must be aware of where this group is coming from as they read what you write. You may, in fact, want to address some of your writing squarely to this group to help them overcome the doubts they have about the Christian faith and the church. If you know people who fit this description, try to learn their feelings, their reasons for their present state of mind and keep this before you as you write.

Closely related to the "doubters" are those with specific spiritual problems. They are basically committed to Christianity, but they are struggling with a problem or problems within their own lives and this may have turned them off from the faith. An example of such a reader might be a Christian who's married to someone to whom the faith means nothing. Or an individual may be attempting to overcome some other situation in his or her life that's become a roadblock to happiness and contentment. You may want to write about some such specific situations. If you do, you'll want to become as familiar as possible with the particulars of such an experience. You will want to study how such situations have been overcome by other people. You may have had personal experience with a similar situation. Be sure you are understanding and helpful in your approach. People with problems are easily put off by judgmental writing or by terminology that's so specifically religious it seems irrelevant to their own life and problems.

A portion of your readership as a Christian writer will be those who are strangers to the faith—the unconverted, or those who have little or no knowledge of what the Christian faith is all about or what it can mean to them. Many magazines feel a definite need for material addressed to this group. If they do and you feel inspired to write for them, you will find a ready market for your writing. However, this is a difficult group to reach, and you need to take a good deal of care to do the kind of writing that will appeal to them. These readers need to be convinced by example of how their lives can be enriched by the Christian faith. You need to show them how others have experienced change and improvement. The approach should be *show* not *tell*. If you are successful, you will have the reward of knowing that this group of outsiders has been reached—one of the most satisfying experiences in the life of a Christian writer.

HUMAN DIFFERENCES

There are other distinctions, of course, among the readers of religious material. These are the differences that exist in all groups of people, but they are equally important to the religious writer. Your readers' occupation, educational level, economic status, the area of the country or the kind of place (urban, rural) in which they live, their racial or ethnic background are all important in your writing. These facts are important not only to know the interests of the reader, but knowing these you can find ways to apply the Christian faith to their daily experiences.

A quarter of a century of sitting behind a desk labeled "editor" has taught me one basic fact about writing that is as applicable in the religious market as anywhere. *In order to write salable material, the writer must have a very specific audience in mind.* The closer you can come to seeing this audience as a single person, the better off you are. After all, once your words have become type on a page, you will be on a one-to-one relationship with your reader. As you sit at your typewriter you should keep this specific audience and preferably one person in mind. If you do, you are a long way on the road to success in being a *published* author who will be read with profit. Christian writing is an evangelism of sorts; to be effective you must have a clear concept of the person you are addressing with your typewriter.

You can find examples of this in your Bible. This is exactly what the Apostle Paul, the prolific writer of the New Testament, did when he sat down and took pen in hand or dictated to a scribe who sat with him in his prison cell. Every letter begins with a salutation such as "to the saints who are at Ephesus" or "to all saints in Christ Jesus who are at Philippi with the bishops and deacons." Paul had a specific solution for specific problems in each of these cities to which he wrote. He also often named people to whom he wanted to be remembered. When we read Paul's epistles today, we must look at the individuals to whom they were addressed before we can understand what he is saying.

Every good editor knows the audience for whom his publication is being produced. Every successful publishing house knows in detail (it's called "market research") the kind of people for whom its books and other materials are being prepared. When an editor reads your material he looks not for the message *he* wants to see or what *he* enjoys reading—instead he looks at everything through the eyes of his readers. Therefore, in order to persuade an editor to consider your material, much less purchase it, you must have a good idea of the person for whom you are writing.

Before you write for a publication, especially if you plan to do a great deal of writing for a particular journal or publisher, find out if any demographic study has been made of their readership. Most magazines do this for the benefit of their advertisers so that they can know whether their product will appeal to the readers or not. This information usually is also available to writers if they ask for it. Take advantage of this to help you get to know your readers. Your editor will be happy to help you in the process as long as you don't make unreasonable demands on his time for the information.

Discovering the particular religious interests of his readers is essential to the religious writer, and I can't stress this too much. On the other hand, I don't want to give the impression that readers of religious material are all that different from other people. They are human beings with the needs and interests common to all of us.

The guidelines you find in other literature for writers about how to appeal to the interests of the reader apply in this field as well. Believers have all of the feelings, needs, emotions, prejudices, and interests that other people do. Much of the material received by editors of religious publications shows that writers haven't learned this lesson too well. Many of the writers of religious articles and books have the impression that in writing for this market one can forget the human factor. If we put our thoughts in the right theological sequence, use the accepted religious formulas, write in the approved religious language, or quote the right Bible verses, our writing will reach the Christian reader. Nothing could be further from the truth! Lack of human interest accounts for a large share of the rejections received by religious writers.

As writers of other chapters of this book point out, the basic rules of good writing apply as much in the religious field as any other. Your writing must be so interesting, so exciting, so vital, that the editor and eventually the reader will read it to the end. These are human beings to whom you are writing. They will respond to your writing only if you meet them where they are, appeal to what they're interested in, manage to make them see the importance of your ideas for *them*.

The diversity of interests among readers of religious books is reflected in the following paragraph which was made into a poster several years ago by the Religious Publishing Division of the Association of American Publishers:

> Religious books are also about love, sex, politics, war, peace, ecology, theology, philosophy, drugs, race, dissent, ethics, technology, morality, revolution, rock, God, beauty, psychology, dogma, the underground, the establishment, death, and . . . life.

Consult the human in yourself as you write. Ask yourself if you would be interested in reading what you've just written. Try to have a very definite person in mind every time you put your fingers on the keys. It's the only way your writing will meet the need of your readers and make a difference to the people out there.

What you write may be just the inspiration needed by a father to help a teenage son or daughter find Christian purpose in life. Your words may be the last bit of stimulus needed to make a busy working mother find time to apply her talents to a Sunday school class. Your article may bring comfort and encouragement to a senior citizen in the loneliness of a nursing home. Who knows where your words will be read, who may be drawn closer to God as a result?

CHAPTER SIX

WRITING TO INSPIRE

by Dina Donohue

Dina Donohue of San Diego, California, has broad experience in both writing and editing in the inspirational field. She has been with Guideposts magazine for nearly thirty years—formerly a senior editor and now a contributing editor. The author of many stories, articles, and children's books, she is a frequent workshop leader at writers' conferences throughout the country. She serves as a judge for numerous writers' contests, including the one that is conducted annually by Guideposts. She also writes book reviews for a national trade book magazine and is an editor with the Don Tanner Literary Associates.

WORDS THAT SING, words that stir, and 65

words that stay make for a memorable story. And *stories* are the heart of inspirational writing.

Many people have been moved by the dramatic account of Joni Eareckson and how she surmounted a tragic disabling accident to become an accomplished artist or by the story of how Corrie ten Boom lived her faith despite great trials during Nazi persecutions and in the years since. Readers have found hope for their own problems in Joni's and Corrie's experiences. True, their lives were exceptionally traumatic, but their stories serve as vivid examples of inspirational writing.

A positive statement that might please my boss of twenty-nine years, Dr. Norman Vincent Peale, the power of positive thinking editor-publisher of *Guideposts* with his wife Ruth: Your inspirational material has a wide market. Religious and secular publications present inspirational poetry, articles, fiction, and books for adults, young people, and children.

WHAT IS INSPIRATIONAL WRITING?

Have you ever finished a story or an article and said to yourself, "I wish I had the perseverance or the compassion or the courage of that author"? If you have, the chances are that you just read an inspirational piece. It is one that appeals to the finer emotions of the reader and challenges him to try to emulate the characters in the story, to be or to do good.

The scope of themes for such writing is impressive. It might be the story of a major league ballplayer's struggle to overcome drug addiction, or the suspenseful account of an injured woman trapped in her home, or how a dedicated teacher salvaged "uneducable" children. These are all themes of recent inspirational stories in *Guideposts*. Usually these problems or dangers were met through a reliance on God, with the author telling how prayer or faith helped in the solution.

It is a question of semantics, perhaps, but inspirational writing doesn't have to be what is generally called "religious" writing. Most inspirational writing is God-centered, but you may have a compelling inspirational story or article that does not mention God or the Bible, prayer or faith. Many religious pieces, concerned with theological issues, church matters, or Bible interpretations, are teaching pieces and do not have the drama of an inspirational story.

When faith does play a part in your story, don't hesitate to present it. But never drag religion in simply to justify yourself as a Christian writer. Spirituality should be evident in your caring, your feelings, your awareness of others. An inspirational story should be as well written as a secular one. You don't have to be a Bible scholar, although some knowledge is helpful, depending on the story you're trying to tell. For the evangelical press, Bible orientation and Bible stress are necessary, but for much of the market they are not.

Using a Bible verse doesn't make your story religious or inspirational. Yet very often it's just such an epigraph that motivates the author or character to achieve his goal. This motivation, plus facts to support it, is important for a well-balanced piece. On the other hand, a story heavy with dogma or theological interpretations will probably not be accepted by most inspirational or religious magazines or publishers.

"Showing" is of paramount importance for all writing, but particularly for the inspirational story. It's easy to write "Alice Scott was lonesome when her husband died. She couldn't get used to living alone in the house. She missed Fred." Sorry, that isn't enough. The reader wants to *see* Alice in action. "Those first few weeks after the funeral were difficult for Alice Scott. Sometimes, coming back from shopping, she'd forget for a moment and call out, 'I'm home, Fred.' She couldn't bear the silence and turned on the radio. She left it on for hours, not listening, just trying to fill the emptiness."

Don't be afraid of honest emotion. Very often it is the ingredient that sets an inspirational story apart from a secular one. Depict fear if it exists or happiness or sorrow when it is appropriate to the theme. As Paul said: *"Rejoice with them that do rejoice, and weep with them that weep"* (Romans 12:15). This doesn't mean that you, the author, should be overly sentimental or maudlin. There is great power in underplaying a sad or happy situation. The imporant thing is to be emotionally honest.

Above all, inspirational writing lets us use our creative talents to help our fellowman and to serve God. Albert Schweitzer once complained, "People are always asking me for something they can do in Africa. But there is so much they can do right where they are." We can serve as missionaries for God through our words.

THE SPECIAL INGREDIENTS

There are three special ingredients for the inspirational piece, whether you are writing for the religious or secular market.

1. *Reader Involvement.* Articles and stories need a theme that relates to the reader's life or problems. One of the first things a writer has to do is bring the reader into the story. This means total involvement—as John Allen of *Reader's Digest* has said, involve "mind, emotions, heart, and senses."

Thus a reader will see herself or friends in the story, will be able to say, "Why, that's exactly how my daughter acts," when she reads about a seventeen-year-old who declares her independence of home influences. The ordeal of a man taken hostage during a robbery may not be anything a reader has ever experienced. Yet if the writing is vivid, the reader becomes involved. He feels the man's fear and shares in his panic. "That might happen to me" is the unspoken thought.

2. *Reader Dividend.* You should provide a practical plus: a message of hope or courage, a how-to that will help the reader in his own life. The story of the teenager might suggest to parents that they need to provide the more mature youngster with more responsibility. The way the man held hostage conquered his fear might help readers overcome their own fears, whatever they may be.

An article in the April 1981 *Moody Monthly* tells how a family is courageously coping with the father's leukemia. It will doubtless give other readers insights on how to handle any serious health problems they may face. The article, "A Faith Leukemia Can't Shake," by Kay Oliver Lewis, has all the ingredients of an inspirational piece.

3. *Spiritual or Moral Value.* For a stronger inspirational effect, add a spiritual or moral plus to your story to give it a dimension that goes beyond information or entertainment. This can be a moving conversion experience, a victory over temptation, or a story in which the author felt the presence of God in a special way. The account should stir some emotional response in the reader.

You don't need to include all three elements in a single story. Since there is an occasional overlapping, two of the three points would serve. But you do need to give specific facts. Show how a character overcame a difficulty—not through a mere "he prayed" but with the actual prayer. "Dear Lord," he cried, "I need help badly. I'm afraid to face my boss tomorrow and tell him I've stolen from petty cash, but I want to get straight with him. Help me to have courage." Be careful to avoid a "preachy" approach—good anecdotes and examples tell a story better than introspective narrative does.

KNOW YOURSELF—YOU, THE WRITER

Who you are is important to your inspirational writing. Ask yourself some questions and answer honestly: Do you like people? Are you concerned about the hungry, the hurting, the lonely—not just theoretically, intellectually, or merely spiritually concerned, but moved to do something to alleviate the distress in some way?

If you feel deeply about someone or some problem, if you want your writing to be more than just a way to gain fame or recognition or money (not that there's anything wrong with that), you are a good candidate for inspirational writing.

As a teenager I had two unhappy experiences with suicides; one was my roommate at boarding school. Because I was disturbed by these unnecessary deaths, when I became a writer I did articles on the subject and on ways to prevent suicide. Likewise, because a friend has a retarded child, I became a volunteer worker to help the retarded. I also wrote stories to try to improve understanding and conditions for them.

Get involved in church and community organizations. Desire and talent aren't enough to be a good writer. Unless we're exceptional, we need contact with others. Personal concern will give us a strong motivation to write inspirational material.

Be involved with life, with people and their problems; listen to the hurting; help if you can. When you're happy, show it in your life and in your writing. When you're unhappy, troubled, learn from it. Help yourself by calling on God or Bible promises or friends or your own strength. Every experience can be a potential story. Yet it has to have appeal and meaning to readers, not just to you. Remember the greatest pitfall of the personal-experience story: conceit. Not everything you think or believe or live through is important or interesting to others. Try to write your story so that you are not the hero. In the inspirational piece, God is the hero. It's important to keep a sense of balance, of humility.

We all have in our own lives and the lives of those about us many happenings that hold ideas for inspirational stories. We need to learn how to find and recognize them.

I gave a *Guideposts* subscription to a friend who's a published author. The first issue she received contained a story about the miraculous escape of a family during a tornado that devastated the countryside. My writer-friend phoned me to say she had had a similar experience but hadn't thought of it as a possible story.

Train yourself to see stories in events about you and in your past. Not all need to be as dramatic as Joni's accident or the suicide of my schoolmate or the tornado. Use the I-remember technique to recall incidents that might have story potential. Start with the words *I remember* and add different situations: I remember a loyal friend, or a day of terror, or the teacher who made the greatest impression on me, or I remember my favorite gift, or my most embarrassing moment. The story possibilities are endless.

You might be surprised at your answers, find stories you never considered. Last year when *Guideposts* was preparing a Christmas book, I used the *I-remember* procedure to recall and write up my visit to an orphanage with my daughter's Girl Scout troop some years ago. One of the little boys to whom we gave toys put his package away without opening it.

"My daddy is looking for a mommy for me," he told me. "When he finds one, I'll play with my toy. Then we'll have Christmas."

From this child I learned a new definition of Christmas: Being with family is "having Christmas."

Short inspirational pieces are welcomed not only at *Guideposts*, but also at many other magazines. Don't neglect them while you're waiting to publish your inspirational novel or to sell your full-length article to a major magazine.

When you find a memory that you think might have universal appeal, it's important to remember in developing it that there must be a single theme and a change, a lesson or a message for the reader. Be careful you don't present a much-ado-about-nothing story that is actually more of a scene than a story. A story usually calls for a problem, a conflict, and a resolution. This is particularly true when you're writing nostalgia material—more about this later.

I've said that you can also find stories in people about you: neighbors, coworkers, family, friends. Develop a keen power of observation, a sense of story, and a concern for others. Then, when you meet people, read a news story, or hear an anecdote, you will automatically ask yourself, "Is it a story? Could it help or inspire readers?"

WALK IN ANOTHER'S SHOES

If you're writing another's story under his byline, be sure you really know your character. *Walk in his shoes* for a while. I've always enjoyed this type of writing for both fiction and articles. I have been a Jewish man whose doctor-son is ashamed of him, a gambler, an unhappy housewife, an Irish bachelor whose mother resents his marrying a widow with two children.

Before writing someone else's story, study his speech patterns. This is where your listening skills help you. If you happen to be a teacher and your character is an uneducated man, let the dialogue be true to your subject, not erudite as you might be.

Conversely, you can write the story of someone who has more formal education than you do. Just be sure you follow the individual's speech patterns. You don't need a college education to write.

I remember a story submitted to *Guideposts* by a prisoner in a women's jail. She had limited education but wrote in a very simple, sincere style. We published the story exactly as she wrote it. It was a lovely story about Gladys, another inmate. Both were serving time for serious crimes. The two women worked in the prison laundry and one chore was washing baby clothes for inmates who had had their children in the prison hospital. Gladys insisted on doing a good rinsing job even when guards yelled at her to hurry. She didn't want the babies to get diaper rash. As Gladys worked, she told the author about God. It moved me that this prisoner, separated from her own children, was concerned for other babies and also took time to share her faith with a fellow-inmate.

Developing an understanding of the other's viewpoint, philosophy, and beliefs is even more important than showing authentic speech patterns and actions true to the other person's lifestyle. The emotional depth of an individual will be revealed in an inspirational story and you want to be as true a reporter as possible. This is particularly important when presenting your subject's religious feelings.

DON'T BE JUST A "HURTING PERSON"

Many authors of inspirational stories are what I term "hurting people." Their motivation to tell their stories is good but, unfortunately, their experiences are often similar to those in hundreds of other manuscripts that appear on editors' desks.

They have survived a disaster and want to share it. They have lost a spouse and want to share it. They have faced trouble or danger and want to share it. There is nothing wrong with this, but sometimes it's necessary to stand away for a while and let the experience take on more dimension, view it from a distance. I often advise such authors that they're too close to their story at this time, and a short wait before writing it might result in a more well-rounded manuscript.

Some editors say, "Write your story, get it out of your system, then put it away and write something else." As you can see, not all editors agree.

I know that editors receive many stories of personal tragedies. Some do get used, but they are the exceptional ones, those with great reader identification and an explicit message of hope.

A book I recently reviewed for a national trade magazine—*Jonathan You Left Too Soon*—was written by one of those hurting people, David B. Biebel, a minister whose three-year-old son became mysteriously ill, deteriorated rapidly, and suddenly died. The author did wait before he told the story of his feelings of guilt, inadequacy, and doubt. By waiting, he was able o give us not only a poignant story of a child's death, but also the story of how a father came to grips with his own soul-searching. The result was a book that is helpful to others who face loss or who counsel those who do.

Not all inspirational stories have to have a happy ending. A story becomes inspirational not because a child was cured or a paralyzed man recovered the use of his limbs, but because the individuals were able to accept their disability or loss and do the best with what they had. When we tell the reader *how* this was accomplished, the reader is helped in his own problem areas. Sometimes he doesn't even need this application: He is inspired just by the sharing of courage and faith and hope.

To be a good inspirational writer, you need an open mind, open heart, and open ears. My 3-L technique can help you here.

LOOK, LISTEN, LEARN

Look! Observe life about you and record unusual attitudes, personalities, and appearances in your notebook (most writers carry one with them to jot down impressions and/or story ideas, quotations, etc.). These can be used to bring life to your fiction. I also look for stories and ideas in newspapers, books, and magazines. I am a great clipper and encourage other writers to be also. Keep an expanding file with subtitles of subjects that interest you. I've written many articles from items that appeared in local papers and even in trade magazines. (Of course, that's just getting the idea. To develop your idea into a story, you have to do homework, get additional information, send a query letter, and obtain an interview.) I also read letters to the editor and the personal columns.

Once, my attention was caught by a notice in the personal column of a newspaper. It read: "Teddy F. J. Merry Christmas, darling, wherever you are. Please write. We love you. Mother and Dad."

As a mother and a grandmother, I was moved by these poignant words and wondered: How could a parent, spouse, or child find a missing person? Intrigued, I researched ways of tracing lost persons and wrote an article "Wherever You Are . . . " showing the work of such agencies as the Salvation Army.

Even after working at *Guideposts* for twenty-nine years and reading thousands of sad stories, I still am moved by a poignant tale. I think readers are also stirred by those who suffer and those who reach out to help them. Recently I read a United Press International story about two terminally ill little boys and their dreams. One wanted to be a police officer, the other a fireman. Both boys had their wishes granted by law enforcement officers, doctors, firemen, and many other caring people who got together and gave the boys special uniforms. Volunteers in the Chris Greicius Make-A-Wish Foundation (named for the first little boy they helped) have made dreams come true for other ill children.

Listen to conversations. Authors, like other people, tend to do much of the talking, but listening can provide not only human interest and information, but also story material. This is true in social life as well as in community and organization work. Be alert in church for anecdotes or stories. You can garner many interesting views from sermons that might spark your interest in writing on the subject. As in all your clippings and notes on quotations, be sure to indicate the source of the material and give credit when necessary.

Listening will also enhance your ability to write realistic dialogue. As a good listener you'll soon notice that people interrupt each other, that some speakers rush their words whereas others pause or repeat certain phrases. An awareness of speech idiosyncrasies is especially helpful when you are writing fiction.

Learn from every experience. Any information you discover can help you as a writer. If you have an area of expertise, study that field for possible stories. For instance, if you've been a nurse or aide in a home for the elderly and have a story or article about such an institution, be sure to state your background in your cover or query letter to a magazine. It gives you the voice of authority. Your work experiences can help greatly in writing fiction as well as articles. I have worked in doctors' offices and in concert management and have used those settings in stories.

Most of the following discussion is aimed at magazine articles but would also apply to other forms of inspirational writing, including books; the categories are similar.

TYPES OF INSPIRATIONAL WRITING

Personal experience.

I like this type and find it easy to write. In this form I include writing someone else's story in the first person under his byline without your name or, depending on the magazine's policy, adding a "with" or "as told to" and then your name.

The most successful personal-experience story evokes warm emotion in the reader, gives a lift to the spirit or hope for the future—makes him feel that life is worthwhile.

Again, to find stories let your mind wander back through your life to isolate experiences that would possibly provide a strong theme. Seek out incidents where you had to make a critical decision or had a problem with motivation, as well as the more dramatic situations.

The personal-experience story has an excellent market with a wide range of publications. Some magazines have special features and even contests from time to time, such as *Today's Christian Woman's* feature, "The Turning Point."

A personal experience should be told in narrative form and show how the problems or events were handled. Often the author, in trouble or sorrow, finds he is unable to help himself and turns to prayer or God. A sense of calm or peace might replace dejection or despair. Use anecdotes and dialogue to advance the story. Avoid sermonizing and preaching. The spiritual point is made through the actions of the individual, not a recitation of beliefs. In other words, use the familiar concept of show, don't tell.

If the the subject of your story warrants anonymity, you may use a pen name with the editor's permission. An editor's note will usually state "name has been changed."

There are a number of special categories within personal-experience writing. They can also be third-person accounts, since there are many ways to present a story. Here are a few of the more popular types.

Recovery-Coping

Stories of recovery from illness, injury, or a handicap are perennially popular with authors, but the market is flooded with such stories, as well as tributes to the dead. This doesn't mean that such stories won't be published, just that they're more difficult to sell. *Yours* might be the one that is exceptional. The September 1981 issue of *Guideposts* carried a story that had the three ingredients for an inspirational piece. It was by Cherry Boone O'Neill entitled "A Different Kind of Weight Problem." Cherry was raised in a Christian home (her father is Pat Boone), but her problem was one of obsessive eating habits that led to a dangerous weight loss.

The important point to remember in telling a story concerned with illness is not to give too many gory medical details, just enough so that the reader knows the situation. It's essential to present all the facts about how you overcame or faced the problem. This Cherry did in her story, seeking and finding help from doctors and scripture.

"I had to learn to accept myself as loved and lovable with all my shortcomings as well as strengths," she wrote. Many teenagers have the same problem, so Cherry's story will have impact on others. An information box giving warning signs of anorexia nervosa and where to find help followed Cherry's personal story.

Involve your reader in the problem, make him care about what happens, let him feel your pain or your victory. Setting scenes, using dialogue to advance the story, and showing conflict will bring your experience to life. It's a story, not a case history to be told in cold, clinical terms.

Self-Help

These may overlap the handicap-coping story but are more often concerned with how you solved a personality problem: overcame fear, loneliness, widowhood, a boring job situation. Some self-help stories deal with problems of addiction: alcohol, drugs, gambling, pornography. The way to overcoming is almost always through the individual's own realization that he has to do something. There may be an outside source to provide impetus: a caring family member, the example of a Christian friend, or a spiritual prodding from devotional or Bible reading. The author should cite how he was influenced, his own determination to change, and the steps he took to achieve the goal. Again, specifics add to the power of the story and provide help for a reader with a similar problem.

Last year, *Insight* magazine printed a story about a young man who was addicted to reading porno books and watching such films. He realized he was wrong and told what he did to break the habit. Prayer played a part in his recovery. The article had the three ingredients for a helpful, inspirational story.

Relationships

The theme of healed relationships is one we like to see in *Guideposts* stories. Other magazines also present them. Such a story is essentially an account of a deteriorating relationship between two individuals or a group of people. Often there is an actual confrontation, followed by alienation. This brings on unhappiness. A story about friction between church members, for example, shows how the participants were able to settle the disagreements. An important word in repairing a broken relationship is "forgiveness."

The key elements of a relationship story are the problem, how it affects the people involved, the decision to try to rectify the situation, facts on how this was done, and the outcome. A relationship story should have an emotional tug and provide help and insight.

This type of story is easy for most of us to write. A story in "The Turning Point" feature I mentioned earlier was about how a wife coped with an older relative who came to live in her home. Subject matter might also come from employer-worker problems or a difficulty with neighbors. We had a story in *Guideposts* that simply concerned a barking dog and how the annoyance was resolved through Christian understanding. Readers can identify with such themes.

Family-relationship stories are popular in Christian publications and also in secular women's magazines. Many books are also written on the subject: how to discipline, coping with a desperately ill child, the problems and joys of adopting older children, caring for aged parents.

Nostalgia

This kind of article is also fairly easy to write if you delve deeply into your background. In a sense, any nostalgia piece is inspirational if it involves the reader in the memory. One grave error is common in would-be nostalgia pieces: The authors relate an experience that has great meaning to them but very little for the reader. Often the problem is simply the way the story has been told, or the details the author has chosen to highlight. A key word to remember for a nostalgia story, as for any other, is *change*. There should be some element of change, whether of habits, beliefs, lifestyle, or simply a change in attitude. It is important that something *happens*.

It isn't enought just to tell us, as so many do, about the wonderful meals your grandmother cooked at Thanksgiving time. Perhaps you've always remembered one special meal because at its end, Grandma had announced that she was returning home to Ireland to live and most of the family would never see her again. Grandma had then asked everyone to join hands while she thanked God for her wonderful family. You must tell how this moved or influenced you so the reader can share your experience, and perhaps learn something applicable to his own life. In this type of writing especially, the author must be aware of the readers he addresses—their ages, interests, backgrounds, spiritual maturity, etc. (See Chapter 5 for a more complete discussion of "who are the readers?")

Adventure

Here is where you would use the 3-L technique to find stories. Inspirational adventure stories are accounts of a person in a dangerous situation: kidnapped, trapped underground, lost in the woods. They usually show how faith helped in a panic situation to calm the person—perhaps through a remembered Bible promise—or how the person was rescued when hope was almost gone. Most often, help came through answered prayer. Sometimes the story is less dramatic but the element of danger or fear is almost always present with a strong sense of suspense.

The market is good. *Guideposts* publishes one adventure story in each issue, many of the Christian magazines use them—often about missionaries in danger—and secular publications like them. Many of those that appear in the latter have inspirational elements. *Reader's Digest* regularly presents adventure stories and also has a special feature, "Drama in Real Life," some of which are staff-written. Be alert for adventure stories when reading your local papers. Recently my local paper had an account of a man who was found unconscious, hidden in a ditch. He had been trapped for several days in the wreckage of his car, which could not be seen from the road. A girl on horseback spotted him. This might be a story from a number of angles.

If the stories are from the United Press International or Associated Press news services, it's harder to be first with your spin-off since other authors and editors have probably also read the item.

Adventure stories have great impact when written in the first person by the one involved, a relative, a friend, or the rescuer. A third-person reporter's account is another popular presentation. Study the magazines for the various styles used.

Art-of-Living

These are also called abstract or thematic pieces since they are based on a specific theme. This kind of article is the least structured of the major types of inspirational writing and can be written in the first or third person. It can be a personal experience or even a bit sermony or introspective. This form of writing explores some facet of living that can be improved or has been improved through ways presented in the article. Subjects explored in art-of-living pieces are such things as the benefits of tears, being bold, laughter, loneliness, gentleness, the importance of leisure time, the joys of walking.

You take a subject you're interested in, explore it, mull it over—for weeks if need be—and collect anecdotes, poems, and quotations. These might be biblical, historical, literary, or personal. When you find such a reference, note the source so you can give credit or get permission to quote, if necessary.

After you've collected enough anecdotes and have a pretty good grasp of your subject, decide what point you want to make. Then prepare a brief outline. Because you've lived with the subject for a while, the article will practically write itself. Very often the application of a Bible verse is how the author found a way to more abundant or successful living. The latter, in fact, can serve as a definition of an art-of-living piece.

Reader's Digest uses this kind of story as do other magazines, although not always under that designation. A query is a good idea since the subject might have been covered recently. Check the *Reader's Guide to Periodical Literature* in your library to see what has been written on the topic. If you have a different approach, the magazine may buy your article.

How-To Articles

Many of the coping-personal experience and even some of the art-of-living pieces have a how-to element. The difference is that most often in the how-to you deal exclusively with action, the doing of something complete with specific steps, often numbered, with descriptions of items needed.

You can also write a how-to article in the first person, using an anecdote to show why and how you started a project, the reason for its importance, then specific directions, and finally a return to the personal with an evaluation of the result. The how-to should inspire readers to follow the same procedure and be as successful as the author.

Some fine inspirational topics in this category are ways to have more effective prayer time; how to conduct a Bible study group; how to raise creative children.

Conversion/Witness

This is an excellent form of inspirational story. There is always a market for an effective conversion/witness piece. Because these stories are emotionally moving and descriptive of the power of Christ to change lives, they have a great potential for leading others to Christ.

Many evangelical magazines want a conversion experience written in the first person, but other publications do use the third-person presentation. Be sure you tell how the subject's life was changed. Show us what kind of person he was before finding God. Let us see the conversion experience and then the changed individual.

Most magazines prefer an anecdotal approach with realistic dialogue. Try not to be overly theological if you're writing for a general magazine. You want to bring your reader closer to God, not alienate him.

Many conversion/witness stories appear in tracts, missionary publications, and youth magazines. The market is especially open for conversion stories of well-known people, both as articles and books.

Famous People

The story of a celebrity is more difficult to do if you don't have credits, but it can be done. For example, you might want to interview Billy Graham and write an article about him. If you have credits as an author, it's easier to arrange an interview. You should have a theme or a story line in mind. And you should read all the biographical information you can find before you ask to do a story.

Write a letter asking for an interview, perhaps saying that you only need an hour's time. State your credits briefly, e.g., "My work has appeared in *Moody Monthly, Christian Herald, Decision,* and other magazines. I also wrote the authorized biography of Roger Williams, published by Cole and Connors."

If you have no credits, you can honestly say, "I am a freelance writer." In both instances, you would tell why you think the individual's story would be of interest and inspiration to readers.

Usually a celebrity story is credited with the "as told to" or "with," especially if it's about the individual's spiritual beliefs. Some celebrities are hesitant to share their faith. New Christians want to do so, and they are easier to approach and write about. This is also true for those who are reaching out to others, such as Charles Colson.

Set forth the problem, tell what it meant to the subject and how he coped with the situation. Sports figures often have fairly similar stories: usually they're meeting defeat in their personal life or on the playing field. They recall what their coach or their parents taught them about Jesus and prayer and, when they turn to Jesus, their life is changed. That's a simplification, but when they tell *how* they overcame defeat or anger, they give the reader help. Sports stories are especially important because they reach the young with a positive, inspirational message.

Personality Profile

Writing this type of story is a good way for a beginning author to break into print. It's usually a feature about someone who serves others in a unique way, although some of the points made about the famous-person story apply here also. Often the profile outlines the achievements of a teacher, missionary, layman, outstanding businessman or woman. Give details of the subject's activities, state why they are important, and explain the impact they have on others. Be specific in the examples you give so that the reader will be able to relate the life of the subject to his own experience.

At *Guideposts* we sometimes present a one-page feature in the third person called "The Quiet People." It tells how an individual reaches out into the community in a creative way to help those less fortunate, following Matthew 6:2. One feature was about a retired carpenter who builds birdhouses and places them outside the windows of nursing-home patients to bring interest into their lives.

Profiles are used as features in many magazines: *Modern Maturity* has a section of short ones, with pictures; *Moody Monthly* has used them, as have a number of trade and secular magazines that spotlight outstanding people. Not all are inspirational in character. When writing about a local individual, don't forget that weekly papers might be your market. For example, friends of mine in San Diego have been written about more than once in features for a local paper. These were inspiring stories of achieving people who in their senior years are still active and reaching out to others.

One profiled a retired doctor, now in his eighties, who still serves as a medical consultant, lectures on health, writes, and continues to take an interest in Korea, where he served as a medical missionary some fifty years ago.

In writing, don't just describe an individual's appearance; show the character's personality through physical mannerisms, actions, and dialogue. Remember, too, that you don't have to present your subject as a saint or hero: Let him be human, with frailities as they exist. Don't tell us about his spiritual orientation; set a scene so we can find out by seeing him in action.

Organization/Service

This is one kind of story through which you can truly serve your fellowman with your writing talents. The story of an organization's work usually is told in the first or third person through the experiences of the founder, a worker, or someone who has been helped. The reporter's style is acceptable at some magazines. Don't take a public relations approach. There is greater empathy when you emphasize the individual, such as in the story I wrote about a halfway house that provided released mental patients with a home and/or training while they adjusted to outside life. I interviewed workers and a few residents and then wrote a third-person presentation about one individual, Ralph. I made him a composite of two young men, to protect his identity. Information about the organization appeared in a box. This method is used because too much data in the body of a story detracts from its dramatic effect.

In the story on missing persons I mentioned earlier, I highlighted two organizations presenting anecdotes of searches. One was instituted by a daughter whose parents had separated before her birth. Now grown, she appealed to the Missing Persons Bureau of the Seamen's Church Institute to help find her father. The man's name was put on an "information wanted" list of missing men that was posted where seamen congregate. The man saw the list. Messages were exchanged and finally the man wrote the chaplain, "Thanks to your organization, I found out, at 67 years of age, and after a period of 25 years, there existed—unknown and undreamed of—not only a daughter, but grandchildren. Thank you. Thank you."

Though an informative, third-person presentation, this article achieved inspirational status.

You may write about well-known organizations such as Youth for Christ, Meals-on-Wheels, Marriage Encounter, or lesser-known ones. You need to write so that your reader will want to be involved in some way: to support the organization, join a similar group, or, at the very least, be emotionally impressed by the story. Again, if it is a local group, don't neglect your neighborhood newspaper.

As you can see, the scope of inspirational writing in magazines alone is great. There is a fairly good market for inspirational devotionals, historical pieces, fillers, travel experiences, juvenile material, poetry, and fiction as well. The three inspirational ingredients I described at the beginning of this chapter apply to these types of writing as well as to inspirational books.

Whatever you write—whether fiction, teaching article, or inspirational—should be the very best you can do. It should educate, entertain, and inform the reader. But, to be inspirational it should have the added goal of helping the reader to be victorious over problems, be a better human being, be closer to God.

You will, I hope, write material that is worthy.

At *Guideposts* I used to pin Bible verses and poems on the cork wall above my desk. They served as guides for my day. One of my favorites was from 1 Peter 4:11 which I paraphrased for myself; it could serve as a guide for all writers: *If you are a speaker, speak in words which seem to come from God; if you are a helper, help as though every action was done at God's orders;* and, added in humility for my guide: *If you are a writer, use every word in God's service.*

CHAPTER SEVEN

HOW TO
GET INTO
PRINT

by Sally E. Stuart

Sally E. Stuart of Portland, Oregon, has been an active freelancer for the last eight years. During that time she has sold nearly 400 articles to 65 different publications. She is the author of three books. To accomplish this she keeps more than 100 manuscripts in the mail most of the time. She is a frequent lecturer and workshop leader at Christian writers' conferences across the country where she teaches a wide variety of subjects. Her class on the "business of writing" deals with manuscript preparation, rights, queries, the new copyright law, and writers' income taxes. She is president of the Oregon Association of Christian Writers, which has some 400 participants, and the editor of their newsletter.

CREATING A PIECE of inspirational writing—

whether it be story, article, poem, or devotional—is only the first step in becoming a professional writer. Real success in this field, as in any other, can be measured only when the piece has been accepted by the editor of a suitable publication and gets into print. Only then can it inspire, minister to those who hurt, or meet a special need, which will be your ultimate goal.

All writers have produced things in the fresh glow of inspiration that they later knew were meant for themselves alone. But they have also penned words they were certain should be shared with the world. The first step toward successful marketing in the religious field is being able to recognize the difference between the two. The most marketable pieces of writing in any genre are those that appeal to or have meaning for the greatest number of readers. In the religious field this usually means non-Christians as well as Christians.

One very important aspect of this that we need to recognize seems to be peculiar to religious writing. Most of us have experienced those times when words came swiftly and surely from somewhere beyond ourselves—seemingly directly from God himself. It's natural to regard such pieces of writing as something special, but this is where caution needs to be applied. Even inspired words—when they come through human hands—are not necessarily ready (or even meant) for publication. It is unwise and unfair to expect a busy editor to accept the first draft (inspired or not) of any piece of writing. Although the thoughts and ideas may be divinely inspired, the arrangement of words is probably not.

Just as a singer cannot expect to become a polished professional on innate talent alone, without hours of practice and development, neither can a writer. We must work on every manuscript until it is, within reasonable limits, the best piece of writing we can produce. A marketable story or article is one that reflects not only a certain amount of inspiration, but meticulous attention to the principles of good writing and manuscript preparation as well. What a shame that we would blame God for our own unpolished manuscripts!

Marketing is the business side of the creative occupation of writer. As in any business, in order to be successful you must learn what is expected of you in the marketplace. Even a beginner can earn the title "professional" if he's willing to learn and function within the prescribed disciplines of the publishing business. This chapter will attempt to make you aware of what's expected and lead you to become a professional Christian writer who will be recognized as such in the religious market.

GETTING READY

The appearance of your manuscript is a prime indication of your professionalism. Although there is no recognized authority on manuscript preparation, editors expect you to follow certain generally accepted guidelines:

1. Your manuscript should be typed on 16# or 20# white bond paper. No colors. No onionskin or erasable bond.
2. Use a good black typewriter ribbon and replace it when it begins to fade. Always keep extras on hand.
3. Either pica or elite type is acceptable, but pica is easier on the editors' eyes. Avoid unusual typefaces. Keep type clean with rubbing alcohol or a commercial type cleaner.
4. Double-space everything in the body of your story or article, and type on only one side of the paper.
5. Establish proper margins. As a general rule, allow one inch at the top, bottom, and on the right with one and a half inches on the left side. Begin the first page just above the middle of the page with the title centered in all capital letters. Drop down four lines and type "By" and your name centered in upper- and lowercase letters. Drop another five or six lines to begin the text. Indent paragraphs uniformly five spaces. Do not use block style.
6. The first page will include the following information in the upper corners. In the left corner, type your name, address, and Social Security number. In the right corner, indicate what rights you are offering (rights will be explained later in this chapter): first rights offered, reprint rights offered, etc. Under that, identify the category: an article, a short story, a how-to filler, etc. The next line gives the number of words: an exact number for fillers up to 1,000 words and an approximate count for longer manuscripts (Exactly 545 words *or* About 1,450 words).
7. Use the same margins for all pages. In the upper left-hand corner, type your last name, and under it, a key word from the title. Type the page number in the upper right-hand corner.
8. The first page should contain no errors, and the rest should be typed as error-free as possible. If you don't have a correction feature on your typewriter, you can erase or correct errors with Liquid Paper. Correction tape is not recommended, as it rubs off with handling.

    After typing, search for errors and correct them. It's permissible to write in a word or make small changes in pencil or type in the space above the line of type. Retype any page with more than three of these corrections.

9. It isn't necessary to count every word in a manuscript, except for fillers. The approximate count can be arrived at by computing the average number of words on each page. Round off this estimate to the nearest fifty (nearest 100 for a book).

10. When mailing, never bind or staple your manuscript. You may use a paper clip. Short manuscripts (up to five pages) can be folded in thirds and sent in a business-size envelope. Those longer than five pages can be folded in half and mailed in a 7x10-inch manila envelope, or sent flat in a 10x13-inch manila envelope. A 6x9 or 9x12 envelope can be inserted flat for the required SASE (self-addressed stamped envelope) that must accompany every manuscript. A postal scale will save many trips to the post office. Be sure to affix the proper postage to both the mailing and the return envelopes.

11. Manuscripts can be sent special fourth class rate: manuscript; this notice must appear on the outside of the envelope. The current rate is 63 cents for the first pound and 23 cents for each additional pound up to seven pounds. After that, it is 14 cents a pound. It's less expensive than first class, but slower, and the post office isn't required to return it if it's undeliverable. (If using this fourth-class rate, write "return postage guaranteed" under your return address.) Also, if a first-class letter is enclosed with a manuscript sent fourth class, an additional first-class stamp must be added and the envelope marked "first-class letter enclosed." First-class mail is more dependable and most professional freelancers prefer it. All of your postage is tax-deductible.

   Note: When sending manuscripts to Canada or other foreign countries, don't use U.S. postage on the return envelope. Instead, enclose International Reply Coupons (available at the post office).

WHERE TO SEND IT

The key to successful marketing is to become familiar with all the possible markets for your material. This subject is covered in detail in Chapter 3, but there are some additional suggestions in order here.

You may find it helpful to compile a card file of the markets you would like to write for, drawing information from all possible sources. Divide the cards into appropriate categories (such as Children, Youth, Women, Family, Inspirational, etc.), and be sure to keep all your information up-to-date.

Contact each publication you'd like to write for and request writer's guidelines and a sample copy. These are usually free to writers or will be sent for an SASE or a small charge. Most market listings will indicate their policy on this.

When you receive the samples and guidelines, spend some time becoming familiar with the periodicals. Try to analyze them and determine their basic purpose; types of articles used; age and educational level of their readers; length of words, paragraphs, and articles; taboos; unique denominational terms or titles; how much is staff-written (check masthead); if they use fiction, poetry, or fillers; if they prefer first or third person; and whether you feel you could write to fit their particular needs. Make notes on the back of the guidelines or on your market cards.

Sample copies can be kept alphabetically in files or boxes, and the guidelines stapled to the sample copy or kept in a loose-leaf notebook with alphabetical dividers. Refer to them often as you continue to familiarize yourself with these possible markets.

If you are overwhelmed by the multiplicity of markets and the task of trying to select the most suitable ones, you may want to begin by sending only to your own denominational publications or others you are reading regularly and are already familiar with. Most religious publications are looking for qualified writers within their own denominational lines who understand their unique slant and needs. Also, selling consistently to the same publications opens the door to recognition and a reputation for good writing that may lead to assignments from those editors.

However, once you've proved that you have the necessary skills to enter the marketplace, you'll want to start expanding your submissions to other publications with similar needs.

Each time you have a piece ready for submission, plan an itinerary or list of publications where you might submit it. Even though you should have a suitable target publication in mind as you complete your manuscript, you'll also want to study your market listings to discover all the other places where your material might meet a need or reach the right audience.

After you have completed this list of appropriate markets, put it into proper order (using the market cards will make it easier), with your original target market and the most logical or best-paying markets at the top, and work down to the lower- and non-paying markets. Although your goal as a freelance writer should be to get paid for what you write, in the beginning you may need to be more concerned with getting into print consistently. Writing even for the nonpaying markets can help you gain experience and a reputation at the outset of your career. Some successful writers also occasionally include submissions to nonpaying markets as part of their writing ministry.

DON'T BE A MAILBOX SITTER!

Once your manuscript is on its way to an editor, you'll be tempted to set up camp next to your mailbox and wait for an enthusiastic acceptance and accompanying check. Don't! The wheels of the publishing business move slowly—often very slowly—so go back to your typewriter, start your next project, and try to forget the one in the mail.

Your market listings or writer's guidelines should give you some indication as to how long you can expect to wait for a reply. For most publications, this varies from two to eight weeks, although some respond faster, and some much slower. (It will be from three to six months for a book.) The question then becomes: Just how long should you wait if you don't hear?

There is no pat answer. First, check the length of time they *say* you can expect to wait, and add mail time. Two months should be long enough for most publications, and it wouldn't be unacceptable to write a *polite* letter of inquiry about your manuscript if you've waited that long with no word. (Be sure to include a SASE.) If your piece is timely or seasonal, follow up much sooner. Be sure to give full details in your letter, including the title, category, date of submission, whom it was addressed to, and the name or pen name used. Keep a carbon copy of your letter.

This letter will usually bring the return of your manuscript, an explanation of why it's being held, or a denial that they ever received it. However, if you fail to get an answer, send a second letter. If there is still no response, you might try calling the editor. In the unlikely event that even a phone call produces no results, send a registered letter withdrawing your manuscript. You may then retype it and submit it elsewhere. A copy of the registered letter in your files frees you of any obligation to the first publisher.

REJECTION SLIPS

You will find yourself in the foregoing situation rarely and are more likely to receive an acceptance or a rejection slip within a reasonable time. Your attitude toward rejections is very important to your survival as a freelancer. Although we all tend to take rejection slips personally in the beginning, a professional writer soon learns to accept them as a normal (though unpleasant) part of the business.

There are many reasons for rejections, most of which have nothing to do with the quality of your writing. The publication may have recently purchased or published something similar, be overstocked, have a low budget, or be recycling old manuscripts. It could be that the editor is prejudiced against your topic or simply had a fight with the spouse that morning.

That itinerary list you prepared before the first submission should be your "hedge" against rejection slips. Each time your manuscript is rejected, get it right back into the mail to the next publication on that list. It's a good idea to set your own deadline for getting a piece back into the mail as soon as possible. From two days to one week is realistic for most writers.

If a piece is rejected several times (especially if you are also receiving negative comments about it), reread it with a critical eye and determine whether you might need to rewrite it or reslant it to fit the remaining publications on your list. However, you should never retire a manuscript as long as you still believe in it or can work it over to make it suitable for another market.

YOUR MARKETING RECORDS

As you will soon discover, it's important to develop an accurate system for keeping track of your submissions. As your output increases, you'll be unable to remember the details of all your submissions and sales. There are any number of methods you might use; find one you're comfortable with that will provide the accuracy you need without becoming too burdensome and time-consuming. It should be a tool, not a tyrant.

Records of submission and return dates, sales, payment, and publication date can be noted on the back of your carbon copy, on the front of the file folder that holds the carbon copy and related correspondence, or on individual 3x5 or 4x6 index cards that contain the manuscript information on the front and a record of submissions and sales on the back.

Another, more complete, method involves the use of a loose-leaf notebook, alphabetical dividers, and one or more sheets of paper for each manuscript inserted alphabetically by title. The individual sheets contain a record of all needed information. At the front of the notebook, include a running list of all submissions of every manuscript (with name of manuscript and publication, and date sent). If you cross out those that are returned and circle any that are sold, you'll know at a glance which ones are still out and when to follow them up with a letter of inquiry.

The notebook can also contain separate pages of postage used, a running list of the year's income, manuscripts sold but not yet paid for, publications sold to, etc.

As you may suspect by now, marketing is a time-consuming process. In fact, it's likely to take as much as 50 per cent of your writing time. That can be frustrating for a creative person, but we need to remember that freelance writing, even in the religious market, is a business and will require the same kind of time demanded by any business to sell its product. It may be encouraging to know that it will go more quickly as you become more familiar with the markets and with your record system. Nevertheless, it's best for your peace of mind if you reconcile yourself from the beginning to the fact that it's going to take time and just accept it as a necessary part of freelancing.

WORKING WITH EDITORS

In the writing business, where you work alone with your typewriter, the editor becomes your first point of contact with the outside publishing world. He or she in a sense becomes your "boss"—the one you have to please or impress. For that reason, it's important to nurture those relationships with editors and discover how to attract and keep their attention.

Much of what has already been said in this chapter applies at this point. An editor will judge you and your ability to meet his needs by the first impression he gets when your manuscript arrives at his desk. Your manuscript will say by its appearance that it came from a careful, professional writer or from a beginner who hasn't bothered to learn even the rudiments of the profession. Therefore it's important to learn and follow all the preceding guidelines for correct manuscript preparation and mailing.

Accuracy is vital and involves correction of misspelled words, typing errors, grammar, and word usage, as well as double-checking all facts in your article.

Your manuscript must be fresh and clean and must look good; it must have no messy corrections, typeovers, staples, staple holes, dates, or stamps from previous submissions. Coffee stains and dog-eared pages also say that your manuscript has already made the rounds of several unimpressed editors.

Because of the importance of that first impression, it might be well to develop a checklist to use in preparing each submission. Start with the basic list at the end of the chapter and add other points that might apply to your particular type of writing.

A careful evaluation of your manuscript against a checklist should guide you smoothly through your initial encounter with an editor, but there are other ways to show him that you know what you're doing. As he reads your manuscript he'll continue to receive messages about your professionalism:

- Have you done your homework? Does this piece of writing fit the purpose and guidelines set out by the periodical? Is it obvious that you have studied his needs—or obvious that you haven't?

- Have you written with a definite target audience in mind? Is it his audience?

- Are you offering him something fresh and new because you know what he's published in recent issues?

- Does your writing reveal careful research, or is it plainly "imaginative fluff" off the top of your head?

- Is your article sharply focused and arranged in a clear and logical order?

After you get past the initial contact with an editor and have established a positive foundation for a professional affiliation, you must continue to build and nurture that association. It can only suffer, and in fact be destroyed, if you react negatively in future encounters. Don't question or argue with an editor's rejection slip or evaluation of your work (or make demands for explanations). Never miss or ignore an editor's deadline for submission of an assignment or revisions.

Occasionally an editor will return a manuscript and suggest you make certain revisions or additions to make it more acceptable for his publication. This does not mean that he's promising to buy it if you make the suggested changes, only that he is interested and is open to looking at it again. For that reason you are not obligated to make the revisions and are free to send it on to another editor who may be happy to accept it as it is.

However, especially for the beginning writer, such suggestions should be seen as personal encouragement that will likely lead to a sale if followed. On the other hand, if you feel you cannot make the changes as outlined, particularly if they reflect a conflicting personal or doctrinal view, you don't have to. In such a case, it's good business to send a cordial note to the editor thanking him for his interest, along with regrets that you won't be able to make the changes on this manuscript. Express your hope that you will be able to work together in the future.

In all your dealings with editors, remember that they're human and treat them accordingly. In the religious market, you'll find that most of them are Christians who are striving to put out a publication and work with writers in a way that will reflect their Christian principles. Approaching them in an honest, direct manner will usually bring an equally honest and direct response. Editors need writers as much as writers need editors, and they're eager to find skilled writers with good manuscripts that will help them put out a quality publication.

WHAT RIGHTS DO YOU SELL?

One of the most confusing aspects of the writing business seems to be the subject of rights, probably because it involves a more technical side of the profession and tends to be couched in "legalese." However, the conscientious writer needs to make a concerted effort to learn and understand the various rights offered in the sale of manuscripts. Following are explanations of the most commonly used terms:

First Rights. This is the right to publish a piece of writing for the first time. Most writers prefer to sell only First Rights to their material, as they may then resell it after it has appeared in print (see Reprint Rights below).

First Rights usually implies one-time use, but it's best to state that in writing at the time of sale.

Serial Rights. Refers to the right to publish a piece in a periodical. ("Serial" here refers to use in a periodical, such as a newspaper or magazine, and not to "serialization" or publication in installments.) The term "Serial Rights" is not used alone but is always used with other terms that specify the limits of use:

> *First Serial Rights.* First use in a periodical. In this case you still own First Book Rights and Second Serial Rights (the same as Reprint Rights).
>
> *First North American Serial Rights.* First use in a periodical in North America. You still retain the rights to sell it in foreign countries other than Canada.
>
> *One-Time Rights.* Gives rights to publish one time only. This usually applies in sales to newspapers. The writer can then resell, outside the first buyer's publication area, after they have published it. One-time rights are also offered in the sale of photo or graphic material.
>
> *All Rights.* This is an outright sale with the publisher buying complete rights; the author forfeits all rights to further use. The buyer may then use it however and as often as he wants without further payment to the author. This includes the right to sell your material to other publications or to use it in anthologies or the like if he so desires. It's not advisable to sell all rights unless there is no further market for the particular piece, or you feel the price or prestige involved merit it. There are few publications in the religious market that pay well enough to justify the sale of all rights.
>
> If you sell all rights, they revert to you after thirty-five years unless you sign a "work-for-hire" contract (to be covered later in this chapter). Note: All Rights (sometimes called Exclusive Rights) cannot be sold unless the transfer is stated specifically in writing.
>
> *Reprint Rights.* The right to reprint work that originally appeared in another publication. First Reprint Rights indicates you are offering second use. The term "Second Rights" is used interchangeably with "Reprint Rights," and either term may be used to indicate any sale beyond First Rights. Although you may be paid slightly less for second use, you aren't required to use the term "First Reprint Rights" at all (simply use Reprint Rights anytime after the original sale). Never offer Reprint Rights until the piece has been published by the First Rights buyer.
>
> *Simultaneous Rights.* Selling the right to print a piece

simultaneously to more than one buyer. This is usually done with nonoverlapping markets, such as denominational publishers, newspapers, regional publications, and the like, that have different reading audiences. Simultaneous Rights are most often offered with timely or seasonal topics that must be published quickly. Never sell Simultaneous Rights unless all parties involved know that you are doing so.

These are the most commonly used rights in the publishing business. You must decide which you will offer on each manuscript and always indicate that in the upper right-hand corner on the first page. Most publications make it known in their market listings which rights they intend or prefer to buy. You will find, however, that many of them are flexible in their terms and will go with what the author is offering.

Another reason you should learn these rights is that if a question should arise in this area, you'll be in a better position to protect your rights if you understand what you're selling and why.

Work-for-Hire

Although the new copyright law, which went into effect January 1, 1978, was designed to better protect the rights of the author, there is one loophole which some publishers are using to continue the former practice of buying All Rights. The "work-for-hire" clause in the new law was intended to apply to work another party commissions you to do, such as work done as a regular employee of a company or on a specific assignment. It was not intended for use by publishers to buy All Rights in their regular dealings with freelancers.

Such editors send work-for-hire contracts to writers when they decide to purchase a piece of writing that has been submitted for publication. The contract says (usually in lengthy legalese) that the piece you wrote was work-for-hire and you are selling them All Rights in and to anything and everything created under that agreement. As mentioned earlier, in this case the rights will not revert to you in thirty-five years as they do when selling All Rights. It is generally agreed that if writers will stick together in refusing to sign such contracts, publishers will be forced to discontinue their use.

Only work-for-hire agreements and the transfer of All Rights must be in writing according to the new law, but you should get any agreement in writing before the sale.

If one of your articles is picked up from a magazine by another publisher, they must negotiate with you to purchase it, not with the first editor (unless you sold All Rights).

Selling Reprint Rights

In the religious market, where only a few publications buy All Rights and payment is generally low, the freelancer has an opportunity to multiply his earnings by selling the Reprint Rights to his work. When you're dealing primarily with denominational publishers whose readerships don't overlap, you'll find that most of them are open to buying reprints. This also provides an opportunity for you to widen your ministry by reaching a greater number of people.

After a piece has been printed and distributed by the first publisher who buys it, you can retype it, have good, clear photocopies made (save the original to make more copies from as needed), and start submitting it to other editors who might be interested. If you still have names on your original itinerary list, continue with it, or go back and find additional appropriate markets.

Although you may send a reprint to more than one editor at a time (since they know you are offering only Reprint Rights), it's better to continue sending to one at a time, unless the piece has an unusually wide, general market potential. Otherwise you tend to flood the market and become your own competition.

If you're interested in selling Reprint Rights but aren't sure what rights you sold originally, write to the publisher asking what rights were purchased and whether you're free to sell Reprint Rights. Many publications that bought All Rights will release you to sell Reprint Rights as long as you inform future buyers that they must carry a prescribed credit line, such as "Used by permission of _____" or "Reprinted from _____"

Other editors will deal only with publications that contact them directly for permission to reprint. In the former case, you will usually receive the full amount paid by the second publication. In the latter case, the first publisher may retain all the payment, split it with you, or sometimes even forward all of it to you. Many editors may refuse to buy reprints if they are required to carry a credit line from the first publisher; therefore, it's still best to retain the rights to everything you write (by selling only First or One-Time Rights to the original publisher) so you'll be free to sell Reprint Rights without restrictions.

You must always indicate on the first page of your manuscript that you are offering Reprint Rights, but it isn't necessary to tell where and when it was published originally unless and until the editor asks.

THE QUERY LETTER

Now that you're familiar with most of the how-tos and wherefores of becoming a professional writer and making a good first impression, it's time to learn how to best catch the attention of a busy editor and save yourself some time and postage in the bargain.

A query is a brief letter to an editor describing a piece of writing you propose to do and asking if he's interested in seeing it. Already a must with most secular publishers, it's becoming a necessary foot in the door in religious markets as well, although you'll still find some editors who say, "No queries."

It also serves as a sample of how well you write. An editor will be able to judge your writing, thinking, and organizational abilities by how well written your query letter is, so let it be a showcase of the best writing you can do.

Sending a query letter is advisable when research and/or an interview is involved or when the periodical prefers or requires one. Most editors don't expect one for fiction, poetry, humor, or fillers. Although you can write a query letter almost any time you wish in order to avoid writing an article without first finding an interested publisher, you should be aware that there are also those editors who insist on seeing only complete manuscripts and will not accept queries.

Before you begin your query letter, go back and study your target periodical. As you go through sample copies checking topics covered, kinds of leads and endings, length of articles, style of writing, and the like, ask yourself if your proposed story or article fits this publication. If it's obvious that it does not, continue your search through other periodicals until you find the most logical target for your query.

Query letters for periodicals generally follow one of two formats. They can consist of an article outline with a short cover letter giving other pertinent information but more commonly take the form of a business letter to the editor. Type it on good, white bond paper or your own professional letterhead stationery; single-space unless it is very short; prepare it as neatly and error-free as possible; and limit it to one page. Address your letter to an editor by name, enclose a SASE, and be sure to keep a carbon copy for your records.

Elements of a Good Query Letter

A query letter, as does the article it precedes, needs a "grabber" opening—something to catch the editor's attention and compel him to read on. Select the most exciting or intriguing aspect of your article and build it into a provocative opening. You may wish to use the actual lead from your proposed article to open your query letter. Follow it with an explanation that this is the lead from an article you'd like to do on your subject and then give the particulars. (In this case a salutation isn't necessary.)

The first paragraph should clearly state the article's subject, indicating a narrow focus on a specific aspect of what may be a broad topic. Make clear to the editor your point of view on the topic: Are you for or against it? greatly interested? personally involved? an onlooker? irate? amused? or setting out to write an objectively balanced report on it?

Try to give some indication why the editor and, ultimately, the reader should care about your subject. What will be the benefit to the reader? Will it help him handle a problem? heal a hurt? inform him? help him grow in his spiritual life or understanding of the scriptures?

Once you have hooked the editor with a strong, appealing opening, fill in the details and provide some samples of what will go into the finished article:

- Quote statistics, if applicable.

- Use quotes from people involved in or related to your subject.

- Include a good anecdote, example, or case history—a story that proves your point.

- Mention authorities you'll use to show that it isn't simply your own idea.

- Throw in enough solid facts to prove that you've done your research and indicate your sources: interviews? case studies? historical documents? firsthand experience? scripture comparisons?

- Don't withhold a surprise ending. Give the editor all the pertinent information but try to whet his appetite for additional details.

Before you bring your query letter to a close, you must give the editor some additional information:

- Mention a catchy title that best conveys the focus of your article.

- Make clear your approach: Will you use first person? third person? how-to? survey? interview?

- Give the approximate length (after checking their market listing to find out their range).

- Let him know when you can have it ready. Make it a designated time *after* you receive his go-ahead.

- Indicate what photographs or art are available.

- Give your qualifications for writing the piece: "I have done extensive research." "I am the mother of three preschoolers [or four teenagers]." "I am a pastor [teacher, nurse, doctor, etc.]." Unless it's a highly technical area, you won't need a degree; just indicate that you're qualified to handle the subject.

● Give a brief rundown if you have professional writing experience. If not, say nothing. Your query letter can say you are a professional—even if you're a beginner.

● State your special skills that relate to the article and indicate any unique resources that might demonstrate your ability to get the story no one else could. Also give your religious or denominational background and state your familiarity with the beliefs of this periodical.

● Reveal your enthusiasm throughout the letter so you can excite the editor about your proposal. Don't try to convince him that this piece came directly from God and he is therefore duty-bound to publish it. God doesn't need an agent!

● Bring your query to a close with the simple question: "Are you interested?"

Write a rough draft of your letter, edit it, rewrite it, and edit it some more. Don't type your final draft until it represents the best writing you can do. You should be as proud of it as of any manuscript.

If you don't receive an answer to your query within one to four weeks, you may send a polite follow-up letter. If the editor turns down your idea, don't let it drop there. Reslant your query to fit a new publication and get it right back out into the mail. Follow up your contact with the first editor as soon as possible by sending him another idea he might like.

On the other hand, if the editor gives you a go-ahead, study his letter carefully, and incorporate the suggestions he may give for changes, additions, or a special slant to better meet the needs of his readers. The editor will also usually indicate whether he's asking you to do the article on speculation or on assignment. "On speculation" means that he will purchase it only if he likes the finished article—he's under no obligation. "On assignment" means he's giving you a definite assignment because he's confident that you can produce a usable article. Some magazines will pay a "kill fee" (up to 50 percent of the full payment) if they decide not to use an assigned piece. This is uncommon in the religious market, as most publications give go-aheads only on speculation.

When you submit the finished article to the editor, be sure to include a cover letter reminding him that this is an article he asked to see, or send along a photocopy of the letter you received from him.

DO YOU NEED AN AGENT?

As you confront the manifold problems that surround marketing, you may well be asking if you need an author's agent to take on this specialized task for you. For the beginning writer, the answer is no. You not only don't need one, but chances are you wouldn't be able to find a reputable agent who would be willing to represent you.

In the secular market, many of the top-paying periodical and book publishers are closed to freelancers who are not represented by an agent. Not so in the religious market. There are virtually no publishers in this field that require the intervention of an agent. And although there are a growing number of Christian agents around the country, most of the religious publishers are reluctant to work with them or actually prefer to deal directly with writers.

Most secular agents aren't familiar with the religious markets and would be of no value to the religious author. Most agents will not handle sales to periodicals only but will wait to take on an author until he has sold a book or two and has additional book-length ideas.

An agent becomes a middleman in the process of finding a buyer for your book and negotiating a fair contract, as well as handling the sale of subsidiary rights, such as paperback, foreign, TV, movie, etc. For these services he charges 10-15 percent of your royalties.

A writer who makes it a point to learn all he can about marketing and the publishing business should be capable of being his own agent in the religious markets. There is much information available on negotiating your own book contracts that will make you knowledgeable enough to handle that aspect. Try to find an experienced book author or writers' organization to advise you on the terms of a contract until you feel confident on your own.

As we come to the end of this chapter, we realize that the rules governing religious writers are really no different from those in other areas of publishing. The standards are high in the Christian marketplace, and there is no place for those who won't strive for professionalism or those who don't understand the uniqueness of the Christian experience.

CHECKLIST FOR MANUSCRIPT SUBMISSIONS

1. Does it look good? Have I used clean white bond? Is it double-spaced?

2. Is the type crisp and black, not faded? No enclosed letters?

3. Are the margins wide enough and consistent throughout the manuscript?

4. Have I included my name, address, Social Security number, rights offered, and the number of words at the top of the first page?

5. Are my last name, key word from the title, and page number typed on all pages after the first? Are all pages in order?

6. Are there any errors on the first page?

7. Have I corrected all errors throughout the manuscript by typing or writing neatly and legibly in the space above the type? Have I retyped every page with more than three corrections?

8. Have I addressed my envelope to the proper editor by name? Are that name and the name of the publication spelled correctly? Are the address and zip code correct?

9. Have I enclosed a SASE with sufficient postage?

10. Have I marked both the mailing and return envelopes with the class of mail (first class or special fourth class rate: manuscript)?

11. Is my return address on the outside of the envelope? If I'm using fourth class, have I typed "Return Postage Guaranteed" under my return address?

12. Have I recorded this submission in my record system?

THE DEADLY SINS OF RELIGIOUS WRITING

The word *sin* is used here in its original meaning. Both the Hebrew *hata* in the Old Testament and the Greek *hamartano* in the New Testament literally mean "to miss the mark." Religious writers who want to hit the mark will do their utmost to avoid these cardinal sins:

1 CLAIMING TO BE INSPIRED BY GOD

All writers, if they obey their impulses at all, are inspired. But to be *inspired by God* is an extremely rare occurrence. When this happens, the spirit of God "breathes in" his message and stimulates the thought but allows the chosen human being to write from his own viewpoint in his own individual style. Those who claim direct divine inspiration often use this as an excuse to avoid polishing their work. Untrained writers, imbued with a burning desire to share "God's message," often tackle writing jobs beyond their ability. Studying and learning their craft step by step before submitting material for publication never occurs to them. They "feel led," so they jot their thoughts down on paper and drop them into the mail with a prayer. Thus God is blamed for mountains of bad writing. He did not inspire it, and it's probably not his will to have it published.

2 PIOUS OBLIVION

Many religious writers think their material is inherently meritorious; since their hearts are in the right place and their subject matter worthy, they assume the writing will take care of itself. Thus they don't appeal to the senses, reach out and grab human interest, or use any of the tools secular writers do to make their work effective. All good inspirational writing is you-the-reader-oriented, carefully designed to draw the reader in and move him to action.

3 RIGHTEOUS RIGOR MORTIS

The stiffness and formality too often typical of religious writing may be the same syndrome that afflicts academics and social scientists—the seriousness and dignity of what they're saying call for an *unnatural* style of writing. Unnecessary use of the passive voice and a consistently wordy and indirect way of saying things will assure that your readers sleep through the message.

4 HEAVENLY HAZE

Writers adrift in this sin are totally unaware of it. They spew out beautiful, flowery phrases and sentences that look great on paper. Those who commit sin # 2 overlook their very human reader in their eagerness to get their message to the world; those lost in the heavenly haze think the whole world is right there with them, enchanted as they are with the words they've just strung together.

Inspirational doesn't mean surrounded by a cloud of haze, and it doesn't mean big wind. Beware of euphonious nonsense and mystic mumbo-jumbo. Do you honestly know what you've just written means?

5 WRITING IN AN UNINTELLIGIBLE LANGUAGE

Christianese, the language spoken only within some sections of the religious community, is usually made up of phrases left over from early British and American revival eras and Old English terms from the King James version of the Bible. At best these cliches clutter the page; at worst they are intimidating gibberish to the reader who has grown up outside the church. You cannot take the reader for granted. Even words like repentance, conviction, agape, escatology, evangelism, and fellowship will not be automatically understood.

Many religious writers are so programmed to speak the jargon of their own inner circle that those outside the group have no idea what they're trying to say. To effectively communicate you must scrutinize every sentence to be certain it is written in language people outside the church can understand— you can't just offer tantalizing hints for the uninitiated.

6 ONE-SIDED ARGUMENTATION

There's nothing wrong with using the printed page for indoctrination—the printed message is often more powerful than the spoken word. It allows the reader to contemplate and absorb thoughts that would be lost in rapid speech. And the written message can be studied privately—an important factor in many cases.

But writers out to convert the world think they are helping their cause by trying to cram their point of view into the reader's mind. They alienate readers with an abundance of angry threats backed up by Bible verses. A preachy, holier-than thou attitude is always self-defeating. And cold, critical, do-as-I-say or "This-is-what-the-Bible-says" copy is the unpardonable sin.

The first step in convincing a reader is to explain your thesis, then, in clear and logical steps, develop your idea and move toward a conclusion. Don't dogmatically propound your way as the only way. Love, sincerity, and genuine concern are the keys to success in Christian advocacy. Readers must be wooed and won, not threatened into conversion.

7 SYRUPY SENTIMENTALISM

Syrupists express themselves in the superlative more often than not—idealistic situations, too-good-to-be-true statements, and unbelievably sweet and kind (or wholly wicked) characters are signs that the writer is bemired in this deadly sin. Other symptoms of this sin are treating good and evil as black and white absolutes, overuse of adjectives and adverbs, and unrealistic situations, conflicts, or personalities. It is dishonest to pretend, in these days of famine, terrorism, and nuclear stockpiles, that the world is flooded with God's rosy light. Life is tough—full of change, loss, and disappointment; people look for and usually find ways to cope. Readers need to know the writer has both feet in the real world.

8 PREACHING ON PAPER

Words on a page are different from preached sermons. The spoken word combines vocal tones with expressions arising out of the speaker's personality. Typed onto paper, the same words may be hollow, meaningless, and full of repetition. Practitioners of this sin are found in two groups in particular; preachers who believe their "inspired" sermons are worthy to be put in article or book form, and religious writers who believe every book or article they write must follow the style of a church school lesson, tract, or sermon.

9 PARROTING KNOWLEDGE NOT YOUR OWN

Originality is one key to success many religious writers fail to try. Without ever thinking it through for themselves, they repeat unendingly the memorized doctrine of their religious group or church. Readers are longing for fresh new approaches to age-old truths. Christian writers must be living what they talk about and loving the people they would write for and about. You need to have been where your readers are; you must let them know you are willing to risk making yourself vulnerable. The truths you promote must first become personal—you must know what you believe and *why*. Study the key tenets of your faith and as you learn from your own life how they work, you will be ready to write.

10 SUICIDAL SUBMISSION

Religious writers, incredibly enough, tend to believe they can approach the writers' market listings alphabetically. If all the A's reject their writing, they proceed to the B's. Differences within the religious society are innumerable and terribly important. An evangelical combs incoming manuscripts for liberal statements. Charismatics are evangelicals but charismatic material will be considered only by their own publishers and flatly refused by all others. Arminian groups guard against Calvinistic statements. Liberals reject Moral Majority material. Some religious publishers accept quotations from Billy Graham, Oral Roberts, Norman Vincent Peale, and the *Living Bible*, while others boycott writers who mention any one or all of these names. Success depends on sending your material to publishers whose points of view you clearly understand.

CHAPTER EIGHT

SOME GOOD
PLACES
TO START

WRITING FOR AND ABOUT YOUR LOCAL CHURCH

by Sue Nichols Spencer

Sue Nichols Spencer lives in Lehigh Acres, Florida, and is a freelance writer and author of Words on Target *and* Write on Target.

Writing, like charity, can begin at home. It can begin in your own church. As a matter of fact, this may be the easiest place to get started, because you will not be competing with scores of professionals.

Since you will be volunteering, you can choose the kind of writing you like to do: factual, narrative, or inspirational. What you do not receive in remuneration will be made up for in good experience. You will not be sending your material to a remote publisher; you will get a speedy response to what you write. This will help you understand your strengths and weaknesses; you will come to see what subjects and styles you handle well and which you should improve or perhaps abandon. After all, we cannot all be poets, we cannot all be journalists. As you write, you will be garnering not only experience but also a folio of your own published works. This could prove an asset in opening new doors for you.

In your church your writing can take one of two directions. You can write for your fellow members to strengthen them in their faith and increase their commitment to the church. Or you can write for outsiders to attract them to the church. Whichever course you decide to pursue, you will want to discuss your plans with your minister or any appropriate governing body before getting under way.

WRITING FOR INSIDERS

There are many opportunities for your fellow church members. Some congregations put out a regular newsletter or newspaper they distribute to members. You could become a reporter or a columnist for it. If your church doesn't have such a paper, you could volunteer to launch one and become its first editor. Writing in this way at a local level could lead to assignments for publications at a broader level, such as a regional newspaper or one of your denomination's national magazines.

Bible study groups are almost always looking for devotionals; you could write poems, prayers, and meditations for them. If you are elected recording secretary of an organization, you will learn how to write in a very orderly manner; if you are elected historian, you could have a field day. In addition to keeping track of the significant things the group is currently doing, you could research its past. Out of your findings, you might develop an illustrated booklet or a slide presentation. You might interest a local historical society or museum in your project, as well as civic groups in the area. Perhaps some organization in your church will want to send a resolution or petition to a larger body—a church council or a secular legislative body. If so, it would give you practice in drafting formal or quasi-legal material.

Although most churches subscribe to an ongoing curriculum for their Sunday school, opportunities for educational writing still abound. Original programs and songs are almost always needed for holidays and annual observations, such as Mother's Day and Lent. Youth groups are on the lookout for fresh ideas and materials as are those planning family and singles camping weekends. Teachers of children's classes usually welcome extra stories that illustrate biblical or lesson truths. Also, churches are offering more and more short-term courses and specialized classes. Sometimes the teachers have difficulty finding either suitable curriculum or lessons when they need them. You may be able to compose just the sort of tailormade material that is needed. And don't forget summertime; it usually ushers in a vacation Bible school with its needs for stories, games, and songs.

If drama interests you, you might like to write and stage one of your own creations. Plays teach and also promote camaraderie. You could dramatize a Bible event or reconstruct a modern event through which a biblical theme radiates. If well done, the play might be offered at your high school or civic center or at a larger gathering of your denomination.

WRITING FOR OUTSIDERS

The principal vehicles for reaching outsiders are the print and electronic media. Newspapers usually run announcements on a church page once a week; TV and radio stations often have a daily feature that telecasts or broadcasts any local announcements submitted. You could become the liaison person between the media and your congregation, supplying news about the worship services, meetings, and activities of your church. The media would also be interested in any contemporary mission projects carried out by your church or unusual stories about any of your members. For example, you could seek coverage if your church sponsored the resettlement of a refugee family, or they would certainly be interested if one of your members made some kind of breakthrough that promised to reduce world hunger or to save an endangered species. The reporters will compose their own stories but you can play an important role by supplying basic information. And of course you could expect coverage if your church invited a person of religious prominence to its pulpit.

Some churches purchase newspaper space and run display ads in order to assure and control their publicity. If yours is one of these, you might try your hand at designing such ads.

Another avenue for contacting outsiders is your church's outreach or evangelistic committee. Often the members of such committees wish they had a leaflet to take with them on visits, a printed piece that would support their verbal message that they could leave with the persons visited. You could fashion a pamphlet that would invite prospective members to consider joining your church on the basis of what it has to offer: its doctrine, its program, its mission, and its fellowship.

Whether you write for insiders or outsiders, you will probably find that one thing leads to another; as one task is completed, another one will surface. As you perfect your craft, you may very well find opportunities beyond those of the local church opening for you.

WRITING BOOK REVIEWS
by Connie Soth

The author lives in Beaverton, Oregon, where she is a freelance columnist and book review writer and teacher.

Reviewing religious books is personal journalism second only to autobiography and poetry. Whether you grew up nurtured in the faith, or met God along the way, your reviews reveal your inner self. A book review *is* personal and it also is *opinion*, not brought down from Mt. Sinai on stone tablets, but worthwhile opinion nevertheless. In direct ratio to your background, formal or experiential education, commitment to God, and practice of your writing craft, your reviews will become ever more informed, skilled, intuitive.

The desire to write book reviews presupposes a prodigious capacity for reading. Three ideal ways to satisfy that appetite are to be a church librarian, a bookseller, or book publisher employee. Many writers move into reviewing from experience on school or university newspapers or because their employer needed writers for the company newsletter.

Writing book reviews is a great way to break into print. An easy market close at hand is your church's service bulletin or newsletter. For the fledgling writer, this Phase One is like writing to please your mother. The church family's noncritical attitude encourages you at the same time it affords you the thrill of your first by-line.

In most cases there is little or no payment for book reviewing unless one is doing it as a column on a regular basis. At first, all that you can expect is the privilege of keeping the book. But, if it is a good book, that is not a bad fee and you are getting practice in writing. There are some journals that pay for longer reviews and several that pay for a group of reviews by one person in each issue. So there is hope after one has experience, but don't expect this to come too soon.

There are several kinds of reviews; the thumbnail sketch is valuable because it forces you to "write tight," appropriate for the bibliographies churches often need. Honing your skill begins here, as you report in a terse line or two what you think about a book.

Then there is the 250- to 500-word review for the church newsletter. Giving title, author, publisher, price—essentials though space-takers—you open a window into the book with provocative, succinct sentences. For fiction, provide a quick, colorful synopsis, but don't give the whole story away; for nonfiction, identify the subject, background the author, tell why the book is best in its field. There is no room for analysis of book or author, only to pique readers' curiosity.

Phase Two: Reconnoiter the local newspaper. Not every newspaper will take a book-review column, but you'll never know unless you ask. In my class, "Getting Ready to Be a Book Reviewer," I advise participants, "Get to know someone in your chosen market." This could mean your paper's church page editor.

Write publicity for your church's functions and deliver the copy in person to the editor. When you've become acquainted, watch for the right moment to tell the editor you also write book reviews. Show samples from your church's publications and give cogent reasons why the newspaper needs your services, making clear that you expect to be paid. A query letter would suffice, but inviting the editor out for lunch and discussion is better. The church/newspaper road seems slow, but as you accumulate experience and your file of published reviews grows, you continually refine your review-writing ability.

Let's say you've now won a place on the local paper. Your column has a catchy title, you've come to an understanding with your editor about payment, and you've learned that nothing makes an editor lose enthusiasm more quickly than a missed deadline—two are fatal. Now you move from word count to column inches. When I began writing "Bookworm's Buffet" for the *Valley Times*, the copyeditor soon educated me on filling twelve column inches. If my copy extended beyond the allotted space, those lines were chopped. Woe to the writer who makes her dazzling point in the two extra lines. I also learned that the editor had no time for "creative editing." She wanted my copy in on time, clean, with no grammatical errors or misspellings. Learning to be my own editor meant becoming sternly objective.

Study *The Religious Writers Marketplace*, which contains listings not found elsewhere. Consult *Writer's Market*'s "Religious" and "Literary and 'Little' " sections. The latter lists publications that want reviews of books from small presses, a good arena for the writer who wants to review secular books as well as religious ones. Most literary magazines pay in copies rather than in money, but by-lines will help you establish a reputation, so query those editors.

Once you have a good backlog of published reviews, proceed to Phase Three. Send two photocopies of your review to the book's publisher with a cover letter requesting advance copies of other books for possible review. Also, send a copy of your review, with a note, to the author, care of the publisher.

In Phase Four, you may receive books in galley proof, uncorrected copies that you either request or receive unsolicited, putting you in direct touch with the team that is working hard to birth a book. They invite your suggestions; they may even follow them. Also study *Publishers Weekly*; learn about projected books for the coming year and write to the publishers, requesting specific titles for review.

Another aspect of reviewing opened for me when I saw a small entry from *Arkenstone*, a Christian literary magazine, in the Evangelical Press Association's directory. I queried the editor, sending samples of my work. Steve Griffith responded affirmatively; now I write essay-reviews up to 3,500 words, and serve as book review editor.

The reviewer of religious books must keep in mind all of the principles of good book reviewing, but in addition take into account some other special features of religious books. What is the theological position or implications of the message of the book? Will it offend the "fundamentalist" reader on one end of the scale or the "liberal" reader at the other end? Is the point of view of the author consistent throughout with accepted religious teaching? Does the writer's message square with biblical teaching on the particular subject or is it critical of the usually accepted biblical position? How will the message of the book affect the religious life of the reader? For what level of religious experience is it written? Is it for "new" Christians or those who have spent a lifetime in the faith? These are some of the questions that a writer of review or religious books will want to face and answer for the potential reader of the review.

Book reviewing can be a career in itself, but you are likely to write more firmly grounded reviews if you also write other things. My "other things" include interviews, poetry, and "think" pieces. Work to improve your knowledge, become adept at research, use words with respect for their sound, feeling, and power. Deepen your dependence on God, knowing that whatever you write will resonate from whatever is happening in your inner being.

WRITING INSPIRATIONAL FILLERS
by Shirley Pope Waite

The author lives in Walla Walla, Washington, and is a freelance writer of many types of materials. She has also led workshops at writers' conferences on the subject of fillers.

Fillers are a great way for the beginning writer to break into print.

Fillers are a smart means by which the established writer can keep something in the mail while working on a book or longer articles.

Fillers are an excellent vehicle for the religious writer to sell to the secular markets.

At one time, fillers were used only to "fill in" that extra space at the bottom of the page. Now they often are a featured part of many magazines or newspapers. Most readers search out these informative and entertaining ideas before turning to longer pieces. Fillers are especially appropriate for religious subjects.

Check the following list. Chances are you have material at your fingertips to fit into one of these filler categories.

1. *Tips and shortcuts*—Everything from recipes to household hints, hobby and outdoor tips, home and shop ideas. Keep your tip brief (50-200 words). Tell the reader how it will save time, energy, etc. Use simple words and short sentences. Enclose a rough picture or sketch if it will clarify. In writing tips and shortcuts for religious publications, stick to subjects that relate to the work of the church—Sunday school teaching, for example. Or tell how to serve a large group such as a church dinner effectively or fast— some shortcuts to efficiency. Or tell how you squeeze in time for prayer or scripture reading on the bus or other public transportation. Publications looking for handicraft ideas include *Bee Hive, Happy Times, Weekly Bible Reader, Reflections,* and *Perspective* (for adult leaders).

2. *Anecdotes*—These are little "slice of life" episodes, usually humorous or very unusual in content and illustrating one of the three "F's" of humanity: Frailties, Foibles, and Frustrations. An anecdote is not a joke but is a story based on an actual happening. Some fictionalizing is permissible, but it should be true to life.

Humor is especially relevant in this type of filler and is appropriate for religious material as well. Several publishers have made collections of humorous incidents related to religion or church, so there is a market here if you can be funny without being sacrilegious.

3. *Personal experiences*—Your life is unique. You have been places, seen things, had encounters that differ from anyone else's. Have you had a unique conversion experience? *Moody Monthly* might be interested in it for their "First Person" feature. Did it occur at a Billy Graham Crusade? If so you may want to send it to his organization's publication *Decision's* column, "Where Are They Now?" Other magazines using personal experience fillers are *Guideposts* ("Fragile Moments"), *Catholic Digest* ("Hearts Are Trumps", "The Perfect Assist"), *Today's Christian Parent* ("Happenings at Our House").

Personal experiences, of course, can become whole books, but what we are talking about here is the short item, telling of just one experience and condensing it to a moment's inspiration in the midst of an unusual experience. Look at some examples from the Bible—such as the widow's mite, or many of the parables of Jesus that contain fewer than fifty words.

4. *Personalities*—Emphasis is on an individual, what he or she is doing or has accomplished. Examples are "People" (*Moody Monthly*), "Saints Alive" (*Christian Herald*), "The Quiet People" (*Guideposts*), "Chosen People" (*Eternity*). Regional magazines and Sunday supplements also are looking for personality fillers about local residents.

It is difficult to describe a personality within filler length, and it will take some hard work at condensing and rewriting to accomplish this, but it can be done. Again, use the Bible as a guide in telling a lot in a brief item.

5. *Problem-solution*—This differs from shortcuts in that it involves two or more people and reflects a change of attitude. It may pertain to disciplining a child, getting along with a neighbor, or a solution to a career or church problem.

6. *Informative pieces*—These usually entail research and are designed to give information: a factual or historical oddity, something going on in the nation, or a letter to the editor. Many church-related magazines call for informative fillers, as do numerous secular publications. Check markets.

7. *Witty sentences*
   a. *Epigrams and quips*—Terse, usually wise sayings defined as a "grain of truth told in a twinkling of an eye."
   b. *Definitions*—Puns or riddles.
   c. *Signs*—Humor may come from the location of the sign. (*Catholic Digest* has a column "Signs of the Times.")
   d. *Things from the press*—Typographical errors, use of wrong words (especially in classifieds), poor arrangement of words which results in humor.
   e. *Cartoon gags*—Many freelancers work with cartoonists, writing the gag that appears under the cartoon.

8. *Contests*—Many secular magazines have contests that require creative ability. *The Saturday Evening Post* features a photo caption contest. Company publications often run contests on subjects such as "How Do You Save Energy in Your Home?" Women's magazines feature recipe contests. Keep alert to these limited filler possibilities.

Poetry, daily devotions, and puzzles are also used as fillers. Daily devotional material is covered next in this chapter, poetry in Chapter Twelve, and puzzles in Chapter Sixteen.

Where do you find fillers? Here are four watchwords. Use them in your own situation.

Observe—people's reactions (both humorous and tragic), funny signs, unusual hobbies.

Listen—to conversations in stores and on buses, children's bright sayings, speakers, sermons.

Read—biographies, books of quotations, magazines, newspapers, newsletters. Most writers are voracious readers.

Search your own experiences—for how-to hints, handicraft ideas, recipes, material for personal-experience fillers. Jot down ideas. Take note of family reactions in given situations. Look for the religious angle in every situation.

Ideas are all around us. Be alert and soon you will have a wealth of material for fillers—a lucrative and fun way to write.

WRITING DAILY DEVOTIONAL MATERIAL
by Mary Lou Redding

The author is managing editor of The Upper Room, *the well-known bimonthly booklet of daily devotional readings.*

Preaching has been described as "filling twenty minutes with holy sound." Some people seem to think that devotional materials are the printed equivalent of that sort of preaching—rhapsodizing in ethereal terms about vague abstractions that have little connection with reality. But devotional writing is not just pleasant-sounding words that make readers feel good inside, verbal stroking. On the contrary, good devotional writing often makes readers not more but *less* comfortable, because it confronts our inertia or resistance and leads us to see where we can be more responsive to God's work in our lives and in the world around us.

Good devotional writing helps readers connect the events of their daily lives with the ongoing activity of God. It causes readers to reflect on ordinary events as a means of understanding supernatural truths. It feeds the interior life, causing readers to examine their commitment to God's ways. As humans, we perceive abstract truths through concrete experiences—and so devotional writing must be concrete. It must be authentic.

In order to be authentic, the writer must choose subjects that she or he knows firsthand. Just as good fiction is that which the reader can identify with, so good devotional writing must cause the reader to see himself or herself. Though the objects and situations you are describing may not be familiar to the reader (and unfamiliar settings may actually intrigue readers), the human reactions and emotions surrounding them must be. The events of daily life may seem too mundane to be the subject for devotional writing, but actually they are the events that best serve the purpose of the writing. When we see God's action in common objects and activities, each encounter with them serves as a reminder of God's work. John wrote to the believers, "That which we have seen, and heard, and looked upon, and our hands have handled . . . that we declare unto you" (1 John 1:3,4, RSV). Devotional writing will be most effective when its subject matter is that which we also have seen, heard, and handled for ourselves.

ANECDOTE FORMATS

Not all devotional material is written in the first person, from actual experience. Many denominations and groups publish daily devotional material. A day's meditation usually consists of a basic anecdote from which a spiritual lesson is drawn, and the anecdote may not be first person. There are several alternatives to the first-person-anecdote format. One of these is retelling a Bible story, fictionalizing it or setting it in modern terms or times. Another is using a familiar phrase, a motto, or a synopsis of a story or poem as a springboard for expansion or contrast. For instance, a quote such as Frost's "Home is the place where, when you have to go there,/ They have to take you in," could be the basis for a discussion of the free and open way God welcomes us, not from necessity but in love.

113

Another common form of anecdote is a contrast or comment on a misstatement. (These are usually from a child; we receive a very large number that fit in this category but use very few.) A fourth form recounts in the third person an adventure or tragedy that happened to someone else. All of these alternative anecdote forms carry with them a dangerous tendency to be entirely abstract, to have very little concrete detail.

Concrete detail abounds in everyday life, and you can train yourself to use the experiences of your daily routine as the basis for good devotional material. The first step in cultivating such a mindset is training yourself to note the details of ordinary events closely and to expect to see God at work through them. You may want to keep a journal in which you record conversations and sensory details. The writing is not the key; the key is deliberate observation. (Human nature being what it is, however, some people can be deliberate only if they set themselves a task of writing about what they intend to observe.) When you consider the events of a day in retrospect to see where God's hand was present, that is meditation. When you look ahead and see how God's ethic of love and service forms your tasks and attitudes, that is meditation. Both kinds of meditation can be written into devotional materials. Until the meditative frame of mind comes naturally, you may find it helpful to use a formula such as the one that follows:

1. Choose an event from your life, something that you experienced with your physical senses, and report it. Write down every detail you can remember, including at least one detail from each of the five senses. Try to re-create the experience so concretely that anyone who read the report would feel the same emotions and sensations that you did.
2. List the characters in the story—a woman, a man, two children, a dog—whatever they were.
3. Analyze the situation in order to classify it. Was it an experience of loss? Success? Family solidarity? Leave-taking? Reconciliation? Rescue? Mistaken identity (when things were not what they seemed)?
4. Look for a spiritual/scriptural parallel. For instance, a story

of loss might be compared to the woman who lost the coin; an experience of failure could be compared to Jesus' conversation with Peter, when Jesus said what Peter learned would be used later to strengthen others; an experience of leave-taking, to Abram leaving Haran for Ur, and so on. The point is, look for ways to link your experience with God's nature or activity as revealed in the Bible.

5. Spell out the connection as clearly as you can. (A corollary of Murphy's Law for writers: Whatever can be misunderstood or misconstrued, will be.)

The result of this exercise will be the rough draft of a devotional piece. (You may also use it to work backward from scripture by listing the Bible characters, analyzing the situation, and looking at your experience for an illustration of the principle presented in the Bible.) Once the rough draft is completed, you face the task of editing. You must choose the details and the ordering of them which most efficiently convey your point. Then you must fit the material to the format of the publication you will submit it to, adding a text, reading, prayer, or whatever else is required. If you are seriously pursuing publication in devotional magazines, inquire about how material is chosen for that publication. For instance, *The Upper Room* tries to balance use of Old Testament and New Testament readings. We work harder to use meditations based on Old Testament texts (other than Psalms) than we do to use a New Testament text (especially a familiar passage such as 1 Corinthians 13 or Matthew 25:24-41). Some daily devotional magazines, such as *Light for Today*, work from a lectionary or use a particular book of the Bible in each issue. Since Christians lean heavily on the New Testament in their study life, most devotional magazines have a dearth of material based on the books of Old Testament history or prophecy, so using these may increase your chances for publication. (In any case, reading the less familiar passages of the Bible in your own prayer and study life will enrich the store of illustrations from which you can draw in your writing. And you may see something about God that you had not seen before as you meditate on less familiar scripture passages.)

Writing good devotional material is a challenge. Writing for daily guides with their strict limitations of length and format is particularly demanding. But you can train yourself to look consciously at daily events to see God revealed. And when you do, you enrich your own sense of God's presence as you make discoveries to share with others.

TEN COMMANDMENTS FOR WRITERS

by Lee Wyndham

1

Love thy subject.

2

Love thy reader.

3

Thou shalt not begin without prior meditation.

4

Thou shalt know thy characters as well as thou knowest thyself—even better!

5

Thou shalt not begin until thou knowest whither thou goest, and have a well-thought-out plan for the journey.

6

Thou shalt STOP when thy story is finished.

7

Thou shalt not worship thy words as images graven in precious marble.

8

Thou shalt make a clear, dark-ribbon copy of thy work.

9

Thou shalt study thy markets diligently, and ONLY THEN send thy manuscript into the world.

10

Thou shalt not brood upon its fate, but set about the workings of thy next project, with goodwill and a high heart.

Part Three

CHAPTER NINE

WRITING THE INSPIRATIONAL ARTICLE

by Georgiana Walker

Georgiana Walker of Glendale, California, a former editor of Family Life To-day, *has had twenty years of editorial experience with Gospel Light Publications. The author of numerous published articles, she often leads workshops on article writing at conferences and seminars for Christian writers. She currently is the director of Christian Writer's Manuscript Services.*

INSPIRATIONAL AND

INSPIRATIONAL AND Christian periodicals offer the article writer a vast variety of markets. A recently published book that scruntinizes the religious marketplace lists more than 500 publications whose editors depend on freelance writers for at least 50 percent of their article needs.

In recent months I've examined dozens of denominational and interdenominational publications and discovered much that is encouraging and significant to the article writer.

Although many of the periodicals are for a general readership, the trend is toward publications for specialized audiences. There are magazines devoted to the particular needs of the clergy, teachers, students, scientists, doctors, publishers. There are publications for different age groups—youngsters, seniors, teenagers, young adults, and middle-agers. Many magazines are designed for families, some for singles. A few periodicals are especially for men, others for women.

With this enormous variety, markets for specialized as well as general-interest articles abound. This does not mean that the religious market is an easy one. On the contrary, editors of today's inspirational and Christian magazines are looking for top-quality writing. They buy with keen discernment.

When you develop a sharply focused article tailored to fit the needs of a specific publication, you are well on the way to receiving an acceptance letter.

WHAT IS AN ARTICLE?

Various definitions describe the article as:

- a short prose composition
- a nonfiction story
- a nonfiction piece that focuses sharply on an individual, an episode, or a theme

Although all of these statements are accurate, their brevity makes them vague. Successful article writers know that in addition to these basic qualifications, a salable article meets these further requirements.

An article is more than a discussion of a general subject. It is a sharply focused story that deals with a narrow aspect of a wide subject.

Max Gunther, a veteran article writer and author of *Writing the Modern Magazine Article*, maintains that the key to success in writing and selling an article is the author's ability to come up with a clear, sharp focus; to develop an article that makes one solid point.

My most frustrating experience as a magazine editor is to read a stack of freelance manuscripts and to discover few—if any—well-focused articles. That's sad. Many of the writers are good with thoughts and good with words, but they tell too much about the broad subject and fail to zero in on one central, sharply focused idea.

Developing a well-focused article demands discipline. The author must be willing to leave the broad, general subject and limit himself to working with that one point he wants to make. As William Zinsser says in his book *On Writing Well,* "Decide what corner of your subject you are going to bite off, and be content to cover it well and stop. You can always come back another day and bite off another corner."

Author Kathleen Winkler demonstrates what "biting off one corner" means in her article "Little White Squares: Who Runs Your Life?" that appeared in *Family Life Today.* In the article Winkler talks about overcommitment—the too-busy life. But instead of dealing with the overall consequences of living with a calendar that is crammed full, she focuses on one question: What does overscheduling do to your marriage?

A great way to learn more about the meaning of focus in article writing is to take a magazine or two that you enjoy reading and to define the focus of three or four articles. First read an article, then go back and examine it, answering for yourself: What one point did the author try to make? Did he succeed? Was the focus fuzzy or sharp? Did any of the material in the article take me away from the author's viewpoint?

I've discovered a formula that's good insurance against fuzzy focus: State your key idea in one sentence. Tape that sentence above your typewriter. Read it often. Use it as a guide to keep every fact, every quote, and every illustration on target.

You'll find that defining your focus *before* you begin to write enables you to choose those items from your research that most effectively support your point of view.

An article is more than the author's view of an idea. It is the author's viewpoint supported by believable evidence.

Quotes, statistics, anecdotes, comparisons—these are the sparks that bring articles to life and make the author's view credible. Art Spikol, a columnist writing about nonfiction in *Writer's Digest,* points out, "A perfectly good writer can strike out . . . because of what isn't in the article. This may take the form of spotty research, an insufficient number of interviews, oversimplification, and so on. Sometimes the problem is lack of examples—anecdotes that illustrate the point."

Good examples help a writer make his point quickly and avoid laborious explanations in general terms. Most general statements demand support and amplification of one kind or another. The skillful use of backup material makes the difference between the professional and the amateur writer. The professional understands the vital need of establishing the validity of his viewpoint by showing the whys behind his thinking. He knows that simply telling what he thinks is not enough.

For example, in "The Transforming Power of Television" by Glenn G. Sparks published recently in *Eternity*, the author examines the question how *does* TV affect us? He writes, "It should come as no surprise that children imitate actions and attitudes they see on TV. . . . But obviously they don't imitate *everything* they see and hear. The important question becomes, 'How do they decide what to imitate?' "

Although earlier in the article Sparks used his own child's behavior as an example, he now moves to authorities in childhood behavior for information as he says, "According to the research of Dr. Albert Bandura, Stanford University, at least two factors are critical for the child's decision. . . ." And so the reader knows the article is giving more than one person's opinion. He's getting the author's view supported by opinions based on research and findings closely related to the thrust of the article.

An article is more than a well-told account of a happening. It is a story told to prove a point.

An article that focuses on a story should use the story for a definite purpose. In "The Man Who Taught Me How to Die" by Wightman Weese, published by *Moody Monthly*, the author tells the story of a loving father, a staunch church member, a friend and encourager of everyone in the community, who dies of cancer.

Told from the viewpoint of the sick man's pastor, the story shows the struggle many Christians have when they attempt to comfort one another during times of suffering and grief. The story provides a powerful answer to the questions, Does trusting God mean you don't cry, you don't talk honestly, you don't express how you really feel?

As the story unfolds, the point is made: Christians can reconcile genuine faith in God with genuine emotions.

A beginning writer might have added his comments to the story, calling attention to the point it established. But Weese, an experienced editor and writer, knew he would only cloud the issue if he moved in to share his feelings. The full impact of the story was allowed to hit the reader without interference.

As Glenn Arnold, teacher of journalism at Wheaton Graduate School, says, "The writer's shadow shouldn't fall across the subject; the subject should be the star." Personal observations usually distract the reader from the point you want the story to make. Let the story do its own work.

An article is more than a collection of facts, more than a series of episodes. It is a structured writing that carries the reader from the beginning to a satisfying conclu-

sion—always moving in the direction chosen by the author.

I particularly remember a "collection" article I returned with a note about the need for structure. The writer was a father and his cover letter explained: "These incidents from the life of our boy show what parenthood is all about."

Wrong. The father had simply put together a series of happenings from the life of his adventurous youngster. The episodes could have been used to make some point about parenthood but they were not. There was no plan, no direction, no point made, no structure to carry the reader to any conclusion.

There is no single way to structure an article so it will make its point most effectively, no magic framework that is right for every idea. Nevertheless, every article must include essential parts in its structure: a *lead* to catch the reader's interest; a *statement of theme* to establish the author's direction; the *body* of the article that presents the evidence and develops the author's viewpoint; and the *conclusion* that leaves the reader thinking, wanting to take action. Examine any well-written article and you'll discover these key parts that make up the article's framework. (Specific patterns for structuring an article are discussed later in this chapter.)

When writing for the Christian market, it is most important to recognize that *an article for a Christian publication is more than a focused, structured, well-illustrated piece of writing that makes a convincing point. An article for a Christian magazine also communicates faith in the reality of God and confidence that biblical principles work in today's world.*

In many articles published by Christian magazines this "sense of the sacred" is not in full view. But look again.

Leaf through a number of Christian periodicals and determine how different writers communicated some aspect of the Christian viewpoint. Look for accounts that show how biblical principles helped individuals make responsible choices. Analyze articles that comment on social injustices. Pinpoint Christian values on display. Find examples of God as man's refuge and strength in difficult situations.

You wouldn't expect an article about basketball's zany Harlem Globetrotters to say much about God's relationship with man. But "America's Team," Bill Wood's article about the Globetrotters in *Athletes in Action*, says a great deal.

Wood focuses on the Trotters' long separations from their families. And when he writes about the loneliness the players suffer he includes a quote from "Fast" Eddie Fields, a new player on the team. Fields says, "Being away from home you are pretty much alone and you need help—someone to talk to. You can talk to God." And veteran player Hubert "Geese" Ausbie, who is known by the Trotters for his nightly Bible studies and gospel music tapes, talkes openly about how God has helped him many times. Especially, he explains how his faith enabled him to accept the death of his mother and the murder of his brother.

It's no mystery why Wood's article qualified for publication in a Christian magazine. His story is not only an entertaining piece about a famous basketball team, it's also a story of faith in action.

WHAT IS A GOOD ARTICLE IDEA?

A few summers ago I led an article-writing workshop at a Christian writers' conference in California's Santa Cruz Mountains. That's where I met Bob and had the fun of looking through his idea notebook. The cover of the brown spiral notebook was in bad shape. But *inside* that book was a gold mine.

Page by page were facts from newspaper stories, thoughts about an argument with a next-door neighbor, observations and opinions about Bob's family, his church, and his college friends. He even had a page of notes from a talk he's had with his granddad on how the senior member of the family was coping with retirement. The last pages listed articles sold and queries out to editors.

That notebook was striking proof to everyone in the workshop that ideas for articles surround the writer. The key is to grab the idea and capture its essence on paper.

Not all of Bob's ideas had article potential. No matter—many of his ideas were great. How can a writer tell the difference.?

Here are five questions that will help you decide whether or not an idea can be developed into a salable article.

1. *Is the idea significant to a large number of people?* Who will care about the idea? If your idea doesn't answer a question that a large number of people are asking, if it isn't relevant to the interests or problems of a specific audience, it doesn't have good article possibility.

Before you spend time gathering material and writing, visualize the specific reader who needs what you want to say. Identify the magazines he's likely to read. Try to be honest as you evaluate: Would the editors of those magazines be interested in my idea?

Experienced writers carefully weigh the significance of an idea against the needs of a definite audience *before* they decide it's worth developing. On the other hand, the beginner often pours his thoughts on paper then asks: Who is this article for? What is a possible market?

2. *Can this idea be narrowed to a sharp focus?* There's that word *focus* again. But you can't talk about article ideas without mentioning focus. That's what provides the specific angle that gives the idea significance for a particular group of people. Focus also gives the writer a sturdy handle for steering an article idea in one direction, the direction that makes his point.

"The Religious Vote" by Jim Castelli in *Commonweal* is a commentary on the massive involvement of religion in the 1980 national elections. A broad subject. The article could be a dull, unfocused collection of election statistics. But Castelli's narrow focus—the historic shifts in religious voting patterns—makes the article move, and it's fascinating reading for the religiously oriented American voter.

3. *Is the idea timely?* Christian periodicals want articles that speak to the current scene. *Eternity* asks for articles "with biblical emphasis on contemporary developments." *Evangelical Beacon* uses "pieces on current issues from an evangelical perspective." *Spiritual Life* wants articles that deal "with the manner in which men and women encounter God and live in His presence in the contemporary world." And so it goes.

Does your idea have special meaning for now? Explain why today's readers want to hear about your idea. Why is it relevant to today's situations? Can the idea be supported with up-to-date information, current research, contemporary opinion? How much has been written about the subject recently? Use the *Readers' Guide to Periodical Literature* at any library to locate articles on your subject that have appeared in secular publications. At a Bible college or seminary library consult *Religious Index One* to discover when and where your subject has been handled in Christian magazines. If too much has been published on your idea during the past year, put it aside for the time being.

4. *Is the idea fresh, the approach unique?* A unique approach is often based on the author's own experiences. For example, "The Spiritual Journey of Jerome Hines" by William Proctor in the *Christian Herald* uses the opera singer's unique career, his difficulties and successes, to communicate the message that God's promises for strength and guidance have powerful meaning for every situation.

Joan Wester Anderson, in her article "Who Me? An Expert?" published in *The Writer* tells how her uncommon experiences as mother of a minimal brain dysfunction child gave her insights that she felt compelled to share with other parents of MBD youngsters. The result? In recent years a number of Joan Anderson's articles dealing with MBD have appeared in Christian as well as secular periodicals.

A fresh idea and a unique approach are good ideas when they truly relate to the needs of others.

5. *Will your idea pass the query-letter test?* There is no better test than writing a query letter to separate the strong ideas from the weak. Attempting to write a query will help you discover:

Is the idea compact enough to be described in a few sentences?

Can you make a convincing sales pitch for the idea? Can you tell the editor why his readers will be interested in your approach to the subject?

Can you state the one key point you want the article to make? Can you give the editor a few details about how you will develop the idea, and maybe a fact or two and an anecdote?

Can you describe some of the sources of material you will use?

If you can do all of these things, get busy. Write that query. Let the editor tell you, "That's a good idea."

RESEARCH

Before you write a query letter, you'll need to get started on research for your article. There are many good sources of material close at hand.

Most writers are well aware of the excellent reference materials available at the public library. But when you write for Christian periodicals there are times when you need to check out additional research possibilities.

I have found the librarian at a nearby seminary most helpful. She introduced me to *Religious Index One* which has proved to be a valuable source of information on religious publications.

Christian high schools, both Protestant and Catholic, often have libraries you can arrange to use. I also discovered that the library of a large Presbyterian church in our city is a good place to look at current issues of the Christian magazines I don't receive at home.

The Christian bookstores in our community are great research spots. I explain why I'm browsing and no one objects. Recently, one of the store managers suggested I take a few books to use at home on a forty-eight-hour consignment. Then, of course, I often buy books because they look too interesting to leave behind on the bookstore shelf.

There are also resource materials you need near your typewriter. I find a reference Bible, concordance, and reliable Bible commentary are necessary tools. I wouldn't know how to operate without the comprehensive index and listings of information in my *Thompson Chain Reference Bible* (B. B. Kirkbride Co., Indianapolis). Examine various Bibles and commentaries before you choose what seems best for your needs.

One word about telephone research. Many times the best quote for your article will come from a telephone conversation, the result of some well-planned questions. Questions by phone can enable you to quote authorities on your subject no matter where they are located.

In doing research for this chapter I called editors of Christian publications to ask four specific questions. It was fast, satisfying research, and I didn't have to leave my desk. Here are the four questions:

1. To what extent do you depend on freelance writers for your article needs?

2. What specific themes are you looking for from freelancers?

3. Do you require a query or do you prefer to receive the fully developed article?

4. What word of advice would you like to give freelance writers?
   Interestingly, the "word of advice" mentioned by *all* editors was "Get information about the needs of our magazine and please read our magazine before submitting a manuscript!"

FROM IDEA TO ARTICLE

Let's say you have a good article idea.

You've gathered facts, anecdotes, and statistics, and everything that you need to bring the idea to life as an article. In fact, you're feeling overwhelmed with all the material you've collected. What now?

It's time to start building, time to put the article parts together in a way that gives the reader the best possible view of your idea.

No matter what type of article you choose to do—interview, personality sketch, how-to, narrative, or whatever—it must have a solid structure. It must feel compact and have a unity and a singleness of purpose that carry the reader to the point you want to make.

Although there is no one way to put an article together, here are a few of the patterns successful writers use to structure an article. Writers use these patterns because they work well, over and over again.

Train-of-thought method. I first heard about the train-of-thought formula for articles in a college journalism class. Years later, in Omer Henry's book *Writing and Selling Magazine Articles* I read his description of the "train" and even ran across a couple of references to the train concept in a writer's magazine. I decided that if the train was good enough to be around all those years I'd better examine it closely. I'm glad I did.

Since then, the train has helped me teach article-writing classes, evaluate stacks of freelance manuscripts, and transform ideas into articles without getting lost in the process.

Visualize a freight train. Snowplow. Locomotive. Boxcars. Caboose. What can this freight train do for you?

Snowplow—captures reader's attention. The snowplow is the lead that literally carries the reader into the article. It may be an anecdote or a quote, maybe a statement or a question. It can even be a paragraph or two. However long, it must arouse the reader's curiosity and keep him reading.

Locomotive—states the theme. Immediately following the lead the author must make a capsule statement that sets the direction and establishes the focus. This capsule sentence gives the reader a concise preview of the author's viewpoint. Examine published articles and you'll find that all-important capsule sentence in the first few paragraphs. That sentence is the locomotive, the power that keeps the article moving on the right track.

Boxcars—carry the evidence that supports the author's viewpoint. The boxcars are the paragraphs in the body of the article that hold the pertinent facts, anecdotes, quotes, and statistics that back up the author's view. These information-carrying cars should be arranged in an order that presents convincing evidence in a logical sequence. As the boxcars move toward the conclusion they help the author state and restate his point in a variety of ways.

Caboose—concludes the article. Often the conclusion is a quote that expresses the theme in a satisfying way. Sometimes it's an anecdote that neatly summarizes the theme. Or it can be a brief restatement of the capsule sentence. However the article ends, the caboose must leave the reader with a satisfying feeling of finality.

The "train" that's helping me write this chapter is lined up against the wall near my desk. It's made of boxes labeled Article Defined, Article Ideas, From Idea to Article, Research, Rewrite, Focus. I'm still shifting material back and forth from one "car" to another. And I will for a while longer. I still haven't decided what will ride in the caboose.

Author Edward Hannibal actually draws the train that helps him write. He explains, "I literally draw a train of linked boxes . . . this very mechanical process is excellent for helping you sort material. I tack the train up on the wall in front of me and write against it." And he goes on to say: "Inside your boxcars, try always to have some kind of . . . action. Trains, after all, are meant to move."

That is the point, to write articles that move readers to a new opinion, a different viewpoint, a satisfying conclusion.

Roller-coaster formula. In this book *Effective Feature Writing,* Clarence Schoenfeld explains the roller-coaster approach to article structure. He says, "Think of your piece as a roller-coaster ride. At each peak you are introducing a new idea . . . then you dive down immediately with a bit of clarification. Then you mount up to another new concept, and coast back down with another explanation."

In the roller-coaster pattern the high points are for making key statements, the generalizations. The valleys are for the specifics, all kinds of supporting evidence. The ups and downs are used to present a logical progression of thought that creates a feeling of continuity. The highs and lows provide variety and change of pace, all the while moving toward that satisfying, speedy downhill run to the conclusion.

Both the train-of-thought and the roller-coaster patterns are based on moving ahead, carrying the reader step by step to the author's conclusion.

Hey! You! See! So? Four words hardly make a formula. But the descriptive "Hey! You! See! So?" used by Walter Campbell in his book *Writing Non-*

fiction provides graphic illustrations of the work each part of an article must do.

Hey!—the lead calling out for the reader's attention.

You!—gives the theme of the piece, the reason the article will be important to the reader.

See!—the body of the article, where the author tells and shows what his viewpoint is all about.

So—is the conclusion that encourages the reader to accept the author's view and take action.

To discover how accurately these four words describe the parts of an article, go through a number of published articles labeling the article parts: Hey! You! See! So? With most articles this exercise will reveal a structure that allows the author to call out to you, tell you his theme, give you the evidence that supports his opinion, then throw the ball to you for the next play.

Put these article patterns to work for you. Each of the patterns can help you build a sturdy article structure that effectively carries your idea from you to the reader.

TIME TO FINALIZE

When the rough drafts of your article are completed and it's time to polish your manuscript for the final typing, change hats. Become more of an editor than a writer.

But before you start editing—and rewriting when necessary—put your article aside a day or two and let the copy cool.

Sometime during that cooling period pick up William Zinsser's book *On Writing Well* (Harper & Row) and *The Elements of Style* by William Strunk, Jr., and E. B. White (Macmillan). The straightforward advice about simplicity, clutter, words, unity, and style is good medicine before any editing and rewriting.

What will you look for as you work on the final draft? What will you listen for as you read each paragraph, each sentence and each word aloud?

Fuzzy focus. Do any illustrations or quotes introduce material that takes the reader off course?

Generalities. Are there spots where specifics are needed to validate a general statement?

Rough spots. Do you need to smooth transitions? Make time and space changes less obvious?

Clutter. Do laborious phrases and long words need to be exchanged for a shorter phrase or word? Do redundancies cloud your meaning with repetition?

Obscure meaning. Does jargon and technical language interfere with your expressing yourself clearly and simply?

As you edit and polish, remember Zinsser's statement: "The secret of good writing is to strip every sentence to its cleanest components."

If you use Bible quotations in your article, be sure you have quoted accurately and that the Bible reference includes identification of version you used. For example, "Proclaim the good tidings . . . (Ps. 68:11, NASB). The NASB explains that the quote is from the *New American Standard Bible.* TLB indicates *The Living Bible.* NIV, the *New International Version.* Editors and readers appreciate this information.

When you are finalizing a manuscript for the Christian market, Margaret Anderson's book *The Christian Writer's Handbook* (Harper & Row) is a valuable tool. Chapter 5, "Disciplines of Style," will help you smooth transitions, choose stronger verbs, check your figures of speech, and much more. Especially note Anderson's comments on specialized terms or jargon. They will help you avoid unfamiliar religious terms that can make your meaning unclear.

Before you send your article on its way to an editor, have a knowledgeable person give it a final reading. It is surprising what an objective pair of eyes can discover.

DO'S AND DON'TS FOR THE CHRISTIAN MARKET

This list of brief admonitions includes valuable guides when you write for the inspirational and Christian markets.

- Do read before you write. Read Christian periodicals. Read the newspaper. Read a sampling of secular magazines. You earn the right to be read when you are informed about needs, problems, and trends in today's world.

- Do be relevant. Readers of Christian magazines want to know what Christianity means for their lives.

- Do show struggle and puzzlement within the life of faith. Readers and editors want realism.

- Do write from the solid base of personal experience and strong conviction. Sincerity kindles response.

- Don't use religious jargon and clichés. A specialized vocabulary obscures meaning, weakens your message.

- Don't preach. Instead, clarify your point with thought-provoking evidence.

- Don't let that good idea grow old. Start now to nurture it with research.

- And—*do write*. Your insights, your experiences, and the light you've discovered that illumines your way can brighten life for others.

As Christ told his disciples, "You are the light of the world. A city on a hill cannot be hidden. Neither do people light a lamp and put it under a bowl. Instead they put it on its stand, and it gives light to everyone in the house. In the same way, let your light shine before men . . ." (Matt. 5:14, 15 NIV).

CHAPTER TEN

WRITING INSPIRATIONAL FICTION

by Lee Roddy

Lee Roddy, who also has written two other chapters in this book, is a prolific fiction writer and teacher in this specialized field. He has been writing and selling fiction since he was fourteen years old. He is currently doing a series of fiction books for a major publisher and has led Writer's Digest workshops on fiction writing.

CHRISTIAN FICTION

CHRISTIAN FICTION is alive and well, as it has been for decades; this field shows every sign of continuing to be a warm, friendly market for new as well as experienced writers. But if you want to write for this steady specialty market, some basics must be understood. Step-by-step, this chapter will tell you what you need to know to write salable Christian fiction.

Major outlets for Christian fiction lie in the weekly take-home Sunday school papers, probably the hungriest fiction market around today. There are other (although fewer) opportunities in the longer novel forms, especially young people's or children's books.

More than twenty-five years ago, I sold my first short stories to a well-established religious house. Just a couple of years ago, the same firm bought three of my adult Christian novels. My published works for this house came to the attention of a major secular book publisher who called to say they'd like me to write an adult novel for them. So it is possible to cross over from the ecclesiastical fiction world to the temporal, or continue to write in both, as I now do. That's because the basics are much the same in both secular and religious fiction publishing, except that the latter requires a spiritual dimension and makes some subjects or details taboo.

THE BASIC FIVE

First, you must understand marketing. Before you write any fiction, you should know which editors might publish it. For if your work doesn't meet an editor's needs, readers will never see your fiction.

Second, you must use the correct mechanical format. An editor can tell at one glance if your fiction is in the proper form. If it doesn't have the accepted professional appearance, the editors will assume you're an amateur. While this is no hindrance in some houses, an attractive manuscript always pays.

Third, you must realize that any short story or novel must have a proper structure—an interior support system.

Fourth, there must be story elements, or ingredients which make the short work or novel appealing and satisfying. This is probably the most difficult part of fiction writing.

Fifth (and perhaps this really should be part of requirement 1), you must know the demographics of your intended readers. You've got to understand who reads your fiction, and why. This is especially critical in the inspirational or religious field.

Let's look at each of these criteria in some detail.

MARKETING: KEY TO SUCCESS

Marketing is covered in Chapter 3, "Where are the Markets?" by Elaine Colvin, but its importance cannot be overemphasized.

Researching markets will show distinct differences in publishing house requirements. For example, a study of *Fiction Writer's Market* and *The Religious Writers Marketplace* shows at least fifty outlets for spiritually oriented short stories. Each house indicates specific guidelines in presenting its weekly, monthly, or quarterly periodicals. Some examples:

"No . . . slang or references to drinking or smoking."

"No erotica, horror, gay/lesbian, fantasy, confession, gothic, etc."

Another publisher avoids "controversial" stories about race, feminism, war, capital punishment, and homosexuality.

Other religious houses won't accept anything about dancing, pornography, card playing, or profanity. Still other Christian publishers list their taboos in short stories as talking animals, science fiction, or Halloween.

On the positive side, many Christian periodicals stress "some aspect of the Christian life," "strong evangelical viewpoints," or "character-building stories that teach Christian truths."

Periodical publishers of short fiction primarily seek to build character and instill Christian values through short stories. Like Jesus' parables, these short works of fiction strive to make a point about the faith through an entertaining narrative devoid of preaching. The theme or moral must be inherent in the story itself.

Your job is to find the spiritual dimensions each house emphasizes and to write for that preference. Research to determine the need should precede the writing of any short story. Research should be sufficiently detailed so that if one house rejects the story, you'll know several possible alternates.

A Christian writing friend once told me, "I spent one hour researching markets for every two hours I wrote." She is today a highly successful author in this specialized field. Write your target publishers and ask for their tip sheets or authors' guides. These are usually free if you enclose an SASE (self-addressed, stamped, envelope).

You must read the publications you hope to sell to. It helps if you enjoy reading and genuinely desire to contribute to a publication. It's usually unwise to try to write for a periodical you can't stand to read—your attitude will show. Editors are sincere in their beliefs and what they present in printed form. Readers are the same. You should be, too.

Remember, the vast amount of material used up weekly, monthly, or quarterly by Christian publishers makes them hungry for good material. Editors can't exist without manuscripts. They need you as much as you need them, but since you're filling their needs, you must write to their requirements. Research will show you how.

In short, a fiction writer must know the markets!

MECHANICS: THE APPEARANCE OF PROFESSIONALISM

Marketing knowledge is a basic requirement for successful Christian fiction writing, and proper mechanical form is the second step.

Since mechanics are discussed in Chapter 7, "How to Get into Print," by Sally Stuart, I'll only stress that format instantly tells an editor a lot about you. For one thing, your first page tells him or her if you've studied your craft enough to know how that page should look. That takes only one glance. Margaret J. Anderson says, "You never get a second chance to make a good first impression."

A longtime editor of one of this country's best-known religious publishing houses told me, "Ninety percent of the material coming in to us is in the wrong form."

When you fail to follow the simple fundamentals of format, your work looks like that of an amateur. Although you may be unpublished, that's no excuse to be unprofessional in submitting your manuscript. Busy editors or readers may not take the time to wade through a first page that doesn't say "professional."

STRUCTURE: THE HIDDEN ESSENTIAL

Structure is basic to everything that possesses form, including writing. You might glance at an airplane, as a writer friend reminded me, and see only the wings and exterior. But if you were going to build an airplane, you'd have to get under the visible, outward shape and study the structure. It's equally true of writing fiction.

All short stories and novels have a beginning, a middle, and an end. This truth is at least as old as Aristotle's observation that a whole is that which has a beginning, a middle, and an end. But ten years of teaching writers' conferences around the country convinces me that most aspiring writers don't grasp this essential principle.

The Three O's

I'll pass along a simple formula taught me by a veteran screenwriter who'd spent more than thirty years in Hollywood.

Divide a piece of paper into thirds so that there's room to equally space out three O's like this:

O   O   O

The left O is the beginning of your short story. It stands for "Objective." Someone or something likeable (such as a dog) becomes your protagonist with an objective worth achieving.

If the lead character has no objective, the writer has no story. So determine first who your principal character is, what he or she wants very much, and for what good reason (motivation).

The middle O stands for "Obstacle(s)." There must be at least one major obstacle preventing the principal character from reaching the objective. In a short story, one obstacle is enough. In longer fiction, the author may shove many obstacles in front of the likeable hero or heroine.

The third O stands for "Outcome," the ending of the story. The last part must show how everything turns out. There are three common endings, which we'll discuss later.

Start with a Problem

To begin your short story, immediately introduce the likeable main character, give him or her a goal or objective, and then throw an obstacle in front of that objective. Presto! You've got an opening, because you have *conflict!*

A word of warning: having read thousands of short stories at writers' conferences, I've found the average writer begins on page four. A short story must begin on page one, preferably in line one, paragraph one, with a problem.

All obstacles arise from one or more of three basic forms of conflicts:

1. Man versus man.

2. Man versus nature.

3. Man versus self.

The first two are external conflicts. In man versus man, our protagonist is pitted against another person. They're competing for the same thing, or the opposing character/antagonist tries to prevent the protagonist from succeeding because it would jeopardize the opponent to let the hero succeed.

Man against nature would include fire, flood, or a host of other environmental obstacles. While a natural obstacle does not think, as an opposing character would, the natural element is no less threatening in its impersonal force.

The third basic form of conflict is internal. It represents struggles with fear, doubt, and a host of other intangible opposing forces. In a Christian short story, the main character may feel a conviction to act in a certain way, but resist. She feels she should make a commitment to serve Christ, or to re-commit her life to God. But fear of losing someone's friendship, or of having to give up certain activities, might create a strong internal struggle.

After the main character and his or her problem are presented in the opening, a struggle or conflict with the obstacle(s) advances the story and provides the body or middle. As the main character seeks to overcome the obstacles and achieve the objective, the reader is intrigued to see how it turns out.

Wrapping It All Up

That brings us to the outcome. The ending must show how the conflict is re-solved and whether the objective is achieved. This is relatively simple, for there are three basic kinds of endings.

1. The *happy ending* is the most common in Christian writing: The main character overcomes the obstacles and reaches the desired objective. In the case of David and Goliath, for instance, the young shepherd boy suc-cessfully defeats the giant Philistine enemy of the Hebrews by hitting him in the forehead with a stone from his sling.

2. The *bittersweet ending* is one in which the main character realizes too late that his or her actions cannot result in a happy ending, so the protag-onist does something noble but at a great price.

Consider the story of Samson, the Bible's strong man. God had a pur-pose for his life, but Samson didn't live up to that purpose. His greatest mis-take was to fall in love with a Philistine woman, Delilah. She persuaded Samson to confess the secret of his strength—his long hair. She clipped his locks, he became weak, and the Philistines made him a slave. He was blind-ed by his captors and thus incapacitated. But his hair grew out, his strength returned, and he had an opportunity to live up to his potential. He pushed apart the two pillars that held up the temple of the Philistines' pagan god. The collapse killed thousands of God's enemies, but Samson also died under the debris. This bittersweet ending is acceptable to readers because they un-derstand why Samson lost his life in this final noble act.

3. Readers rarely like the *unhappy or sad ending*, but they'll accept one if the writer has properly prepared them.

For instance, the Bible tells how Solomon became the wisest man who ever lived. At Solomon's request, God granted the Hebrew king great wis-dom so he could properly rule his people. But Solomon violated God's laws by marrying many foreign wives and allowing them to have their own pagan deities. In his old age, Solomon himself fell into idolatry.

The scriptures cite Solomon's sin of idolatry for God's displeasure. God's punishment was to take Solomon's kingdom from the son who was to rule after him. But this sad fate for the world's wisest man is acceptable because the readers understand why it had to be.

Once you have the three O's clearly in mind—you've decided what the story is about, from the opening through the body to the conclusion—you must flesh out your structure with the proper elements.

STORY ELEMENTS—THE HARDEST PART OF GOOD FICTION

Before starting to make a cake from scratch, the wise baker would read the recipe and line up all the necessary ingredients to be sure they're on hand. These would then be mixed in the proper order and stirred, and the mixture would finally be poured into the pan that gives shape to the finished product.

As you gather the basics to go into your fiction "cake," use this checklist for your "recipe."

1. In a single sentence, what's this story about?

2. What's the theme or point I'm trying to make?

3. Is conflict evident from the beginning?

4. Have I planned a high point or climax for the story?

5. Do I know how the story will end?

The answers to these questions will give you a grasp of the whole story so you'll be better able to set up the most crucial part, the opening.

The Vital First Sentence

A story should open fast and run hard from there. Here are some examples of my early published openings from denominational take-home papers:

> The entire cabin trembled with the knocking at the door. I sat bolt upright in bed and groped for the light switch.
> ("Crown Fire," *Catholic Boy*)

It was the day after Charlie Higgins was bitten by a rabid skunk that Grandpa Morton came to stay with us awhile. ("Eli of the Ladies' Polecat Patrol," *Sunday Pix*)

Ken Smathers stared at his boss. So that's how it was done! A penny here, two cents there, maybe a nickel here—and the customer never knew. ("Checkstand Cheat," *Sunday Digest*)

In each of these stories the main character is introduced with a problem or a hint of one. After that, the objective is quickly presented and the other story ingredients (which I'll explain momentarily) are worked in as smoothly and rapidly as possible. After an editor had read the first 500 words, I don't think he or she—even today—would put any of those manuscripts aside. Yet some of those examples are nearly twenty-five years old. Good story-telling elements don't age.

Remember this is the most crucial part—unless the editor likes the first page or so, the story may never be read. So you must take great care to see that the opening is exactly right. This can be done by asking yourself certain questions:

1. Will my story entertain from the very beginning?

2. Will my first page have eye appeal, look easy to read?

3. Remembering editor Joe Bayly's comment, "You don't need to eat all of an egg to know it's bad," have I planned an opening taste that will make it impossible not to eat the whole thing?

Opening Elements

A friend of mine began his highly successful writing career as a reader for one of New York's major short fiction publishers. He was paid fifty cents for each unsolicited manuscript he read. If he recommended a story which the magazine published, my reading friend received an additional five dollars. It was to his advantage to find the five-dollar stories.

He quickly learned that if he didn't like the first 500 words (roughly two pages) there was no sense reading further. He promptly rejected the manuscript. However, if he liked the opening, he'd steal a glance at the ending to see if it seemed to wrap up well. If he was still interested, he put the manuscript aside to read through later. This usually turned out to be worth five dollars to him.

He passed along the questions he expected to find answered in the first page or two of a short story. These opening elements are critical to all good fiction.

1. Viewpoint character: Am I telling this story from the right point of view? It may not be the main character. Consider Dr. Watson and Sherlock Holmes.
2. Locale: Where's this story taking place?
3. Time: Is it past, present, or future?
4. Mood: Is it light drama, humorous, etc?
5. Description: Are people and places described briefly, but vividly enough so the readers can picture the characters, locale, and time period?
6. Immediacy: Is something happening or about to happen that draws the reader into the story?
7. Characters: Is the protagonist introduced at once, made likeable, and immediately plunged into trouble?
   Who's the opposing character?
   Who're the other necessary characters?
8. Motivation: What does the main character want very much and for good reason? What motivates the opposing character to make him or her clash with the main character? What motivates all other people in the story? Everyone's motivation must be believable.
9. Conflict: Is this going to be a conflict of attitudes or a physical conflict?
10. Confrontation: Do I know what the main characters are going to do so they're in direct conflict at once?
11. Stakes: What's the reward for success and penalty for failure for the two principal characters?
12. Decision: What decision does the lead character make that sets the story in motion?
13. Action: What's the initial action taken as a result of that decision?
14. Progression: What are the logical results of this action? What reaction does it cause in the other characters?
15. Cliff-hanger: Have I plotted my opening so that the reader can't quit at the end of the first 500 words?
16. Scene: All major scenes must be shown, not told. Narration is for lesser points—all important scenes should be re-created: visualized for the reader, complete with dialogue. Smaller scenes may also be briefly re-created, or shown as though they were happening in front of the reader.
17. Words: Have I chosen active words (especially verbs) instead of passive?
18. Dialogue: Is there believable dialogue on the first page, preferably showing conflict? Try to work characterization

into the way each one speaks. Use it to advance the story and build conflict. Aim to have dialogue begin on page one if possible. Read dialogue aloud to be sure it's natural and believable.

19. Plant: If I'm going to need something later to make the story turn out logically, have I planted that fact early? Remember: "Plant it now; pay it off later."

20. Crisis and Climax: Have I planned my opening so that it will lead to a rousing crisis? Have I planned my climax so the reader will be satisfied?

It's never easy to get so many vital elements into the beginning of a story. Rise to the challenge and fun of writing a strong opening.

Middle Elements

One of my writing instructors used to say that the writer should "Lead an elephant down an alley so he can't turn back." A good story moves logically and smoothly from an intriguing opening with all necessary elements to the place where there is no turning back. No matter what the obstacles are, the author can't quit, and his main character can't stop, either. Hopefully, the reader will stick around to see what happens.

By now, you should have at least two compelling characters in conflict. The principal character has a worthwhile objective and good motivation, with some obstacles. In the center or body of the story, you develop the protagonist's struggle to overcome those obstacles.

What he or she does in this struggle provides the suspense (will he or she succeed or fail?) and keeps the interest high. Usually, the chief character struggles and fails, eventually coming to a crisis where all seems lost. This can be achieved by using a checklist for middle elements.

1. Inspirational: Is my protagonist acting in a way that shows character development? If she or he is tempted to do wrong, am I showing wholesome, inspirational character traits that will eventually cause my hero or heroine to do right?

2. Complications: Am I giving my main character difficulties that could prevent him from achieving the objective?

3. Black Hat: Is the opposing character (the Black Hat of old-time Westerns) winning all the battles? He should be at this point.

4. Theme: Am I telling an entertaining story wrapped around a kernel of truth so that my point, moral, or

theme will be clear without preaching when I reach the end?

5. Compassion: Am I building reader concern for the principal person struggling against increasingly heavy odds?

6. Back story: Have I kept the exposition brief in the front of the story so I can enlarge upon it here, either as back story or (rarely) in a brief flashback? Back story is defined as narration (usually in the form of the protagonist's thoughts) that provides important information about something that happened before the story opened. Back story may also be presented in dialogue (for example, in which the protagonist and another character briefly discuss previous events). Flashbacks are re-created scenes complete with dialogue wherein the protagonist relives something that happened earlier. Most editors I've talked to discourage flashbacks in favor of the tighter, shorter back-story technique. The guiding principle is: *Never get between the reader and the story.*

7. Movement: Does the story move? Does each event lead logically to the next?

8. Essentials: Have I kept only what's absolutely necessary to tell this story? The secret of editing is to ask, "If I cut this scene, paragraph, or word, will the story still stand?" If so, cut it.

9. Spiritual: Have I included a spiritual dimension (a spiritual truth that builds character and faith) which is a natural part of the narrative? Too many writers want to preach; the reader wants to be entertained.

10. Crisis: Have I built my story so that the main character has come to a crisis where it seems he or she can't win? If so, I'm ready for the final part of the narrative.

Ending Elements

This section of the story should be short, showing how the main character snatched success from failure and, by his or her own actions, satisfactorily resolved the conflict.

Just because you're writing an inspirational story doesn't mean there can be divine intervention. Aspiring religious writers sometimes bring in an angelic cavalry, complete with miracles. I don't know of any publisher who will accept that kind of an ending. A satisfying fiction work must be resolved in its own terms or the reader will not accept it. It is entirely permissible, however, to have the protagonist pray or otherwise call upon his or her faith in this crisis. In fact, this is an excellent opportunity to show how that person's spiritual resources helped resolve the problem and achieve the objective. Just remember that the ending must be logical, sans miracles, for today's reader of any age.

The ending should show (not tell) whether the main character achieved the first O in our plotting: objective. But that includes some other elements which can also be determined by a checklist.

1. Objective: Did my protagonist succeed in achieving the original goal? If not, is that failure clearly explained and logical?
2. Climax: Following the crisis, did I have a climactic scene, a high point, which I'd planned earlier?
3. Payoffs: Did I reward the good and punish the wrongdoer?
4. Spiritual: Did I prove my theme in such a way that there's a spiritual dimension that helps build character and faith, without being obvious or preaching? Remember, all well-told stories are allegorical.
5. Plants: Did I pay off any plants made earlier?
6. Ravels: Did I tie up all loose ends neatly?
7. Resolution: Did the Black Hat win all the battles only to have the White Hat win the war? Above all, is the reader satisfied with the ending?

The above guidelines have helped me write marketable manuscripts for many years. And they work equally well in short stories and novels. In a short story, of course, there may be fewer elements, and fewer obstacles to be overcome for the principal character to reach his or her objective before the outcome. A novel allows much more conflict and many more details.

THE INSPIRATIONAL/RELIGIOUS NOVEL

I hear two basic remarks from people who've written short fiction but are hesitant to tackle a novel: "I could never write anything as long as 50,000 words," or "I'd like to write a novel but I don't have time."

I challenge both assumptions. A novel is easy to write (in my opinion) when viewed as a larger work to be done one word at a time using the structure and elements of short fiction. As for time, everyone has twenty-four hours a day. You can surely discipline yourself to write at least one page—or about fifteen minutes daily. This actual writing time must be in addition to plotting, planning, researching, and so forth.

Most people find the time daily to brush their teeth, comb their hair, shave, eat three meals, and do other routine things. Your novel must be given priority among those daily activities. I suggest a set time to write, just as we generally arise at a certain hour, eat at specific times, and do chores on a regular schedule.

One page a day, Monday through Friday, will produce more than 300 pages in a year. A standard-length novel for most Christian houses I know about will run from 160 to 200 pages. So you should be able to write at least one novel annually, including rewrites and polishes.

If you produce four pages (1,000 words) a day, about an hour's work at the typewriter, you'll have 5,000 words a week (Monday through Friday) or 22,000 words a month. In ten weeks a novel can be completed. Allowing for rewrites and polishes, it's possible to produce four short novels annually. So why not begin now to plan your novel?

Here are some pointers on writing a short novel for the religious/inspirational market.

HOW TO GET A HANDLE ON YOUR NOVEL

The paperback novel is today enjoying a hefty share of shelf space. *Publishers Weekly* surveyed 500 US bookstores and found that 69 percent of sales are paperback books.

Most mass-market paperback novels today are "formula," although some publishers might like to deny that. The close study of mass paperbacks, however, will show that stories follow a fairly set format. The reason for that is simple: Readers like consistency. This is escape or entertainment reading for fun. A reader who prefers romances, for example, wants to know that each book purchased will have familiar conflicts between a heroine and the eligible man she will eventually marry. Western buffs like the seven basic plots common to that field. The gothic is the most highly structured of all popular novels; the basic story line is always very similar to all others in that genre.

The first thing to do in getting a handle on your novel is to choose the genre you prefer. As I write this, romances (according to Silhouette Books' editor-in-chief, who's bringing out a line of inspirational novels including "God and country" or traditional elements) have 30 percent of the vast paperback field.

Let's consider writing a novel with a spiritual dimension for this extremely popular romance field. Twelve chapters is about standard although ten chapters may be used.

Writing a Romance

The heroine is usually uprooted from her normal environment for some reason. She meets at least one eligible man, a few years older than she, to whom she is attracted. But there are conflicts, which continue through the next-to-last chapter of the novel. Only in the last chapter does the heroine discover her hero really loves her. There's always a happy ending.

To make this a religious/inspirational romance, we must include some elements of faith. The usual sensuous details common to mass-market romances must be played down. A good general rule of thumb is to follow the way the Bible handles such matters, minus the outdated words.

The scriptures deal with almost every sexual issue, including incest (Lot and his daughters), rape (Tamar II by Amnon), adultery (David and Bathsheba), propositioning (Potiphar's wife of Joseph), prostitution (Judah and Tamar I), and even coitus *interruptus* (Onan and Tamar I). For more examples of how the Bible treated sex, read Genesis, Leviticus and the Song of Solomon.

Since love and romance are common to all humans, there are millions of Christians who would buy romantic novels with a spiritual dimension.

Let's assume you've got an idea for such a novel and want to outline it before beginning the actual writing. Here's how it can be done:

Before You Start

Ask yourself, "In one sentence, what's this book about?"

The answer provides the single cohesive line on which the entire novel should then be built.

Ask next, "What's the comment I want to make about life?" This becomes the theme or the point the author wants to make; the kernel of truth wrapped in the entertainment shell. This probably will involve some aspect of faith; perhaps some spiritual observation based on a biblical truth.

From here, you must choose characters suitable for the story. Remember that people are mostly interested in other people. Your novel will succeed in direct relation to how much the reader cares about your characters.

Give some thought to the locale of the romance. Readers prefer exotic places. But if you've never been anywhere more exciting than your hometown, you may successfully use that background if you can make it intriguing in some way. Basically, readers are more interested in the conflict between the heroine and hero and in the way they work out their relationship than in the background.

Many romances are contemporary because that's what most romance publishers now prefer. However, you may also set your romances in a wide assortment of historical periods. Biblical fiction has a ready market in the religious book field, but any historical period requires extensive research. Are you willing to tackle that plus writing a novel based on your findings?

The Mechanics of a Novel

Some authors can plot a novel entirely in their minds. Most of us have to do it the hard way: by outlining everything. Let's assume that's your situation. Where do you start?

You check publishers' requirements and determine that a 50,000-word manuscript is preferred. That means you're limited to ten or twelve chapters. Twelve chapters will make each chapter slightly shorter than ten chapters would. We think most people prefer shorter chapters, so we choose twelve chapters and divide them into 50,000 words. That works out to about 4,200 words per chapter. At 250 words per page, we'll need just under seventeen pages average per chapter.

We are not strictly bound to this format, but unless we stick close to these limits, we'll end up with a novel that is too long or too short. To keep them in line, all chapters will be as close to the seventeen-page limit as possible. If one chapter runs twenty pages, we'll try to cut the next back to fourteen.

Structure of the Novel

Our romance is now ready to be structured. We divide the sheet of paper into three O's and determine what goes under each.

Objective? Let's say the heroine is uncertain about marrying her wealthy hometown fiancé so she takes a trip somewhere to think it over. Then she'll decide if she wants to marry him or not.

Obstacles? Besides her internal conflict, the uncertainty of her feelings about her fiancé, she meets and is attracted to another man. He becomes our hero. We root for this man and woman to marry. But they can't seem to get along; they're constantly in conflict. There is also another woman who has obvious designs on the hero. This woman is beautiful and sophisticated; she has everything our heroine seems to lack in looks and experience. And, just to complicate the situation, the fiancé also shows up so all four principal characters can be brought into even greater conflict as we near the crisis and climax of our novel.

Outcome? After some earlier love scenes which give readers the romantic interludes they want (with inevitable misunderstandings or conflicts following), we come to the twelfth and last chapter. Then, and only then, does the heroine learn the hero really loves her. She chooses him over her original fiancé and the two principals presumably live happily ever after.

The other woman is explained away when the heroine learns that the hero never cared for the other woman. She was the aggressor, but he only loved the heroine. She had misunderstood the hero's intentions toward her rival just as the heroine hadn't believed the hero really loved her until this final chapter.

This simple formula has been repeated countless times with endless variations, and will continue to be repeated because the basic plot has reader appeal, and individual authors can make each telling fresh and distinctive.

Diagram Your Chapter

There is one final thing to do before you start writing a novel. Take twelve **147** sheets of paper, one for each chapter, and make notes like this:

CHAPTER 1—*What's the purpose of this chapter?*
> To introduce heroine and fiancé, start the conflict and show the reason she's changing environment.

CHAPTER 2—*What's the purpose of this chapter?*
> To show how heroine meets hero, throw them into conflict, and introduce the other woman.

Chapter 3 and the remaining chapters must be considered with the same question—"What's the purpose?" The answers will change as the story progresses. The critical chapters will be the last two:

CHAPTER 11—*What's the purpose of this chapter?*
> To show the hero and heroine having a major misunderstanding and seemingly irreconcilable differences.

CHAPTER 12—*What's the purpose of this chapter?*
> To show how the hero confesses his love and he and the heroine get together.

Opening Elements in the Novel

Remembering that the first page or two may be all an editor reads, let's try to put our best elements right up front where they'll hook the potential buyer. Let's consider our checklist from the short story to see what's applicable for our romantic novel.

Since this is an inspirational story, let's make the spiritual dimension an integral part of the problem. So we summarize our story in a single sentence this way:

The story of a young woman of spiritual convictions who dreamed of love and security, but is attracted to a struggling young lawyer who can offer her little but love and faith.

Theme: A romance based on faith will bring both happiness and security because the priorities are right.

High point: A misunderstanding is cleared up and the heroine is confident that her faith helped her make the right decision.

Direction and goal: The story is going to end with the heroine finding happiness through her faith and doing what the faith tells her to do. She'll marry the right guy.

Checklist of Opening Elements

See how the story begins to take shape as we follow our guidelines? Now let's make sure we've got all the ingredients for the opening by going over our earlier checklist for short fiction.

1. *Viewpoint?* The heroine's, because that's required in contemporary romances.
2. *Locale?* We begin in a small midwest town and quickly move to Hawaii where the rest of the story unfolds.
3. *Time?* A contemporary romance means it's got to take place now. So, like the viewpoint, that's easily settled.
4. *Mood?* Light drama.
5. *Description?* Make up the four principal characters along the rather strict guidelines laid down by the most popular romance publishing houses. Basically, the heroine is not beautiful but can be striking, and she is definitely physically appealing. The hero does not have to be dark and handsome, but he must be tall. The other characters are also "stock," as guidelines show.

   The locale should be described (along with the two principal characters' clothes) because readers want to vicariously share the sights. But feed the description in bite-size pieces. For even though the readers want escape and entertainment, they don't want paragraph after paragraph of descriptive words about sunsets and daffodils—things that are after all only part of the background. Remember, the conflict's the thing!
6. *Immediacy?* The sooner you introduce the protagonist and plunge her into conflict, the better the possibilities of selling your work. Try for the first page or even the first paragraph, although romances (like gothics) do allow a slower opening than I personally like. I recommend starting the conflict in the first paragraph.
7. *Characters?* We could open with the heroine and her fian-

cé just as they're starting a serious quarrel. In a novel, I like all main characters introduced by the end of the third chapter. Never spring an important person late in the story. Plant them early if you're going to need them near the end to resolve the conflict.

8. *Motivation?* The heroine wants love and the security she's never had, but can attain by marrying a wealthy and successful businessman she's not sure she loves. Her uncertainty about her fiance causes her to leave her small-town, ho-hum existence to at least taste something else before she decides about marrying. The hero: Is barely able to support himself, because his religious faith and philanthropic nature have prompted him to become a store-front lawyer helping poor native Hawaiians. Other man (fiance): Thinks he loves the heroine and anticipates a promotion if he marries her because the heroine's late father worked for the boss and the boss is very fond of the heroine. Other woman: In rebellion against her wealthy uncle-guardian, she flirts dangerously with being disinherited for becoming involved with the hero's "cause," which intrigues her and drives her uncle wild.

9. *Conflicts?* There will be many conflicts of attitudes, plus some internal ones as the heroine fights the very human yearnings of her body, which oppose her determination to wait for marriage. Our virgin heroine will be tempted, but not yield to any man. She'll also have conflicts with the beautiful, sophisticated other woman. As much as possible, we'll remember, "No conflict, no scene."

10. *Confrontations?* In spite of the mutual attraction between the hero and the heroine, they seem to clash about almost everything. These confrontations are relieved by brief periods of romance, which always end up in another disagreement or misunderstanding. The path of true love, of course, never runs smooth. There will also be confrontations with the other woman and the fiancé as the story builds toward the crisis.

11. *Stakes?* This is what each stands to gain or lose. Heroine: Loses security if she doesn't marry her wealthy fiance. If she wins the hero's love, they will have only their intrinsic faith to sustain them in a practical world. Other man (fiance): Loses his promotion if he doesn't win and wed the heroine by deadline. Other woman: Stands to be disinherited if she continues working with the hero, whom she loves, but both of them can win a prestigious place in

the community and her uncle's good graces if she can persuade the hero to marry her, give up his present work, and become a part of her uncle's established law firm. For each, failure to achieve their immediate goals will affect their ultimate objectives.

12. *Decision?* The girl's decision to leave her fiancé and small town for a while is the precipitating event that advances the conflict and the story.

13. *Action?* She follows through on her decision, going to a new environment where she promptly meets the hero, with whom she quickly comes in conflict.

14. *Progression?* Our protagonist will decide to stay in Hawaii, thereby giving her an opportunity to repeatedly come in contact with the hero. A series of events would give us an opportunity to show the islands—culture, people, scenes, etc.—as the story progresses.

15. *Cliff-hanger?* We must try to end each chapter with a surprise, an unanswered question, twist, problem, or situation that makes the reader immediately turn to the next chapter. An example might involve the other woman and our heroine, with the former saying at the end of one chapter (untruthfully, as it later turns out):

"Surely he's told you by now? He and I are going to be married!"

16. *Scene?* A novel has major and minor scenes—re-created visualizations with dialogue—that represent a single episode (remember: "Show it—don't tell it"). Keep asking yourself, "What's the purpose of this scene?" "What's the problem?" "Is there conflict?" "What's the decision that leads to action?"

With that in mind, we'd have major scenes in this romance (1) where heroine breaks up with her fiance (2) where heroine meets the hero (3) their confrontations which show obstacles to love (4) conflicts with the fiance when he reappears on the scene (5) and especially in the last chapter where the hero tells the heroine he loves her. Minor scenes would include the other woman's lying to the heroine about the hero's intentions toward the other woman, her catching our heroine in an awkward or embarrassing situation, etc. The crisis, or dark moment would naturally be a major scene just before the resolution where we see the happy ending.

17. *Words?* Concentrate on keeping everything happening in the "now." Avoid passive verbs and flashbacks. If there

must be back-story inserts, keep them brief and use "had" as infrequently as possible.

18. *Dialogue?* Dialogue (in addition to the uses described earlier) helps break up the "gray" look of a page and makes a story easier to read. In this novel, we'll use dialogue that reflects:

> Heroine's faith, internal and external struggles, her blue-collar background with low self-esteem (a common characteristic in romances where the heroine never thinks the hero can really love her) and her Cinderella hopes. We'll also use dialogue to show how she's learning to cope with the independent, adventuresome spirit inside her.

Dialogue will be similarly used for all the other characters to show their background, education, personality, etc. For example, the other woman in a romance is often sultry-voiced (reflecting the sophistication of her wealth, her exclusive women's college background, and sensuality). There's a trend away from such "stock" characters, but dialogue will still tell us a lot about anyone's background and personality.

19. *Plant?* To keep our spiritual dimension, it's essential to show early on that the heroine's faith is important to her so that when she's finally tempted almost beyond endurance, her faith carries her through.

20. *Crisis and climax?* The logical crisis is where the heroine has misunderstood the hero and she almost makes the wrong decision. But the climactic scene shows her realizing her error, and the two principal characters confess their love. As for the other two principals, the old movies always had them fall in love. But whether this is practical in our story remains to be seen. Maybe they were meant for each other, but maybe they're too selfish to fully care about anyone else. The logical conclusion to their machinations is probably to leave them alone. Anyway, our concern is for the hero and heroine, whose final scene together will be in a beautiful Hawaiian setting that promises rainbows forever. After all, this is a romance!

Middle Elements in the Novel

Go back to the short story elements for this section and apply those ten points to the novel now being plotted. Perhaps only number 3, about the Black Hat, needs explanation here. Since romances have no real villains, we'll call the fiancé and the other woman the Black Hats. Their scheming and actions will constitute the opposition to the "good guys," the hero and heroine.

Ending Elements

Again using the points given for the short story, answer the questions posed there. Enough has been revealed in plotting our novel to this point that the answers to the seven ending elements can logically be inserted in our novel.

The only element that might need elaboration is number 4: Spiritual. Here we must show how the heroine's faith inspired her to triumph over all her problems and lead to the happy ending.

And there you have a novel in the rough outline form that most of us use in our early efforts and some of us throughout our writing career. Continue to use an outline as long as it works for you. It works for me, and it has worked for many of my students.

Now you can try it yourself, going on to the fun part of authoring a novel—the actual writing. These mechanics and structural aspects of plotting should not limit your creativity. It should inspire the writing of the novel itself to know that it has everything it needs—besides your writing ability—to be salable. The same basics apply to most genre writing so you can go forward with confidence.

CHILDREN'S NOVELS

You may want to try a younger readers' novel. The structure and elements of effective juvenile fiction are the same as for adults (already detailed in this chapter). Let's consider what else is necessary to be successful in this market.

It is essential to know the characteristics of the age group of readers you want to reach. The finest guidelines I've ever seen were from *Ideashop* (©1975 by Standard Publishing Company). A child's physical, mental, social, and spiritual characteristics change dramatically from one year to the next. You must know the details of this to hit your target.

There are some helpful books on children's needs that can give you additional insight on age characteristics. Children have about seven basic needs: (1) security (2) belonging (3) loving and being loved (4) achieving (5) knowing (6) playing and (7) aesthetic satisfaction. Your writing should fill at least one and preferably several of those needs.

Of course, the whole purpose in writing fiction is to entertain. When you write for children you can tell a rousing good story that not only entertains, but also makes a spiritual point or gives a moral without preaching. However, the subject matter and the protagonist must be suitable for the age group you want to reach. Additionally, you'll need to limit your novel to about 25,000 words. Again, I'd suggest twelve chapters. These would naturally be shorter, about 2,000 words each. That figures out to about eight pages with 250 words to the page.

After you've understood these basics, you must learn something about yourself. For example, I can only write for readers in the junior and senior high age levels. All my protagonists are in this category because I'm comfortable writing for this age group.

My short stories and novels fall into two types: humor (which goes great with the younger readers) and what one religious editor called "crisis adventure." This includes a series of adventurous mysteries and a couple novels in which there is a cliffhanger every eight pages or so. You'll have to discover what *you* like to write for the juvenile market and aim at those publishers that need your product.

You'll have more girl readers than boys. Research over the years has taught me that girls love horse novels and boys love dog stories. Girls will read boys' stories but not vice versa, usually. I've sold many boy-dog short stories with spiritual emphasis and my girl-horse Christian novel, *The Taming of Cheetah,* was the first of my books to go into foreign languages.

The juvenile market also allows a writer to present history and Christian heritage in an exciting and enjoyable way. I became intrigued with Hawaii's religious history. So I wrote a high adventure novel about a fifteen-year-old boy searching for his long-lost twin brother among the whaleships and missionaries of Hawaii, circa 1850. The first printing of *Search for the Avenger* was sold out in a few months.

There is a fairly new market for teenage romances under the heading of Young Adult. If you can remember the bittersweet pain of "puppy love," you may be able to write a novel for this market of girl readers aged twelve to sixteen although a spiritual slant isn't presently sought.

Another possibility is a spiritual treatment of the issues facing so many kids today—drugs, alcoholic parents, divorce, an awakening sexuality. Judy Blume has meaningfully dealt with some such issues in the secular market, but as far as I know, nobody has tried it from a religious slant. However, since kids (whether they're believers or not) all face the same problems of growing up, there should be a hungry market out there for a novelist who can handle these troublesome topics from the Christian perspective.

There is one problem with writing inspirational novels for the juvenile market: Many publishers don't pay an advance. This usually works to the beginner's advantage, since professionals tend to move on and leave the field to aspiring novelists. But there is one good feature to writing novels for this market, too.

Most children's novels tend to be carried on a publisher's list longer than adult novels. Consider how many children's books have been around for decades. You may not make a lot of money, but there are other rewards in writing for this market, and your children's novel may be around for many years to come. So why not try writing one?

Your success as a writer of character-building novels for young people will depend partly upon your interests and a great deal on your desire to communicate your faith to young readers. But it's well worth doing.

For when you write a young person's novel from a Christian perspective, you may reach farther than you'd ever dreamed. Just remember that kids like action, adventure, humor, and mystery. Editors want stories that build character and painlessly teach biblical truths through spiritual (internal) conflict and external struggles involving other characters and forces.

WHO READS CHRISTIAN FICTION?

The final thing to remember about Christian fiction is the demographics. You must keep your readers in mind. For a detailed discussion of getting to know your readers, see Chapter 5, "Who are the Readers?" by William Gentz.

In the take-home papers, all ages and both sexes are the ultimate consumers. But adults make the decisions on what youngsters will read, as they do in what mature readers will see in print.

Several religious periodical houses offer free information about their writing requirements for the various age groups. These guidelines show marked changes in needs from one age period to the next. It is imperative that a writer for this periodical market obtain and study closely the requirements, interests, and general demographics of the publications' readers.

The book buyer is far easier to profile. From the Christian Booksellers Association and other sources, we know a great deal about the book purchaser.

The basic market is female, aged twenty-six to forty-eight. As in the secular book world, women purchase at least 75 percent of all books, fiction and nonfiction.

The age spread of book buyers suggests a woman who is in the years of romance, early marriage, and early career through the start of grandmotherhood. It isn't clear why women seem to stop buying books about the time their children are grown. Many theories exist, but the important thing to remember is that book buyers are fairly young, and they are women.

SUMMARY

Christian fiction is alive and well today, particularly in the short-story form. It has been around for many years, and shows every sign of continuing. But to write for this specialized market, you must become a market specialist, follow the proper mechanical format, master the structure, learn the elements and where they fit, and know your reader. If you can do all that, always wrapping your entertainment story around a core of spiritual truth, the publishers and readers are waiting for you.

CHAPTER ELEVEN

WRITING THE INSPIRATIONAL BOOK

by Lee Roddy

Lee Roddy has publishing credits in the book field that include twenty-five ti-tles, fiction and nonfiction. Among these are five books also produced as motion pic-tures and one book that became a popular TV series: The Life and Times of Grizzly Adams. *He frequently teaches book writing at Christian writers conferences.*

·SOONER OR LATER, most religious/inspira-
tional writers want to write a book. If this is your desire, how do you go
about it? I've answered this question again and again at writers' conferences
all over the United States. And as the letters, autographed copies, and joy-
ous phone calls I've received testify, I've helped many a student sell his first
book to this specialized market. In this chapter I'll share the step-by-step
guidelines that have helped me get contracts for a couple dozen books in this
field.

Religious books come in all shapes and sizes, and cover a multitude of
subjects. (In Chapter 10 we considered the special problems of writing and
marketing fiction; in this chapter we'll concentrate on the most clearly salable kinds of books—nonfiction.) There are three easy-to-sell books for aspiring authors: the self-help or how-to, the "testimony" or inspirational
autobiography/biography, and the reference or study book. No matter
which of these types of book you decide to write, there are professional approaches to take. Let's explain the process in steps.

STEP 1: SELF-INVENTORY

Begin by asking yourself such questions as: "Do I read religious and
inspirational books? Do I understand Christ's message? What are my motives in writing for this market?" You can't expect to write well a type of book
you don't already read and enjoy. It's impossible to write sincerely unless
you have the inner faith required to meet the needs of this market. If money
comes before ministry in your writing motive, you probably won't be successful in this field.

The next important questions are: "How good a writer am I? Am I
willing to learn my craft?" Surprisingly, some aspiring writers cannot write
a simple declarative sentence. Some don't have the necessary command of
the language. Writing isn't easy. If it were, there'd be no need for you or me.
Most people (even those with the natural aptitude) won't pay the price required to write successfully for the hungry, hurting people waiting for what
only you can say.

The price? Hours of writing. Make a commitment to write at least one
page daily, Monday through Friday. Even at this rate, you'll complete a 200-
page manuscript in less than a year. Price? Hours of reading. Read! Read everything, especially in your field of interest. But read analytically, asking
yourself the question that can turn us from readers to writers. Ask, "Could I

have written this?" And when you say, "Yes, and I could have written it better," you're on your way to becoming a writer.

That's what got me started. As a teenager on the farm, I read every spare moment and often exclaimed, "I could have written that better." It wasn't always true, as I found out when I tried, but the belief spurred me to write. And since my first draft was never as concise and polished as the model I strove to improve on, I learned revision is an essential part of craft.

Another question on the self-inventory concerns your research skills. Do you know how to use the library? Unless you're writing your own testimony, your book will probably require some research. You may need to spend weeks searching indexes and card catalogs, studying books and periodicals, taking notes, and then organizing your material. Do you know how to find the facts that aren't in print yet? Authors often interview authorities for up-to-the-minute information, as well as relevant quotes and anecdotes.

Also ask yourself, "Do I have any special qualifications for writing in this field?" Your credentials could include a degree, a job, or a life-changing experience—anything that makes you an "authority." Have you taught classes? Has your writing been published? Although it's not an absolute requirement, publishers are usually more receptive to authors who've proved they can write salable material. Writing articles will not only give you valuable firsthand experience with the publishing world of deadlines, proofs, and that strange breed known as editors, but will also develop your skills in researching, writing, and revising.

The next question is one I heard W. Clement Stone, the self-made millionaire, ask members of Dr. Robert Schuller's Garden Grove Community Church. "If you could do anything you wanted that didn't violate the laws of God or the rights of your fellow men—what would it be?" If you dream big (and all aspiring writers should), you're thinking of something bigger than yourself. As Dr. Schuller has said, "If you can do it by yourself, God probably isn't in it." Dare to dream so big that only God's Holy Spirit can accomplish that goal through your writing.

Finally, ask yourself this question: "If you knew you couldn't fail, what would you write?" This may be a type of writing, such as children's literature, romance novels, or self-help books, or it may be something specific, "I'd write a book about . . . ." Whatever your abilities, it makes sense to begin with what you like, care about, and believe in.

Once you've inventoried yourself, you have some personal guidelines for writing a book. Now you need a good idea. But what *is* a good idea?

STEP 2: IDEAS AND HOW TO TEST THEM

Ideas are like seeds. Ninety percent of book ideas are no good, just as great numbers of seeds are produced in almost every living thing, but few grow to fruition. The problem is determining how likely a seed-thought is to produce a publishable nonfiction book.

There are some simple tests for this. Jim Hefley, who with his wife Marti has written many popular Christian books, asks, "Who wants to read about that?" To develop a publishing perspective, ask yourself, "Are there many people who would care enough to pay money for this book?" Remember a book today costs anywhere from $4.95 to $14.95 and up.

Surveys show people buy Christian books for very specific, "self-centered" reasons. The buyer needs help from a spiritual or biblical perspective. She may need to deal with a problem, heal a hurt, grow spiritually, be inspired, or even be entertained. Would your book meet any of these needs?

The idea doesn't need to be new. As the Preacher in Ecclesiastes noted, "There is no new thing under the sun." Old truths come alive in new stories. For instance, the biblical parable of forgiveness has been treated in thousands of books, yet it's so central to Christianity that it can be written about forever. However, what's written must shed new light, offer a new approach, and say something that hasn't been said over and over before.

In teaching and writing over the years, I've developed what I call the BERT (Benefit, Entertainment, Relevance, and Timeliness) test for book ideas.

Most nonfiction Christian books promptly offer a reader benefit. In fact, the title should do this and the first chapter should plunge right into this promise. At the very least, the opening should offer hope to the reader, make him feel his life will be better for reading this book.

Next comes entertainment. Most publishers specify a "popular style"—nonacademic and easy to read. Entertainment, in its original sense, means "to hold the mind." Jesus' parables held their audience, and still do today, because he spoke the people's language. Unlike the scribes and Pharisees, Jesus used stories from everyday life to explain universal truths. Most people aren't interested in big words and elaborate theories. They want simple answers for their own lives.

Relevance is a key selling point. A relevant approach appeals to the reader's self-interest. What you say must *matter* to the reader—not just to you.

Finally, the timeliness of the topic is crucial. If you want to be timely, don't just read the Bible, read the newspaper. It's been said, "This is a *now* generation," but concern for relevant, contemporary subjects isn't limited to any age group. Christian books today zero in on the problems of coping with or overcoming obstacles of the moment.

Once you've given your idea these tests, the book must be boiled down to a single sentence to sell your idea to a publisher; for example, the hardcover reference book I did in 1981: "A unique review of all named women in the Bible aimed at making their lives relevant to present-day readers." I knew women wanted scriptural answers to their problems, and I showed how the thoughts and emotions of Bible women can be directly helpful to the women of today.

The key words are "unique" and "relevant." A number of Bible-women books were already on the market when this idea came to me, but none had the slant mine took. *Intimate Portraits of Women in the Bible* was sold the first time out through a query letter.

But before you start mailing off query letters, look for a publisher who'll care about the kind of book you're planning.

STEP 3: GET TO KNOW THE PUBLISHERS

It's important to find out why a publishing house exists. Is it denominational or nondenominational? Does it have a specific ministry? What are its basic beliefs? Are any subjects taboo? If your book is charismatic (i.e., Pentecostal) don't send it to Moody or Broadman (Southern Baptist) or others who do not hold that belief.

For example, in the case of the Bible women book I mentioned earlier, I had more than just a good idea. Everything I knew about marketing a book went into that project. Research into what various houses had published, who their readers were, and what seemed to be lacking from their catalogs narrowed the choice down. Then, although some publishers still frown on the practice, I made multiple submissions to the most likely markets.

Always find out if your target house publishes fiction and nonfiction, does reprints only, publishes only certain types of material, and even whether the house will accept unsolicited manuscripts or if queries are first required. You can track down this information in several ways:

1. Study the market guides listed in Chapter 3 of this book.

2. Write for publishers' catalogs to see what subjects different houses are bringing out.

3. Write for editorial guidelines, enclosing a self-addressed, stamped envelope (SASE).

4. Go to your local Christian bookstore and ask to look at R.R. Bowker's *Religious Books in Print*, which shows what various publishers have already done.

Once you discover a publisher whose editorial policies and spiritual beliefs seem compatible with your idea, you're ready to write a query letter.

STEP 4: A QUERY MEANS SELLING

The right way to approach an editor begins with what's politely called a "query letter," but is really a carefully written sales effort. In it, the author sells the editor on the book idea and involves the house in developing the project. Since Chapter 7 of this book covers queries, we'll omit the details here. Just be sure you give enough information for the editor to make a decision. Include your idea-boiled-down-to-a-sentence to explain the purpose of your book. Stress how your book is different, why it's needed, and who you see as the audience. Give your working title and mention any special qualifications you have for writing this book. Finally, offer to provide an annotated outline and sample chapters upon return of your SASE indicating their interest.

If your idea and your query are good, the editor will reply with a cautious indication that he or she is willing to see your book proposal on spec, or speculation. In other words, the house doesn't guarantee to buy it, but there is an interest in seeing how you develop your idea.

Sometimes you'll get a response like th one I got on my one-page query about the Bible women idea. Leslie H. Stobbe, of Christian Herald books, whom I'd met at a writers' conference and who knew my credits replied: "You've got yourself a publisher for *Bible Women: Human Like Me*. Now we need to get together on size of book, delivery date, and financial terms. The team is really enthusiastic."

My working title, given above, was later changed by the publisher to *Intimate Portraits*. But that's the way this book started.

Of course, it wasn't quite as simple as the editorial director's letter indicated. First I had to develop a book proposal. This consists of an outline and sample chapter, and is primarily for the benefit of the team, the in-house editorial board.

STEP 5: A BOOK PROPOSAL

The team Les mentioned in his letter is a vital part of the industry today. An editor doesn't make a book-buying decision on his own. What's generally known as an editorial committee makes the final decision. The committee is not made up exclusively of editors, as the name indicates. Representatives of just about every department of the company sit on the committee, and it's always heavily weighted with marketing people. That means salesmen.

If the marketing people don't think the book will sell well—"pay its own way"—it probably won't be published.

Thus, in preparing a book proposal, it's essential to concentrate on the sales or market potential for that title.

Publishers want to know:

- What's the proposed book about?

- What's different about it?

- What's the intended market? Do you have any special insight into the book's potential market?

- What are your qualifications to write it?

- Are your knowledge, talent, and skill likely to produce a marketable book manuscript?

- What personal and/or organizational contacts do you have that will help promote the book?

- What does the marketing department consider a realistic estimate of sales the first year?

To answer these questions satisfactorily, you must prepare a package that will show the publisher why this is a marketable book. This means a book proposal with its emphasis on marketing/sales, promotion, competition (hopefully, little or none), and why the book's unique. Somewhere in there, of course, the book must be well written and have significance—*mean* something to prospective buyers.

The hard part, of course, is keeping all this vital material brief and pointed. At most, four pages (double-spaced) should be used for all this data, including an outline and/or a concise description of the book itself.

A book proposal is market-oriented, but it also illustrates the author's writing skills. So at least one sample chapter is a necessary part of the package.

I've asked many editors what they want in the way of a sample. The usual reply is, "At least the first chapter and preferably the first three." The first chapter shows if you know how to start the book off, hook the reader and draw him or her into it. The next two chapters give him a chance to see how you're going to develop the material.

Some editors also want to see the ending. "This shows the author has a 'handle' on the whole book and knows where he's going," one editor explained. "If the author can wrap everything up neatly, then the middle usually isn't going to be much off the mark." However, unless an editor asks for specific chapters as samples, go ahead and write the first three.

STEP 6: OUTLINING YOUR BOOK

You are now ready to concentrate on outlining your book prior to writing a sample chapter or more. But since each type of book has specific disciplines, we need to examine them to make sure the idea is professionally presented.

The self-help or how-to book remains the most popular in the Christian field. It's also the easiest to outline and write. Self-help covers subjects like coping with/or overcoming family problems, money difficulties, personal struggles, and so forth. The approach must be from a biblical perspective, offering help on a contemporary subject, in a popular writing style. It should motivate and be spiritually sound.

I've found the easy way to outline a self-help book is to ask myself some questions and then answer them, as: "In a single sentence, what's the purpose of this book?" or "What must the reader know to be able to successfully accomplish what my book teaches?" Here's how we might outline a book on dealing with midlife crisis, for example:

Chapter 1: Your single-sentence summary of the book's objective followed by an overview of what the book will cover. Quotes, anecdotes, statistics, and other data which support the basic premise or theme are included. A reader benefit or hope is extended, ending with a tie-in to the second chapter.

Chapter 2: A single-sentence summary premise answers the question, "What's the purpose of this chapter?" For instance:

Chapter 2: Proves that attitude is the critical factor in any mid-life crisis.

Every chapter in the outline should be summarized in a single forceful sentence, followed by more anecdotes, quotes, and other supporting data. Continue this way through every chapter.

The "step-by-step" method is a good way of conveying both self-help and how-to information. It's easy for the reader to grasp—and for you to keep on track—that way. Your steps can be presented openly, as in this chapter, where the steps are named and numbered; or it can be handled more subtly, as David Enlow and Arthur Moss demonstrate in *How to Change Your World in Twelve Weeks*, where the step-by-step guidelines are implicit, integrated into the text.

The final chapter should be a logical summation, a wrap-up of all that's gone before. Hope should be reaffirmed. The final chapter should end on a positive, upbeat note, challenging the reader to try the book's principles.

Now that we have an outline, a blueprint of what the entire final project will contain, it's easier to begin writing sample chapters one through three.

STEP 7: WRITING THE SAMPLE FIRST CHAPTER

Open with something which grabs the reader's attention. It's been said many times, but it's important to stress: If the first person who reads that first sentence and first page isn't impressed, that may be all that's ever read. Even if you bypass the first readers and go directly to the decision-making editor with your query and book proposal, the first 500 words are absolutely crucial. You may need to rewrite your opening material several times.

Just make sure it hooks the reader, gets to the subject promptly, and makes clear the benefits of reading the book.

Once you've finished your sample chapter or chapters, polish them and make sure the manuscript is professional and eye-appealing. You can refer to Chapter 7 for tips on standard formats. Double-check your outline of the remaining chapters to be sure they all tie together. Then send everything off to the publisher who has expressed an interest.

STEP 8: MAILING YOUR PACKAGE

Of course, you're going to send the book proposal to the editor with whom you've been dealing. But sometimes the manuscript ends up on another person's desk. So you should provide a couple of aids.

On the outside of the envelope write, "Requested Material." The first sentence of the inside covering letter should begin, "Per your request, I'm enclosing the sample chapter and outline of my proposed nonfiction book," and include your working title. This should get the material where it belongs without undue delay.

In the meantime, don't wait for the editor's reaction to your book proposal. Go ahead and write the rough draft of the book's balance. Even though there's good advice from many quarters to the effect that you shouldn't write a book without a commitment, unless you have a proven track record, many publishers like to see a complete manuscript before making a decision. Another good reason to write the draft is to prove that you can really do it—writing a book takes stamina and dedication. But if you can discipline yourself to write four pages daily, your output will be about 1,000 words, or 22,000 words a month. In many cases that's almost half what your finished book will be, so you can finish the rough draft in two months. However, don't rewrite until you hear from the editor. He or she may have input or suggestions about what the house would like included. Whatever you do, don't just sit around and wait.

If you haven't heard from your publisher after two months, write a polite letter inquiring about the status of your manuscript. If the house isn't interested, the sooner you know, the sooner the right publisher for your book can be found. Keep the project active.

But assuming you get a favorable response and a contract is offered, what next?

STEP 9: A CONTRACT

When you receive your first contract, the natural inclination is to sign anything they offer you. Don't do that. If the publisher really wants your book, they'll negotiate.

Remember, all contracts favor the publisher, so don't sign away your copyright. Stipulate that the copyright be in your name. The publisher bought the right to publish the book, not to own it.

Strike out the clause that gives the publisher the right to your next book. If you sold one, you can sell another. By the time your next book is ready, you may be able to command a better deal if you're a free agent.

Contracts often specify that the author participate in promotion of the book, so even if you're scared to death of audiences, learn to speak. Your book will get extra exposure and you can probably sell some autographed copies to your audience.

Finally, consider getting qualified outside counsel. It may not be practical to hire a lawyer (and not just any lawyer would do), but if you don't read carefully, you may sign a bad contract.

Once the contract is signed, the manuscript polished and mailed, what should you do? Perhaps you should try your hand at the second most popular Christian book, the "testimony" or inspirational autobiography/biography.

THE TESTIMONY, OR INSPIRATIONAL AUTOBIOGRAPHY

You may have had an unusual personal experience that qualifies you to write an inspirational autobiography. That, incidentally, is my term. In Christian circles, these are usually called "testimonies," but unless there is an inspirational element to the life story, nobody's going to care enough to buy the book.

It isn't enough that the story be about someone who had real difficulties to overcome. There must be something *inspiring* in the subject's life. Excellence in the abstract is hard to aspire to, but when human beings like ourselves achieve spiritual awareness or greatness of character, we're inspired by their example. And unless the subject is a famous personality whose name alone would attract readers, the book buyer still has self-interest in mind when shelling out for the title. "What's in it for me?" is a perfectly legitimate question.

One good answer is the emotional lift the reader gets from reading the other person's life story. A biographical story must warm the heart and bring tears to the eyes. The reader should be left saying, "After reading that person's story, my life doesn't seem so bad. If that person did it with God's help, then I can do it." At the end of this chapter you'll find information on writing biographies, so we'll concentrate here on autobiographies.

The best test of whether your life story is worth writing about is to go back to the original idea test: "Who wants to read about *my* life?" Also ask, "Do I really have something to say that will benefit others?"

Since you're writing for a religious audience, your theme must have a spiritual dimension. Perhaps your life was harsh and full of troubles, far from the understanding of God. Somehow, in your struggles against very difficult odds, you encountered God. This changed your life. Since then, you've been a different person. By implication, the reader could also have his or her life changed by learning the spiritual lessons in your life.

In outlining the inspirational autobiography, it's best to open with a dramatic incident, complete with dialogue and a re-created scene. Make it live again. Then, having firmly hooked your readers, go back to earlier parts of your life and come forward. Don't jump back and forth after the initial opening drama.

There are some major pitfalls to be avoided in writing either your autobiography or a biography. The main one is the tendency to narrate. "Don't tell it—show it!" is a famous and meaningful writer's commandment. Make the scenes live again. Make the reader hear, feel, smell, taste, and touch the important people, places, and things in your life.

Another important consideration in writing an autobiography is condensation to the essentials. You can't tell a five-decade life in detail in 200 manuscript pages. Concentrate on the essentials: major turning points, events which shaped you, and so forth.

If nobody is likely to care about your life beyond immediate family and friends, perhaps you should collaborate on someone else's autobiography. This is a never-ending field of opportunity and through it you can touch countless lives.

COLLABORATING ON THE AUTOBIOGRAPHY

It's been my privilege to work with many nationally and internationally known Christians whose stories needed to be told. Sometimes my involvement in writing their stories is unknown to any but the subject and a few others. That's true of several authors I know who wrote books about popular personalities. Sometimes there wasn't even an "as told to" or "with" credit to the real author. Just remember that unless the listed author (who is probably well known or even famous) is recognized as a writer, that biography or autobiography was probably written by someone else. I've done more of these collaborative manuscripts than any other type.

Perhaps you know someone who has a stirring life story or specific adventure that involved his or her faith. I've met dozens of such people: refugees from communism, people who've survived terrorist takeovers, or who learned to overcome their handicaps, etc. You may arrange to collaborate on that person's autobiography.

Assuming you've found a suitable subject and you're ready to begin, what next? Although it can be outlined the same way as an autobiography, a collaboration is not nearly as simple as writing your own life story.

There will be some severe pitfalls to avoid up front. The average subject simply wants to sit down and narrate his or her life story. It has been my experience that this tendency cannot be overcome by explanation. So I've learned to let the subject talk into the recorder. Later, going over the typed transcript of the tapes, I'll highlight with a colored marker those events that seem the stuff of high drama. Then I hold a second session and ask—no, insist politely—that the subject re-create those parts.

It's painful. One person later told a banquet crowd where I was introduced, "Lee made me relive every hard part of my life." Another man said, "It hurt, but I was purged. For the first time since it happened, I'm free of the terrible feelings I've had about that event."

In outlining the book, you will almost surely run into other major problems. The subject will not have correctly given the chronology of events, and later will bring that to your attention. "You've got that wrong. This didn't happen until two years after that. You've got it backwards."

Of course, you can strongly request a chronology before the first taping session begins. But that doesn't work, I've found. No matter how I stress the importance of a chronology, the person either will not submit one at all, or it will be incorrect. Somehow the blame always falls upon the writer, so there's nothing to do but expect to have that happen and go on from there.

After the chronology problems have been ironed out, the subject always, always has second thoughts. "I know I said I wanted to tell everything as it really happened, but if we put that part in, it'll hurt my mother, wife, children, etc." So it's omitted.

Unfortunately, so are some of the high points of your book. There's the case of a well-known Christian speaker who kept her divorce out of a second book. Another subject's board of advisers refused to allow any mention of the person's ulcers. The board was quoted as saying it feared the constituency would not understand that a Christian leader could have such a human health problem.

On the other hand, sometimes the collaborator must omit episodes the subject wants to include. The person can't understand why you'd want to leave out a favorite childhood memory, for instance. I explain it this way: "You've now lived fifty years. We've got two hundred or so pages. Only the important, life-changing parts of your life can be presented in those few pages. Our thrust must be to show the events that shaped you, the people who influenced you, and why it all ties in with the spiritual dimension of your life. If you were a reader, which parts of your life would you most want to know about?"

If collaborating on another's autobiography is sometimes frustrating, it's also extremely rewarding. You feel good knowing another person's life story is out on the bookshelves ready to help and inspire readers, because you cared enough to write that subject's story as his own.

Perhaps you don't know of anyone who'd be a suitable subject for an inspirational autobiography. If you know how to research and find a need, you might consider writing for the reference and study market.

WRITING THE REFERENCE OR STUDY BOOK

Another major area of book publishing, particularly in Christian houses, is reference material. Under this classification you'll find such things as biblical commentaries, Bible dictionaries, encyclopedic volumes on such subjects as world religions and church history, Bible background books of geography or archeology, and so forth. This is not usually an area a writer should tackle unless he or she has the necessary education or background to handle the subject. Also, writers in this field are usually assigned the subject by the publisher. However, if you do have the experience or knowledge, this is a fruitful field. Some large houses have one editor who does nothing but search out new ideas and new subjects for reference books. It's worth looking into.

E. Stanley Jones, the famous missionary statesman, once commented, "If God shows you a need, that's his way of inviting you to do something about it." What helped you grow spiritually? What do you seem to need to help you grow? Answering those questions may provide the seed idea for a new reference or study book.

If you've read this far, you're probably a serious candidate for writing a religious or inspirational book. If you have spiritual values and beliefs, you can share those ideas in a book. It is an awesome responsiblity, for almost any successful book in this field will reach more people than many pastors touch in a lifetime from the pulpit.

Your book will minister where you can never go, in places you'll perhaps never hear about. I have letters from readers whose lives were totally changed as a result of reading some of the books I've written for this field.

Why shouldn't you do the same, or better?

If you've met the criteria outlined in this chapter and others in this book, you can do it. You *can* do it! The only thing that'll stop you is yourself: fears, self-doubt, inaction.

Everyone knows something well enough to write a self-help or how-to book. Life makes us all experts in some field. We can write our own testimony if enough people will be inspired by reading it. Or we can write someone else's story and inspire readers to let God help them through a tough spot—through life.

There's no question you can if you'll hang in there and persevere. The only question is, will you?

Then what's holding you back? "Behold, now is the accepted time," Jesus said. Today's the day to begin writing your religious/inspirational book. Only time will show how effective your book really was, but it may bear fruit beyond your wildest dreams.

WRITING BIOGRAPHY FOR THE CHRISTIAN MARKET
by Dorothy Nafus Morrison

The author lives in Beaverton, Oregon, and has published many biographies, specializing in those for young people.

As a writer you may be interested in biography and in the Christian market, but you wonder whether the two can be combined. You may rest assured—many religious book houses, perhaps most of them, have a place for the life of a real person in their lists. Although their standards are similar to those of any quality publisher, they do have some special requirements.

CHOOSING A SUBJECT

Obviously, your first problem is finding a person to write about. Scan church magazines, scientific magazines, textbooks, and encyclopedias for ideas, considering not only missionaries and clergymen, but also scientists, teachers, sociologists, and many others. Florence Nightingale, Luther Burbank, Henry Schoolcraft—many people like these are welcome if they haven't been done too often. The religious market both limits and expands the field of biography, because it rejects those whose lives do not exemplify its ideals, while it accepts subjects who are known in the religious field but not quite important enough for general publication.

Before deciding, ask yourself the same questions you would ask if you were aiming at a general publisher. How many biographies exist about this individual? Are there enough sources of information, with lively enough content, on which to base an interesting account?

In addition, you should consider two special points:

1. Has this subject had positive impact? Christian houses are not interested in fascinating rascals but in people who have made the world a better place in which to live.

2. Could clergymen and church librarians conscientiously recommend this life story? They would probably shy away from a picturesque fur trader who succeeded in mapping important new trails, but mistreated the Indians and lived with a succession of mistresses. However great the contribution, if the individual's personal life was unsavory, you should look elsewhere.

TYPES OF BIOGRAPHY

With a subject in mind, you will next consider what kind of biography to write. There are three main types, all acceptable to a religious publisher. They are the factual, which tells only facts; the fictionalized, which sticks to the main facts but adds "made-up" dialogue and scenes; and the biographical novel, which tells a story about a real subject, using fictitious dialogue, scenes, characters, and events.

The choice depends on the way you write best, on the flow of events, and on available sources. If the story is exciting and you can find enough lively material, a factual biography will work well. If sources are skimpy, you are almost forced to fictionalize. If the life was humdrum, a biographical novel may give it spark. The Christian market is open to all these forms with one reservation—a really far-fetched novel that has little relation to actual events, or one that relies on scandalmongering. These will have little chance here.

Books are not the only outlet. Religious magazines often use biographical sketches, which can be fictionalized or not, and can cover an entire life, or a few incidents, or perhaps only one. Short sketches sold to periodicals can be a useful byproduct of material you have gathered for a book. Since length and other requirements vary, you will save precious time by first examining the magazine, then tailoring your submission to fit.

RESEARCH

Whatever the form, plan to do a great deal of research, keeping accurate notes and recording all sources by title, author, and page. This is important, for if you once lose track of a reference, it may be hideously difficult to find it again.

Cherish the wonderful, rambling, and circumstantial accounts in some letters and journals, for they bring the time and place to life. You will of course include general information about living conditions, travel, historical events, and ideas, but the religious market will also want references to its own movements—the cultural accomplishments of a pope, formation of new sects, migrations of persecuted minorities. The subject of a religious biography need not be generally known but his or her life should be of some significance in the ongoing expansion of Christianity in the world.

In all your reading be alert for bias and other flaws. Was this letter written by a rival? A disappointed suitor? A relative? Has this out-of-print biography been discredited by newly discovered journals? You need not eliminate all doubtful sources, but for this market, which aims for a high level of accuracy, you should use special care.

THE WRITING

When you come to the actual writing, remember the editors of Christian houses want a lively, fair, well-balanced account, not a dull chronicle or piece of propaganda. Their goal is to inspire and to produce an upbeat effect, which requires enthusiasm from you. Write in scenes, vary the pace, include suspense if possible. If you have a novel, it must stand up as quality fiction. If your work is factual, avoid a dull, journalistic recital of chronological events. Rather, think through your subject's life, discover the motivating wellsprings, evaluate the impact of major events and then tell the story with verve and style from your own individual point of view. Try to portray a rounded character who has both faults and virtues. Avoid both iconoclasm and adulation. Use the Bible an an example in writing biography. Note that the faults and failures in the lives of the greatest heroes—David, Moses, Jacob, Abraham, etc.—are not glossed over. However, in spite of these, their faith in God and accomplishments for him come through in the story.

Since you are striving for accuracy, if your work is factual, you cannot make up anything or rearrange events; and if it is fictionalized, you should take the trouble to portray a believable and correct historical setting. If you use the trappings of scholarship, such as footnotes, be sure they refer to legitimate sources, not to discredited theories or works of fiction. To your readers, many of whom will have no information except that in your book, the little reference marks may look like the Gospel itself, but a canny editor might check them out.

Before submitting your final manuscript, you will probably want to add an introduction or author's note. This will give you a chance to explain whether you have hewn to the rigid line of truth, or invented dialogue, or rearranged events. Although most Christian houses will accept fictionalizations, they don't want to be misled.

In short, biography for this market demands the best writing of which you are capable—sincere, vivid, sturdy—on a topic that is in tune with Christian ideals. If you can make it, you have a right to the glow of honest pride.

❧ CHAPTER TWELVE

WRITING INSPIRATIONAL POETRY

by Viola Jacobson Berg

Viola Jacobson Berg of Malverne, Long Island, New York, has had more than 1,700 poems published since she began writing poetry in 1966. She is the author of seven published books and has prepared two others for publication in the future. Her most notable contribution to the field of help for religious writers is Pathways for the Poet, *a poetry manual. She has conducted poetry workshops in Wisconsin, Washington, D.C., California, and Arkansas. She is a feature writer for* Jean's Journal, *a poetry magazine. Several of her poems have been set to music. She has also taught high school classes in poetry writing and appreciation.*

What is a poem?
Who can really know
What bit of music
Makes the spirit glow?

—*Pathways for the Poet**

POETRY EXPRESSES emotion, observation,

and conviction in such a way that it penetrates the heart of the reader.

Poets are not born with fully matured and perfected talent. They may have inherited a special sensitivity, an extra awareness, and an impelling desire to share themselves, but the ability to use language well is a skill that has to be developed and honed.

Writing poetry requires a vital interest in words, an instinctive desire to arrange them in original ways, relate a sense of wonder, capture a bit of mystery.

Where do ideas come from? A sensitive spirit can find poetry wherever he looks—in the wag of a puppy's tail, in a loaf of freshly baked bread, in a dandelion boldly pushing its way through a crack in the sidewalk, in an old trunk in the attic, through eyes of pain, of joy, of sorrow, of faith.

The poet's success depends not so much, however, on the ability to see, to hear, and to think clearly, as on the ability to relate personal responses with authenticity and skill.

More Christian poets are vitally needed to write positive messages of encouragement, inspiration, and compassion, with conviction and eloquence, to offer to a disillusioned world grown weary of shifting standards and unanswered questions. The Christian poet has a decided advantage for he has access to the source of all wisdom, the one who has promised to help and direct his child in all his ways (Prov. 3:6, James 1:5). If poetry is to throb with vitality, the poet must experience a personal, active relationship with the giver and sustainer of life. Editors are quick to recognize a poem that may have a proper skeleton, even an attractive form, but no pulse.

Christians, then, should be the best poets in the world. Through the medium of words a poet can be a means of sharing the faith, a channel to aid in the building of God's kingdom. What a privilege! What a challenge! What an incentive to strive tirelessly for excellence!

* All poems in this chapter are by the author.

DEVELOPING A POEM

A poem starts with an idea, sometimes with a feeling. From this intangible beginning the creative urge is triggered. The desire for expression is so great, the emotional involvement so intense, that the poet is propelled by his own enthusiasm to transform feeling into phrases, message into metaphors, articulation into art.

Each poet creates a poem in his own way. *How* to do it cannot be taught. A teacher can suggest, encourage, offer guidelines, share helpful ideas, but the spark must come from within the poet. The fact is that when God created man in his own image, he put within man the exciting potential for creativity and the urge to use it. Poetry is one avenue for sharing that potential.

The poems that really communicate and continue to live on are the ones in which the poet has interwoven beauty of thought with beauty of form. The greatest poems of all have embraced worthy ideas concerning universal themes—faith, struggle, hope, brotherhood, truth, quest for fulfillment, conflict, love. The poet must know his subject, his own emotions, and his own abilities well enough to go far below the surface message of the words.

Sound and sense have always been inseparable. In addition to combining sound and sense, the poet must also convey the real and the imaginary, the spiritual and the practical, while accepting the double challenge of mastering content and form. Carefully chosen verbs can do the work of both a verb and an adverb. Words that appeal to the five senses will guarantee reader response. Excessive adjectives and adverbs weaken a poem. Connotative words add richness and overtones of meaning to a poem.

Contractions may be used in humorous verse, but are not considered desirable in serious poems. Ideas are best expressed by simple words, as they do not call attention to themselves and distract from the flow of thought.

Pictures made with words are worth many words and foster reader participation in the poetic experience. A line should not end with a weak word. Save the strongest line for last. Lines should be kept short, not more than five feet. Correct grammar and spelling are basic. Rare exceptions are in some forms of nonsense verse.

Well written verse finds greater acceptance than mediocre poetry. Inspirational verse has proved a blessing to millions. Some editors, however, will consider only poetry. (Further explanation of the distinguishing factors of verse and poetry is given later in the chapter.)

Verse can be meticulously manufactured at any time. A determined writer can follow the comparatively simple rules of pattern and form, incorporate his message, and turn out a finished and satisfactory arrangement of words. Verse is written primarily by the intellect.

True poetry, however, comes from a source more profound than the mind. A poem is the unfolding of a desire, a wish so deep, or a yearning so strong that it just has to be captured in words, and prose is not good enough. An inner urge drives the poet to convey his feeling, using the tools of his art.

Every poem is different, having its own origin; occasionally by quick impulse, and other times through exhausting labor. But when a poet is caught up in the creative process, he joyfully surrenders to the overwhelming power that drives him to draw upon his own "beyondness." He is transported into another world (Christians are uniquely able to do this) where his thoughts can come forth clean-edged and pure. An intuitive light mysteriously enables him to transcend the usual limitations for a little while.

In order to work toward the ideal marriage of sound and sense, the poet should strive to perfect his attitude of mind and spirit. The greater balance he has of intellect and emotion, the greater treasures of wisdom and discernment he can store in his mind, the more he grows in understanding and compassion, the more he will be able to draw on this experience—make a composite of it, refine it, and then to bring forth poems that are truly his own.

The writing of a poem comes, in the end, to a matter of dedication. One cannot write from the surface out. It takes depth to write to depth, and the poet who is willing to go deeply into himself achieves the undiluted sincerity that gives conviction to his poems. The farther one reaches into oneself, the more one will have in common with great poetry. There is truth in such poetry which corresponds to universal truth.

As a poet's experience broadens, his own developing personality will gradually find its own shape, choose its own path much as a river makes its own channel. His own style will emerge from his own uniqueness. No poet ever need imitate another, for he has his own message to share and his own way of sharing it.

KEY INGREDIENTS OF A POEM

Editors are meticulous in selecting poems for their publications, and each editor has his own standard for judging excellence in poetry. Acknowledging that editors are as variable as poets and that we all have a right to our own modes and tastes, how are poets to know how to get an editor's attention? A true poem is composed of four major ingredients.

Content. Worthy content. As Christians we have the epitome of worth to write about. Every subject, not only things commonly thought of as spiritual, is grist for the poet's pen. We are told in Philippians 4:8 to set our minds deliberately on things that are true, honorable, just, pure, lovely, and gracious. A poet is also faced with the challenge of dealing with trials, injustice, and heartaches. Within all of these realms the poet has unlimited scope to use his art for the blessing and benefit of others.

Beauty. Of expression, if nothing else. No one deliberately writes an ugly poem. Poets have the opportunity to be their own interpreters of the beautiful, of painting their own picture. They are artists with words, and true artists build beauty into every endeavor.

Craftsmanship. Within this area, verse is separated from poetry, gold is refined, rough stones are polished. The various tools of the poet are used to enhance and improve his work. Craftsmanship will be dealt with more fully later in this chapter.

Originality. Obvious, of course, but so vital—that fresh approach, the unexpected twist, clever wordplay, something unique from the poet's own creative resources to distinguish his poem as different. A poem may be perfect in structure, correct in doctrine, but quite unexciting because it is too ordinary. This kind of effort does nothing to impress an editor who receives hundreds of poems to review every week. One of the greatest services a poet can perform for himself is to become an original thinker.

MAJOR CLASSIFICATIONS OF POETRY

An aspirant who strives for excellence in the art should be familiar with the major categories of poetry, both from deliberate study and from personal experience in each. The styles and patterns of poetry branch out in challenging directions from whatever base a beginner chooses for his first effort. Following are descriptions and examples of the five main poetry classifications—versatile pathways for the poet that will broaden his skills.

Patterned—Rhymed. The most structured type of poetry has both a definite meter plus a rhyme scheme. Among literary treasures we find a wealth of ballads, elegies, epics, odes, and sagas, most of which have made use of rhythm and rhyme.

We have come to take for granted such standards as the Burns stanza, the Browning sestet, the Spenserian stanza and sonnet, the heroic couplet, the Swinburne octave, the Omar stanza, Poulter's measure, the rhyme royal of Chaucer and Shakespeare, and the familiar Shakespearean sonnet. Twentieth-century poets have continued to create new and unusual patterns.

A pattern-rhyme form presents a double challenge, for the message must be written to fit happily and comfortably within its confines. The following example is representative of rhythm-rhyme poetry. It's written in tetrameter tercets, and an identical refrain ends each stanza.

WRITE ABOUT THE LORD

Christians, get your pencils out;
Share your joy and sing and shout;
Tell the world what life's about—
Write about the Lord!

Reach the world of needy men;
Write with passion in your pen;
Tell them Christ will come again—
Write about the Lord!

Give your work an edge, a tooth;
Pierce the consciences of youth;
Point the way to Light, to Truth—
Write about the Lord!

Write for presidents and kings;
Write with hope and write with wings;
Write until your message sings—
Write about the Lord!

The consistent rhythm and the rhyme combinations contribute immensely to the effectiveness of the poem. The reader is carried along by its smooth beat, and his ears gradually anticipate the rhyme pattern.

Patterned—Unrhymed. This form is less structured and is characterized by syllable count or numbered poetic feet. Though a smaller group in number, this category is growing all the time.

Some of these delightful unrhymed patterns have come down to us from antiquity, mostly of oriental derivation, e.g., the haiku. This thirteenth-century Japanese form, which creates a vivid image in three short lines of 5-7-5 syllable count (or less), is designed to capture a beautiful moment in nature as it happens. In the last twenty-five years, syllable-count poetry forms have mushroomed and have found a substantial place in the poetry scene.

A beautiful pattern to illustrate patterned-unrhymed poetry is the Campion form, named after the seventeenth-century English poet Thomas Campion. Each four-line stanza is composed of a first line written in trimeter (three feet), the second and third in tetrameter (four feet), and the fourth in dimeter (two feet). Note this example:

BREAD OF HEAVEN

Creator of the cliffs,
the crags, and awesome towering mounts,
is Himself the firm, unchanging
Rock of Ages.

He who made the seas,
the oceans' depths, the crashing waves,
is Himself the overflowing
Living Water.

He who gave the seed
that granaries might be filled with wheat,
is Himself the satisfying
Bread of Heaven.

When appealing content, imagery, and beauty are woven into the message and the pattern is followed exactly, the writer will have created a jewel of a poem. There is a challenge in writing a form and a profound satisfaction in mastering it.

Blank Verse. Blank verse is unrhymed, but it does have meter. Almost every poet of literary note has tried this form and many have produced their best work in it. Mediative poetry and poetic drama are at their best in this form. Depth of emotion and purity of thought are unhampered by the necessity for rhyme.

In this stanza from "Tired Wings," note the smoothness of the lines. The poem is truly "itself" in blank verse.

He earned his peace, this youth of tender years,
His time of striving over; signs of war
Erased forever in the dew-kissed dawn,
For he has crossed the valley to the day.

The rhythm is pleasing and soothing for either silent or oral reading. Blank verse is endowed with its own characteristic grandeur and simplicity. This category is a prime example of the importance of meter in poetry. Its rhythm enhances the presentation of the message.

Free Verse. Free verse is so called because of its complete freedom from rhyme and from any fixed form or precise meter. But free verse does have definite characteristics without which it would not be poetry.

This immensely popular style of writing is built on cadence and a delicate sense of balance. The recurring beat of the line is completely absent. The unit in free verse is not the foot, as in metrical verse, but the *strophe*, meaning a round or a unit of thought.

Determination of the line length is based on words in natural stress groupings. The end of a cadenced line comes where a pause or falling inflection of the voice would naturally come in reading or speaking. Therefore, a line of free verse, with few exceptions, ends on a strong word. The next line starts with an unstressed syllable and leads again through the next grouping of words, which by their meaning and association belong together.

A sense of balance is a prime requisite. Free verse can have no awkward lines. It can have no weak ones. One idea should be treated as concisely, as powerfully, and as beautifully as possible. Any phrases that are not needed to further the message should be eliminated because they weaken it.

The following poem, "Prayer of a Lamp," illustrates these various points:

Cleanse me, Lord,
with the abrasive of your discipline
and the polishing cloth
of your holiness,
that the glass in my chimney
might be clear and spotless;
trim my wick
that the charred edges
of selfishness and pride
shall be cut away.

Then fill me, Lord,
with the oil of your spirit;
place me in a needy pot of your choosing;
light my wick with your flame
that I might be on fire
for thee.

Free verse is not easy to write. A poet must introduce his idea, develop the message, and then conclude, as in metrical poetry, with his strongest point. Without some degree of figurative language the effort is just prose.

Light Verse. Humor is a great asset in life, and light verse is an intriguing part of the poetry picture. We are creatures with a sense of humor, and I'm sure the Lord has one. How dull and dry every day would be if we did not have the capacity to recognize humorous situations around us, to enjoy the whimsical and the ridiculous.

Light verse demands precision and art. The poet amuses his readers by applying charm, inventive imagination, and an easy approach. He makes his point in an entertaining way without trying to be ha-ha funny. Often a dry wit is the most effective. A play on words, a touch of irony, a breath of fantasy, a tongue-in-cheek effect, a sly pun—all make for interesting reading. The light-verse writer automatically employs rhyme and rhythm. For instance, a limerick wouldn't be a limerick without its enjoyable bouncy rhythm and its anticipated rhyme.

A writer who can create verse that produces a chuckle or a smile has accomplished something worthwhile. Excellent light verse is sought by editors of religious material, too. Humor is a matter of individual taste, but it encompasses such a wide field that any situation at all that strikes a poet as funny can be raw material for imaginative treatment. With a sense of humor, the poet can even laugh at himself. The following verse was used by a church bulletin publishing house and featured on its back cover for Father's Day.

FULL CIRCLE

It took twenty years
Of living and tears

Before I could really see why
That the dad I thought dumb
Wasn't really a crumb;
He was actually wiser than I.

Now with wisdom mature
I'm deserving, I'm sure,
To be honored as sage and as saint;
But it's my turn to groan,
I've a son of my own
Who is just as convinced that I ain't.

A BRIEF STUDY OF RHYME

Ideas should never be sacrificed to rhyme. If we purposely write rhymed poetry, the rhyme pattern must be regular. Good rhyming is a series of pleasant sounds that add to the pleasure and the message of the poem. It also
adds emphasis to the meaning by giving an emotional accent. Rhyme does
not make a poem; it simply enhances it.

In light verse and in children's poetry, rhyming is obvious and is expected. It's basic to the structure, and without rhyming, both kinds of verse
would be limp and lifeless. Without inversions, rhyming in serious verse
complements the easy flow of the poem without taking attention away from
the message.

Rhyming patterns vary from the simplest verse patterns to those that
apply to the poem as a unit.

The term *perfect rhyme* is applied to those rhymes that are as near identical repetition in sound endings as we are able to produce, the recurrence of
identical sounds from the last stressed vowel to the end of the line.

Correct rhyming is judged by the ear and not by spelling. This eliminates words that look alike but are pronounced differently. The following
words, which have identical end spellings, have three different ending
sounds, so they are not rhymes: through, plough, and rough.

The most common bad rhyming is trite rhyming or the use of overworked rhyme pairs, such as *spring* and *sing; life* and *strife; trees* and *breeze;
love* and *dove*, etc. A serious poet will avoid the trite and think of more original rhyming pairs.

It is poor writing to use two sets of rhyming words in the same stanza
that use the same vowel, such as *meet-greet* and *feel-real*. This makes the vowel sound appear overdone and is a bit confusing, as well as totally unnecessary—it's easy to avoid.

Unintentional rhyme, a rhyme that pops up where it's not expected,
produces something of a jarring effect. Words or phrases should be rearranged to correct this.

If a poet uses rhyme, he should know enough about rhyming to do it correctly. A rhymed poem, well written, will insure an editor's consideration. If tritely or badly rhymed, it would not have a chance.

Poetry is not dependent on rhyme to make it so. The many devices and tricks of rhyming are tools the poet uses to enhance his efforts and to make his poems more musical. A beginning poet should not try the variations until he has mastered conventional rhyme, and until his writing experience qualifies him to venture further.

A LOOK AT THE MOST USED METERS

Our language contains many natural rhythms and patterns of expression. Exact terms are needed to identify these recognizable rhythms. *Meter* describes the sequence of the stressed and unstressed syllables.

Two-foot Meters

Iambic meter most closely resembles speech and is the easiest and most natural to write. The *iamb* begins with an unstressed syllable and is followed by a stressed syllable. Each pair of syllables in this order (‿ ——) is counted as one iambic *foot*.

The following example of iambic meter is written in *tetrameter*. The four stressed syllables in each line are underlined.

The <u>silence</u> <u>of</u> the <u>April</u> <u>dawn</u>
Rests <u>lightly</u> <u>on</u> the <u>waiting</u> <u>hills.</u>

Trochaic meter is the opposite of iambic. The stressed syllable comes first, followed by the unstressed syllable (—— ‿). Each pair of syllables in this order makes up a *trochee*.

<u>Marching,</u> <u>ever</u> <u>always</u> <u>marching;</u>
<u>Minutes</u> <u>march</u> to <u>form</u> the <u>hours.</u>

In the first line above, each of the four words is a perfect trochee. The second line begins and ends with trochee words, and the trochees in between are made up of separate words.

Three-foot Meters

In *dactylic* meter the stress falls on the first syllable, followed by two unstressed syllables (—— ‿ ‿). Three-foot meters are more lively and rhythmic than two-foot meters, as only one out of three syllables is accented. This example shows four dactyls to the line.

> If one as fragile as you are esteemable,
> Could it be possible I am redeemable?

In *amphibrachic* meter the stressed syllable is in the center of the foot, surrounded by an unstressed syllable on either side ($\cup$——$\cup$). Each line in the example contains six syllables—two amphibrachs.

> While searching for springtime,
> I found a brave jonquil.

In *anapestic* meter the stressed syllable follows the two unstressed syllables ($\cup$ $\cup$ ——). Three anapests make up each line below:

> As we search in the Scriptures for light,
> We will find He illumines our path.

Consistency of meter is important, of course, or the rhythm will be lost. An interesting point arises here: It is possible that too much meter could produce a monotonous jingle. As soon as a poet has had enough experience to know what he is doing, he can quite naturally substitute one foot for another if the feet are of the same rhythm.

THE POET'S TOOLBOX

Figurative language is one of the strongest distinguishing factors that separate poetry from verse. Verse has only a literal surface meaning. A true poem, however, cannot be taken literally. The meaning becomes clear through the exercise of our imagination and by calling on our deeper understanding. Imagery makes a poem come alive and intensifies the emotional appeal. By using his tools, a writer can lift his efforts out of the novice category into a deeper dimension.

Metaphor and *simile* are both standards of comparison. A simile is generally recognized by the use of *like, as,* and *than.* Its comparison, therefore, is pointed out or expressed.

> A sunbeam, *like* a warming blanket . . .
> Some words are soft *as* sheerest wool . . .

Metaphor, the more powerful of the two, is an implied comparison, and is more direct and dramatic.

Time is a villain, chasing its prey . . .
April is a flirt, changeable and coy . . .

Beyond everything else, a poet needs a command of metaphor. It is a springboard to profound thinking, more evocative and gripping than mere description.

A *symbol* means more than it says and directs thought to encompass all the connotations that radiate from the symbol itself. All of the following will be recognized immediately as powerful symbols: Job, Scrooge, the *Titanic*, Waterloo, Rock of Ages, Thomas, Jonah, to name a few. More than one meaning can emerge from a single symbol, and an entire poem can be symbolic of a deeper concept.

Allusion is closely related to symbol, usually referring to well-known names or events from history, culture, or literature. Each of the following has a significance of its own the reader will recognize: The spirit of '76, Custer's last stand, the Golden Rule, Sodom and Gomorrah, the Promised Land. When allusions are appropriately chosen, they add depth to a poem with a minimum of words.

Allegory is described as the art of double meanings; it relays a parallel. Usually applied to longer poems, allegory involves concepts that illustrate a spiritual or philosophical truth. *Pilgrim's Progress* is an allegory in prose.

Paradox is a seeming contradiction that expresses a deeper truth. For example: "We listen, but we have not heard; we see, and yet are blind." Two ideas, which seem to contradict each other, actually combine to make a point. Because of the nature of spiritual truths, many are expressed as paradoxes.

He that loveth his life shall lose it; and he that hateth
his life shall keep it unto life eternal. (John 12:25 KJV)

An *oxymoron* is a type of paradox that is apparently contradictory in its terms, such as generous miser, young octogenarian, tiny mountain. A careful choice of adjective and noun is needed to make meaningful and appropriate combinations.

The term *pathetic fallacy* is used to describe the poetic practice of attributing human characteristics to inanimate objects. A fallacy it may be, but poets through all the centuries have delighted in this keen and spontaneous metaphorical expression: calling the air "kindly"; the cold "cruel"; the sun "friendly"; the sea "angry." Pathetic fallacy is a clever guise of imaginative writing.

Related to metaphor and pathetic fallacy, *personification* attributes human characteristics to abstractions or things not human, and allows them to talk, think, feel, respond. Situations and personalities can also be involved. Personification can take over an entire poem. Church buildings can get lonely, glowing lamps can praise God, flowers can smile, faith can look for a home.

Also related to personification is *apostrophe*, a means by which the poet addresses an absent person as if he were there, an object as though it could understand, and an inanimate substance as if it had life. Examples: Moses, a rosebush, the darkness. Under the subhead, "The Poets Toolbox" "tool" usually refers to the figures of speech rather than individual words.

Hyperbole, an image of overstatement, is an extravagant exaggeration that gives force and intensity to a poem. This tool must be used with care; but used with discretion, it adds emphasis and power. Note this example from "Elegy to the American Legion": "Graves cannot contain their spirits, halt their feet from keeping time." This is quite an exaggeration and a lot to expect from buried soldiers, but the poet makes his point.

The opposite of hyperbole, *understatement*, is a subtle form of imagery that relates a truth in a unique way. This tool can take various forms, such as bypassing the obvious and expected reaction for a lesser and sometimes ridiculous one. It can also involve irony or satire with striking effect.

Another figure of speech, *metonymy*, uses a feature or characteristic of a thing to stand for the thing itself. Example: "The gold is lost, the music ended. He didn't live; he just pretended." The gold and the music are representative of everything beautiful, valuable, and meaningful in life.

Very closely related is *synecdoche* in which a part is used to represent the whole: "A host of hungry *faces* waited expectantly in the breadline." Phrasing it this way presents a more striking and dramatic picture.

Zoomorphism is assigning an appropriate part of an animal to God's person in order to convey some truth about God. "But unto you that fear my name shall the sun of righteousness arise with healing in his wings" (Mal. 4:2a KJV). The wing image, associated with birds, illustrates the abilities of an all-powerful God to transcend human limitations.

Anthropomorphism assigns an appropriate part of man's body to God's person in order to convey some truth about God; " . . . underneath are the everlasting arms" (Deut. 33:27b KJV). God's care for his children is symbolized as "everlasting arms," a parallel we can understand.

Alliteration is a device of sound that can take many forms and that can cast a pleasant though intangible spell upon the reader. Alliteration is a repetition of the same beginning letter or sound in words succeeding each other at close intervals. Probably the most familiar illustration of this tool is found in the tongue twister "Peter Piper picked a peck of pickled peppers."

Old English poetry centered around alliteration. Notice in this illustration of Old English alliteration how the first three accents in each line begin with the same sound. This quatrain is entitled "The Organist."

> Mastery of mystery, musing and gay;
> Tasteful and tender, so tuneful his air;

Gone are the ghosts and the guilt of the day;
Soothing so softly, his song is a prayer.

One of the popular variations repeats the same word at the beginning of a series of lines.

An oddity referred to as *concrete poetry* has been employed with effect for centuries. With a little planning and thought, poetic material can be arranged into the typographical shape of the subject matter, for instance: a tree, cross, book, lamp, or star. This unusual presentation of the poem appeals to the eye as well as to the ear and the mind.

Words rich in *connotation* suggest or imply additional shades of meaning beyond their dictionary definition. In poetry we seek to appeal to something much deeper than the intellect; something that will set off a chain reaction in the reader's consciousness.

Onomatopoeia is the simplest and probably the oldest of language devices; it involves the making or forming of a word by imitating a sound. Some of the most common words not only imitate the sound they represent but also suggest the sense and action of the word. Examples: *crunch, crackle, crash, squeak, hiss, twitter, fizz, bubble, honk, mumble, hush.* This device magically ties sound and meaning together.

Parallelism is the setting up of counterparts of phrasing or the matching of ideas. In poetry this is accomplished by balance and repetition. The King James Version of the Bible derives much of its rhetorical and rhythmical power from accumulating parallel structures. For example, see Ecc. 3:1-8.

A *refrain* is a line or lines repeated at intervals throughout a poem for emphasis and to tie the poem together. It is used most commonly at ends of stanzas, many times as a shortened line, and often is also the title, as in the poem, "Write about the Lord" discussed earlier.

Parody is a fun kind of writing that mimics the work of another. Generally it can be of two types—comic parody, which is close to burlesque, and literary or critical parody, which imitates more closely the parodied author's style.

Satire is defined by Webster as a literary work holding up human vices and follies to ridicule or scorn. The tone varies from poet to poet—solemn, sarcastic, biting, teasing, or pompous.

All of the poet's tools are also used to some degree by prose writers, but the tools that involve imagery are the poet's special treasures. The more effectively he knows how to use all these devices, the better his poetry will be.

PITFALLS TO AVOID

One of the best ways for poets to strengthen their skills is to develop a sensitive awareness of what not to do. Every writer will fall into these traps from time to time, but a lot of problems will be avoided if we learn to screen our own efforts, watching for the following vulnerable areas.

False emotionalism and insincerity. These weaknesses surface when a poet deliberately writes about a subject in an emotional way. Straining for an effect by using words like "ecstasy" will not do it. Good poetry is never written to be purposely sentimental or overwhelming. When a writer strains too hard to produce emotion or reaction, he has a tendency to overemphasize everything. This fault can be traced to insincerity or to the lack of experience in writing with depth. The backbone of a poem must be fortified with a believable, workable message or it will not have the staying power to survive.

While scripturally true and poetically correct, the following four lines tend to be dogmatic; the conclusion too neatly packaged. No real depth is here, just trite statements rehashed and served on a small spoon.

> With Christ all things are possible;
> He cures the sick and heals the dumb.
> He spares not trouble but He gives
> Assurance we shall overcome.

The next poem does not try to deal with theology or religious themes per se but shows instead a miraculous power at work.

THE CONQUEROR

> Resentments,
> jealousy,
> selfishness,
> pettiness,
> where did they go?
>
> Somehow
> they all lost their grip
> on me—
> vanished!
>
> And all because
> I am wading in love,
> knee-deep!

One vital difference is in the "showing" and not the "telling."

Vagueness/muddiness. If a pool of water is clear, the bottom can be seen at one hundred feet. A mud puddle might be only an inch deep, but you cannot see the bottom. A poet should learn the difference between depth and muddiness in poetry. Depth brings a second dimension to poetry, elaborates on a concept, triggers the mind to recognize analogous comparisons. Muddiness begins and ends with vague, incomplete thoughts that have no clear focus.

Following is one example of a deeper dimension in poetry. As the episode unfolds, the readers see beyond its surface tale and relate its symbolism to situations within their own experience.

CASTES OF YELLOW

I'm just a humble dandelion
Blooming in the grass,
Beaming cheer to one and all,
Smiling as they pass.

But something happened yesterday
Which made my gold heart bleed:
A buttercup informed me that
I'm really just a weed.

I cried at first, but then I knew
That I was not to blame;
So I'll enjoy the sun and rain
And blossom, just the same.

No muddiness here. Depth and clarity combine to make the message come alive.

Forced rhyming. A word that is obviously put in for a rhyme should never be used. Words placed at the ends of lines just for their rhyming value mark the writer as one who mistakes rhyme for poetry.

Padding. It's almost as bad to pad a line with extra syllables to prevent the rhyme word from getting there too soon. Each word in the line should carry its own weight of meaning, and not be put in to fill up the space until one gets to the rhyme.

Misuse of images. An image must be carefully chosen and be an integral part of the message. Farfetched imagery and mixed images should not be used for they will only confuse the reader. If a number of images are used, they must have a definite relationship to one another and to the theme.

In the following poem, for example, the impact of the snowflake analogy is weakened by the last two lines where the poet brings in a different image. The reader is forced to shift mental gears in order to follow the final point.

How good God is
(knowing the limitations of his creation),
to provide each human snowflake
fallen into the common drift
of frozen anonymity
with its own opportunity to thaw,
find its own identity,
and decide upon its own
Genesis.

On the other hand, this next poem correlates and intertwines its related images throughout its entirety, from the title to the last word, combining to produce a strong poem and a complete picture.

IN THE KING'S ARMY

The Great Commander
who sees all
knows the soul-searing struggles,
the agony of waiting for orders,
the battles in secret,
the boring guard duty,
the humbling discipline of KP,
the obedience with which we take the point,
the price in spilled blood,
and the heartache of the mopping-up operations
after we reach the hill.

God promotes
his own generals.

Shallowness and fragmentation. Some writers produce material of dubious quality because they get carried away with the outer form and work so hard at being different that clarity and meaning suffer. Rather than offer a message that flows, they present bits and fragments, loosely held together, leaving the reader with shallow disjointed clues from which to draw his own conclusions. A good poem should reflect both depth of content and a cohesive presentation.

Moralizing. This approach is resented and turns readers away. The writer must build his moral into the message without being obvious. To be safe, don't moralize at all. There are better ways to make your point.

Staleness. If the reader feels he has read your message a dozen times before, you may be sure he won't respond to it. The subject might be very familiar, but the treatment of it must be new. Care is needed to relay the poet's experience vividly so that his enthusiasm will create its own freshness.

Diffuseness. Going off in all directions seriously weakens a poem. Good poetry is condensed, and the focus is kept central and clear.

Pomposity. If readers feel they are being preached to, and a poet addresses his readers from a self-appointed position of superiority, you may be sure that poet will lose his audience. A gracious, common-ground approach opens doors of communication and will find a sympathetic response.

Generalizations. Never say *tree* when you can call it a *blue spruce* or a *sugar maple*, or write of a *flower* when *begonia* or *carnation* is more striking. A poet cannot create sharp mental images by using generalities; he must use specifics.

Misused or inadequate vocabulary. Above all else, a poet's vocabulary should not be ordinary, meager, or secondhand. Originality and accuracy of wording give the poet's message the best chance of being appreciated. Triteness and tired poeticisms will turn off the reader. Obsolete and archaic words should be avoided. A poet who deliberately uses words that are not easily understood is working against himself and the impression he is trying to create.

Poets, beware! Never fall into the trap of assuming that cuteness is automatically cleverness or that daring to be different is necessarily excellence. If in editing our own poems we check carefully to see if we are guilty of these weaknesses, we can avoid these pitfalls.

Christian writer, do you realize that the God who made us is a poet? Who do you suppose inspired David, the singer of sweet songs, and Solomon, and Isaiah, and John? He can also inspire you to communicate to mankind those life-giving, life-changing truths about himself that we need so desperately to know. But first, the heralds of his message would do well to wait upon their God; to seek counsel at his feet; to acknowledge their need of his special touch.

TOUCH ME, LORD

Creator of all life-producing words,
who spoke the worlds into being,
whose command breathed life into the dust,

whose *content* fills all of time and space
        from eternity to eternity,
        whose being upholds all things
        by the word of his power;

whose *beauty* is as bright as the morning star,
        pure as the lily of the valley,
        the fairest of ten thousand
        to my soul;

whose *craftsmanship* creates masterpieces
        like violets and Matterhorns,
        polishes rough stones into jewels,
        transforms tears into joy;

whose *originality* devises uniqueness for each snowflake,
        designed mustard seeds and little lambs
        as well as mountains and planets and galaxies,
        authored redeeming love
        for aliens and prodigals,
        and found a way to save my soul;

    I bow before you, the Living Word;

worship you, the Greatest Revelation;
acknowledge you, the Perfect Poem;
and as I kneel before you, O God,
craving your special touch,
by your grace
would you stretch forth
the tip of your finger
and write something beautiful
in me?

As you pick up your pen, remember God is depending on you to share that "something beautiful" with others. He has called you to fulfill a mission close to his heart.

While you are struggling up your own poetic hill, keep yourself open to new ideas. Be willing to accept criticism and, above all, continue learning. I suggest you secure a good resource book on poetry, such as my *Pathways for the Poet*. This book is especially helpful regarding the disciplines and tools of the art and offers a great number of poetry patterns plus examples, both rhymed and unrhymed.

There are no shortcuts to excellence. No amount of "holy inspiration" can take the place of plain hard work. A successful poet needs both.

After you have studied, practiced, and prepared yourself, don't be timid. Think of yourself as a modern Joshua. Pick up your ram's horn trumpet and circle the walls of the publishing world with sample volleys. If the first six charges, packed with appeal, excellence, technique, relevance, vitality, and impact, hurled toward the Jericho walls don't result in an opening, don't give up. Bear down with your seventh onslaught, the often underestimated missile of perseverance. This continuing volley will wear down those seemingly formidable walls. The entire fortress may not come tumbling down, but at some opportune moment, in some needy crevice, a crack just big enough for you will open. As you take your first steps within the city gates, the reward of knowing you are on your way will be yours.

❧ *Part Four*

CHAPTER THIRTEEN

WRITING FOR CHILDREN AND YOUTH

by Patricia C. McKissack

Patricia McKissack of St. Louis, Missouri, is the children's book developer at Concordia Publishing House. As a part-time teacher of writing at the University of Missouri School of Continuing Education, she works with beginning students interested in writing for children. She is also a writer, guest lecturer, and consultant for the Learning Institute based in Palo Alto, California. She has led workshops for children's writers at several Christian writers' conferences.

IF YOU WANT to write religious materials for chil- dren, your decision couldn't come at a better time. During recent years there has been a steady pattern of growth in the religious publishing industry, and among the leading products in development and sales have been religious materials for children.

Research within the industry shows that parochial school enrollment is increasing; Sunday school attendance is up in most areas; parents are deeply concerned about the spiritual growth and development of their children; church librarians are being allotted more money to stock children's products; and in many communities, churches are the primary source of competent day care and preschools. Never before has there been such a demand for religious materials to service the home, school, and churches. Now more than ever, religious publishers are prepared to meet these demands. For the Christian writer with knowledge of and personal identification with biblical content and concepts, and a genuine interest in the young audience, this is good news.

This chapter is designed to encourage writers to build on their desire to communicate the "Good News" to young readers, and to offer an apprenticeship, albeit a brief one, in the craft of writing for this specific religious market.

Good writing doesn't happen by chance and it doesn't materialize by will. It is the mastery of technique, the coordination of talent and skill and the balance of personal drive and patience that separate scribblers from communicators, whether they are saints or sinners, writing for children or adults. Writers! Learn your craft!

EXORCISE THE DEMONS

Writers are constantly being worried by mental demons. Procrastination is the prince. His purpose is to seize every opportunity to prey on the writer's isolation and plant seeds of doubt, preoccupy his mind with visions of the future, and fool him into believing something is being done when in reality his "doing" amounts to little more than busywork.

Exorcise this mental demon by establishing a writing schedule, flexible enough to accommodate changes without frustration. Organize a comfortable work area away from distracting noises. Then, set goals, attainable and realistic. *I will write 500 words today. I will finish this project in two weeks.* A regular routine will reward you with measurable results and a sense of accomplishment.

EVALUATE IDEAS

If you work regularly on your writing, ideas will begin to form. There are two kinds of ideas: the Athena Idea, which springs forth fully grown and overflowing with wisdom, and the more common Mustard Seed Idea, which starts small—usually as a scene, the name of a character, an experience, a question. Whether it bursts forth in full bloom or matures slowly, every idea should be evaluated to see if it is worthy of development.

When your manuscript is sent to a publisher, you won't be there to explain your idea. Therefore, a manuscript must have a voice of its own; it must speak with authority and express with confidence what it is. Your intentions must be clear to the reader, and the promised benefits delivered. A well-thought-out idea is the foundation on which a writer begins.

Be careful not to spend too much time thinking about an idea. At some point the writer must master the idea or the idea will master the writer.

THE "SEW" METHOD

Writing without purpose or direction is usually unproductive. Beginning writers know what they want to write, but know very little about what readers want to read or what publishers want to produce. Successful writers know their audience and their market. How do you get this information?

At a recent workshop Walter Wangerin, Jr., the award-winning author of *The Book of the Dun Cow* (Harper & Row), introduced the SEW method of preparation: study, experimentation, and watchfulness (observation). He advised beginning writers "to *study* the religious publishing industry." Order catalogs from publishers and review the kinds of material they produce. Read the authorities in Christian education, child psychology, and pediatrics. Visit schools and Sunday schools; talk to teachers and librarians, and listen to the people who have made their careers working with children. Parents, of course, are also a primary source of information.

Wangerin encouraged writers not to limit themselves to any specific type of writing. "*Experiment* with a number of literary forms." Experimentation gives you valuable experience, and experience strengthens your confidence.

Twenty-five years ago a Christian writer was limited to writing curriculum, Bible stories, or prayer books for children. Today a writer can choose to write an easy-to-read for the very young child or a novel for the high school student. Religious publishers have expanded their lines to include nonfiction, fiction, poetry, drama, and history for a more diverse, demanding readership.

Since children are your target audience, you must spend time with them, learning about their world and how they perceive it. *Watch* things with the eyes of a child, and you'll be better prepared to share those experiences convincingly in your writing.

CATEGORIES OF RELIGIOUS MATERIALS FOR CHILDREN

In the religious market there are seven basic categories of children's products:

The pure Bible story

Bible-based materials

Religious concepts and moral instruction

Fictional stories/nonfictional stories

Prayer/devotionals

The seasonals

The activity

Examine these categories carefully and use the SEW method to familiarize yourself with the features of each.

The Pure Bible Story

The one book that is unrivaled for Christian authenticity and authority is the Bible, but the language is too difficult for young children to read and understand. Bible stories make an excellent preview to actual Bible reading, and that's why they're the all-time favorite of those who are concerned about assuring biblical knowledge. Youngsters of all ages love them and will read them.

Most religious publishers and many secular houses feature one or more Bible story books in their catalogs, and bookstores devote an entire section to this category. Order catalogs from publishers and study their Bible story line. Be a frequent visitor to bookstores and church libraries: Good writers are first good readers; learn to read with a critical eye and analyze the techniques a writer used. One excellent way to develop critical skills is to review books for a local newspaper or a church bulletin.

Some Bible story books contain brief retellings of major biblical events from the Old and/or New Testaments (strictly adhering to scripture) while others contain excerpts from the life and teachings of Jesus or other Bible characters, e.g.: *Women in the Bible, The Prophets, The Kings,* etc. Some writers choose to retell a Bible story in prose, whereas others prefer poetry. Experiment with a variety of literary forms until you establish your own style.

The market for the large, all-inclusive volume of Bible stories is limited, but a well-written Bible story will always be considered in the curriculum, vacation Bible school, and magazine markets.

Bible-based Materials

Not all retellings are the pure Bible story. Frequently, fictional characters are added for reader interest and detail. For example, in retelling the familiar Bible story "The Feeding of the Five Thousand," a writer might name the boy with the loaves and fishes, establish him in a family, and give him a personality. This allows the author to use dialogue, description, and action not in the actual biblical account. A reasonable amount of fiction gives the story life and color and a ring of reality that will interest children. It's usually acceptable as long as the actual account is not changed. For example, in the same story, it would be totally unacceptable if the boy brought cheese and fruit instead of loaves and fishes.

Fiction used in connection with the Bible may bother publishers who service a more fundamental market; therefore, study the Bible-based materials that have been produced, and by whom. The Arch Books produced by Concordia make use of Bible stories retold in poetry from a fictional character's point of view. But these books don't conflict with the scriptural account or make the Bible seem like fiction: that is the key to their success.

How much fiction or fantasy you wish to inject in retelling a Bible story is a personal decision. It's a difficult formula to master, but it can be done successfully. As a Christian writer you have an obligation to make sure your young readers are not confused about what the Bible actually says. Teachers and parents often complain that they have to "unteach" many things children have read in a book or seen on television.

Before submitting your manuscript for publication, share it with teachers and children. Carefully observe their reactions. If there is the slightest hint of confusion about what is fact and what is fiction, you might need to rewrite or change your approach. And examine the requirements of each publisher before sending your manuscript. Some will not consider a fictionalized Bible story; others will.

Religious Concepts and Moral Instruction

During childhood years questions arise such as, How can God be everywhere at the same time? Why can't I see God? What happens when I die? These questions trouble adults as well; parents feel inadequate to answer and seek help in explaining these abstract concepts and beliefs to their children in a simple but intelligent manner.

The language in such products should be simple, freeing the young reader and the adult to concentrate on grasping the concept behind the words. Two books to study are *God and Me* and *You and Me,* by Florence Parry Heide. Each book simplifies a religious concept in a satisfying and appealing way: how God can be everywhere and not be seen, and why we are so much alike yet so different.

Select a religious concept to simplify it. The results will either lead you to try something else or will open a up a new area of writing for you.

It is necessary to study the theological references regarding a concept to get an interpretation that will sell to a specific publisher. However, every writer of a concept book—or any children's book, for that matter—must spend time with the real thing—children! How do children think? Watch how they play. Watch how they delight in the simplest things around them. If you are fortunate enough to have a small friend who's willing to invite you into his special world, your experiences will be enjoyable and they will be invaluable in determining the proper approach to use in explaining a religious concept.

Stories: Fiction/Nonfiction

Remember back a few years ago when there were only a few products on the grocery shelf? Selection was easy. Today supermarkets are larger than ever, with countless varieties of products stocked on the shelves. Children's books are no different. The choices are myriad.

One of the growing areas in the Christian market is fiction and nonfiction for children. Young readers of all ages enjoy stories about other children from the past, present, and future, or about interesting adults. Study the mysteries, sports, animal stories, folktales, legends, fantasies, adventures, historical novels, and biographies that have become a part of contemporary religious literature for children. If you write a fast-moving, action-packed story with characters who solve their problems realistically, it will stand as good a chance as any of being accepted for publication. It doesn't matter to children if the story contains a religious theme as long as it's interesting and is presented in a manner that says *now*. Please note that publishers are mostly concerned that the religion isn't tacked on as an afterthought—for example, a Bible passage placed at the top of each chapter. The religion should be an integral part of the story, without being preachy and didactic; children like to discover rather than be *told* what to think and believe.

The success rate of materials of this type varies from publisher to publisher and depends largely on their primary market. It's a growing area of development in the publishing industry and a promising avenue for the Christian writer. Somewhere out there is a religious Judy Blume. Every religious publisher is looking for her—or him.

The Seasonal

Dorothy Van Woerkom, author of two seasonal classics for children, *Journeys to Bethlehem* and *Stepka and the Magic Fire*, responded to a letter I wrote asking her about writing: "We celebrate Christ's birth because without it the gates of heaven would still be closed to us . . . We celebrate Christ's resurrection because without it his life would have been only our hope and not our salvation. It's natural, then, that the most popular Christian literature is the seasonals."

Seasonals in the religious market usually mean Christmas and Easter but sometimes include Advent, Epiphany, Lent and Pentecost.

Publishers are always interested in a manuscript that presents a beautiful account of Christ's birth and the glory of his resurrection for children. But how does a writer improve on the biblical account?

In Van Woerkom's *Journeys to Bethlehem*, she focused on the points of view of the various people converging on Bethlehem at that time. In her *A Hundred Angels Singing*, she describes the thoughts of a modern child who compares what's going on at her Christmas Eve celebration with things that happened at the first Christmas. In both books—one traditional, one contemporary—all the elements of the biblical account are accurately presented. This is the most important feature.

In *From*, Beverly Beckmann used thirty-seven words to explain the resurrection, and Carol Greene used the metamorphosis of a butterfly to tell the story of the resurrection in *A Truly Remarkable Day*. Inspirational poetry, religious folk themes, and analogies are often used to retell these important stories in a fresh and appealing manner.

I couldn't agree with Van Woerkom more when she says, "The religious seasons are constantly being renewed for us through the imaginative and creative approaches of authors who are willing to explore them in a new and exciting way."

Writers who SEW with consistency will be aware of market needs in this area and find new and interesting ways to present an old story.

The time schedule for seasonal books usually runs eighteen months in advance of projected release. In the magazine market, seasonal items should be submitted six months before the actual season.

Prayer Devotionals

A top priority for Christian educators and parents is to teach their children to pray. If children can feel comfortable with praying they will do it more often and with a better understanding of why it is important in their lives. If they know that God hears prayers whether whispered by a bedside or shouted out in glee, the idea of God, the unseen father, protector, and provider, is much more meaningful.

Prayer books and devotionals that help children get started in their personal prayer life are standard among publishers.

Whenever possible, listen to the prayers of children and keep a notebook handy to jot down some of their candid remarks. Talk to children about how they talk to God. When do they pray? Why do they pray? Where? All these questions will give you the framework of a prayer/devotional.

Study what's in the marketplace. Examine some of the standards, such as *Little Visits with God*, by Allan Hart Jahsmann or the prayer books *A Child's Garden of Prayers*, *Holiday Prayers for Children*, and *Little Folded Hands*. Some of these books were published more than twenty-five years ago, but they are still being used and enjoyed by thousands of children.

The Activity

The activity—dot-to-dot, cut and paste, coloring pages, word puzzles, mazes, etc.—featured in magazines, newspapers, and books are very popular items. The economical price tag attracts the teacher who's looking for products to buy in quantity as handouts, and parents like them because they offer hours of constructive entertainment. The best benefit is that while the children are playing and having fun they are also learning Bible characters, places, events. Who says Bible study can't be fun?

There must be hundreds of these products on the market, but there's a constant market for more.

A good activity must be challenging, usually a level above the age group for which it is intended, but in the religious market there must be a clear-cut benefit, something that's learned at the conclusion of the activity.

THE WRITING PROCESS

No doubt you've spent a lot of time—too much time—*thinking* about your decision to write. Now it's time to do something about it. Writers write!

Once you've selected a category, it must be matched with the correct format. The format is determined by the kind of book you want to write. A big mistake beginning writers make is saying, "This book is for all ages." A writer must choose a specific age group and write in a format using the vocabulary and word count within that format. That's not to say once the book is published its sale and distribution will be limited to that targeted age group only, but when writing, you must have a clearly defined audience and format before proceeding.

Some authors argue that writing within a given format limits their creativity. I quote Dr. Harley Swiggum, writer of The Bethel Bible Series and respected teacher and lecturer: ". . . You [the writer] can break the rules if you learned the rules in the first place. Picasso mastered the techniques of the classical artists before he broke from the traditions and started the new school of modern art . . ." In the beginning, learn by the rules. Your creative genius will not be stifled, and your writing will be strengthened.

Selecting the Correct Format

The physical and mental growth and development of children from birth to adolescence is startling. Ask any parent who has to replace new shoes before the soles on the last pair are hardly worn, or a grandparent who is confronted with "I'd rather do it myself. I can, you know."

Children who had to sit passively and listen to a story in September can, by June, read a complete book all by themselves. To young children everything is new and exciting. Everything is full of wonder and surprise. Their world is constantly expanding, and their interests change as they gain confidence in their ability.

You must be aware of these changes when writing for specific age groups, and the reading level and the interest level of the reader must be suited for the format you use.

Easy-to-Reads

The easy-to-read, sometimes called the "easy reader" or "beginning reader," is not a picture book, nor is it a textbook that attempts to teach the child to read. It is a book to help and encourage primary-age children (five-to-seven-year-olds) to read by themselves. Teachers and librarians call them enrichment or supplementary reading. Children call them "a book I can read by myself."

An easy-to-read has to be true to the promise it makes. If the child has to ask an adult or an older child how to pronounce every other word, it's not an easy reader.

The characteristics of an easy reader are:

- a vocabulary that is very simple. (Publishers who produce this type of book usually have guidelines and word lists available on request.)

- short, concrete sentences that usually read subject, verb, object. (See sample page from an I Can Read.)

- pages that do not exceed six through nine lines in length.

The writer should rely heavily on rhythm and the natural flow of words. Avoid awkward construction and remember your reader is just learning how to read. Keep characters to a maximum of four. Bible stories work well in this format, because the child is comfortable with the familiar names and the sequence of the story.

Picture Books

The picture book is a story told through the interaction of words and pictures. No, you don't have to be an artist to write a picture book. In most houses, teams are established: a writer and an illustrator who complement each other and an editor who coordinates their efforts.

The text and the illustrations are of equal importance, although the balance may vary with each story. The writer should remember that the words need not tell everything, because the idea is to give the reader room to use his own imagination.

Picture books are usually designed for the very young reader; however, older children enjoy them, too. The subjects may be Bible stories, a contemporary story, a seasonal, or perhaps a Bible-based story. Some picture books contain no copy, whereas others have as many as 1,500 words or more.

Picture book illustrating is a highly technical process and a marketing consideration. Two unknowns are rarely teamed, and price objective, size, number of pages, etc., are important parts of the design process. A writer should not illustrate or have a manuscript illustrated. It's unnecessary and a waste of time and money. If the manuscript is appropriate for a publisher's market, the editor will recognize what it is and assign it to an illustrator who will know just what to do with it. Strange though it may seem, authors and illustrators don't usually know each other. One picture book author said, 'I'm always surprised when I see how the illustrator pictures my words. That's the most exciting part of my work." Remember the illustrations don't sell the manuscript, the copy does.

Read-to Books

Children like to be read to by an older child, parent, or teacher. Since there is a difference between what a child can read at any given age and what he can understand and enjoy through listening, the writer must take this into consideration and write accordingly.

The lap book (so called because children sit on a lap and listen while being read to) is not as heavily illustrated as the picture book. Your choice of words need not be as restricted as in the easy-to-read or the picture book. A good lap book is one that's enjoyed by both the reader and the listener. The length will vary, but will usually range from 2,500 to 3,500 words. Unless you're writing for a specific series with a definite word count, don't trouble yourself with length. Tell the story, keep the characters limited, watch your transitions, and make sure the dialogue is expressive and clear. Make sure the listener knows what's happening at all times. Avoid lengthy description and keep the action moving.

Tape your manuscript and listen to the rhythm. If you use words that are difficult, define them in the story. *Flying Feathers* is a Slavic folktale rewritten by Mary Kentra Ericsson. In the text she uses the term *opanke*, an unfamiliar word to young readers and most adults. See how she explains it without interrupting the narrative:

> Nika threw up her arms and shouted with excitement. She turned her body around trying to watch the feathers as they disappeared in the valley below.
>
> Then she took off her opanke and held the soft shoes in her hands so she could run faster and get back to Baba and tell her she had done her bidding.

Concept Books

Concept books are really picture books that are not for the very young child, but for older children between seven and ten years of age.

During this age children are full of wonderful imagination; they have been described as "pure imagination." Can you imagine a green crow? a square circle? a tiny dinosaur? Or perhaps you have become like the adults Mary Watkins describes, " . . . we laugh at and scorn those who waste their time dealing with imagination."

In a child's world full of wonder and surprise, anything and everything is possible—it need only be "thought."

In a wonderful story called *Mr. God, This Is Anna* (Ballantine Books), Fynn, the author, tells how Anna, his four-year-old friend, gave him a wonderful lesson in imagination.

> One night, on our usual walk, she asked for the chalk. She knelt down on the pavement and drew a large red circle. "Pretend that's me," she said. Outside the circle she liberal-

ly sprinkled a number of dots. About the same number of dots were sprinkled inside the circle. Looking around, she pointed to a tree. "That," she said, "is that there," and she pointed to a dot outside the circle and marked it with a cross. Then, pointing to a dot inside the circle, she said, "That is that dot outside the circle, and that is the tree," and with her finger on the tree dot inside the circle, she continued with, "And that's the tree inside me."

Up to this point everything has been perfectly logical; it is within the realm of adult comprehension. But Anna didn't stop there: She invited Fynn into her world.

> "And that," she exclaimed in triumph, laying her finger on another dot inside the circle, "is a . . . is a . . . flying elephant. But where is it outside? Where is it, Fynn?"
> "There ain't no such beastie, so it can't be outside," I explained. "Well, then, how did it get into my head? "She sat back on her heels and stared at me.

How would you have answered Anna?
As adults we frequently move from the abstract to the concrete in our reasoning. Children have the ability to move from the concrete to the abstract because their imagination is so active and free of limitations. If a writer can learn to think like a child, explaining a difficult concept such as Why can't I see God? becomes *possible*.

Florence Parry Heide is probably one of the most prolific writers in this genre; she has more than six concept books in print. I asked Heide what she would say to a beginning writer interested in concept books. She responded in a letter:

> In writing concept books for the religious market, I have tried to instill in young children's minds a sense of wonder and joy. Since they find it difficult to grasp abstractions, I try to find ways to present an idea in terms they can understand: using simple language is not enough. The idea itself must be scaled to their size.
>
> I try to use specific examples of their familiar surroundings to lead them into the idea itself. However, to stick too closely to the physical world is counterproductive: their imaginations must take strong forward steps.
>
> Perhaps, then, leading from the particular to the general, from concrete to abstract, is the answer. This is what I tried to do in *God and Me*:

There is a curve in the road ahead.
I cannot see what is around the corner
until I walk that far.

There is a garden there, and a swing.
I cannot see the garden.
I cannot see the swing.
I will see them when I turn the corner.

And on to the abstract:

Some things I cannot ever see.
I cannot see yesterday, or tomorrow.
I cannot see the song of a bird,
but the bird sings.
I cannot see God,
But God is there.

Just as there are many messages, there are many methods. I speak here only of my own approach.

Joann and Ben Marxhausen skillfully combine an analogy and colorful artwork in their *Thank God for Circles* and *Three-In One: A Picture of God*. Circles explain the everlastingness of God and an apple explains the trinity.

Pre-Teen Books

Wally Ambruster, author of *Noodles D'Jour*, says, "Mothers are people who bear children. Children are often hardest to bear twelve years after they are born." How true!

The pre-teen years are often stormy for the child and the adults in their lives. Pre-teens are searching for identity and life goals. They don't like to be forced to read, nor do they like "preachy" material. What they do like and expect in a book is honesty combined with strong characters and fast-moving action.

For this age group there are two choices. The *first novel* is positioned for the lower age range (fourth and fifth grade), and the *juvenile novel* for the older end of the age range (sixth to eighth). The first novel is longer than a storybook but not as long as a novel. It's usually the first full-length book a child will read on his own, at about age ten.

The elements of a good first novel or juvenile novel are:

- a length of no more than 25,000 words.

- lots of action and good character development. Children this age like to know their characters on a personal basis and relate to them, reference: friends, sisters, brothers, teachers, etc.

- dialogue that is believable.

- plot that is challenging and exciting but not overwhelming.

- a vocabulary that is at the higher level of the reading/interest group.

A good juvenile novel has the same features of any adult novel or work of fiction. The juvenile fiction writer should use the same techniques but make adjustments for audience interest and reading level.

Series Books

Once a group of characters takes hold, readers want more stories about them and publishers try to accommodate them. *The Sugar Hill Gang, The Goosehill Gang*, and the *Haley Adventure Stories* are examples of successful series. The Haley stories began as a single title and are now a set of eight books. Mary Christian, the author of *The Goosehill Gang*, began her series much the same way.

Mary Christian's characters are real and believable, yet they are fictional. "How do you develop them?" I asked her in a recent interview. She responded:

> Most series are written with one dominant character and a secondary cast of followers, usually flat characters. However, I found that for me, particularly for a Christian series, I preferred to create characters of varying and complementary talents. They are each well rounded with both weaknesses and strengths. One or the other may be dominant in a single episode, but each of them has been the major character sometime during the series.
>
> I feel this not only strengthens the series by having "real" people involved but also demonstrates the Christian concept that we are all beautiful and important in God's eyes.

It's important for a writer to make the characters and the setting as real as possible. Consistency is also important. Mary Christian says:

> Series generally take place in a single location with at least

some of the same people each time. To avoid inconsistencies over the three-year period of production [fourteen books], I kept biographical sketches of each character, adding information as it was revealed. It included the family tree, character traits, descriptions, hobbies, talents, etc.

I made a map of Goosehill so I knew exactly how far it was from Tubby's to the nearest hamburger stand, from Beth's to the bookstore, and where their houses were in relation to each other. As characters were introduced, I located them on my map.

I knew then whether the gang had to turn east or west, whether they were on Elm or Oak, and whether they could see the bandstand from City Hall.

Although you may not begin a book with a series in mind, the characters and the setting should be established in the beginning so that they can become a part of an ongoing story. Do not write a complete series; one book is all that's needed. The editor determines whether the project will become a series. Many series are not written by the same author but are illustrated by the same person to insure continuity.

If you're interested in writing for a series, write to the publisher for guidelines.

CHOOSING A PUBLISHER

Selecting the right publisher is as important as the writing process and can save a writer time and expensive postage. Choose a publisher whose philosophy is the same as your own.

Editors are responsible for selecting manuscripts based on editorial policy or corporate mission. Generally, children's products have one or more objectives: to entertain, to inform, or to teach or strengthen a skill, e.g., reading. Editors expect one or more of these features to be self-evident, but in addition to these, the Christian editor has more specific objectives, including but not limited to the following:

- to assist children in developing a strong faith through a personal identification with biblical characters, content, and concepts.

- to encourage children to grow naturally into a lifestyle that reflects Christian beliefs (in some cases the beliefs of a denomination).

- to offer children the Christian alternative in the problem-solving and decision-making process.

- to strengthen family unity through materials that offer an opportunity for children to share in the worship process.

With this information and with the help of other publishing aids, journals, and instructional books such as this one, you should be able to select the right publisher. Here is where your perseverance and tenacity will play an important role. Rejections will come; this is part of the publishing process, but as soon as a manuscript is returned, have an envelope addressed and be ready to send it out again. What one publisher can't use, another might have a slot for immediately. You'll never know if you keep it filed in your drawer.

THE CHALLENGE

I imagine that Jesus' receiving the children had a humbling effect on the religious pedants around him. In those days children were to be seen and not heard, but Jesus knew their minds and hearts.

"Let the children come to me," he said. And I'm sure they came, running, laughing, bursting with joy. And we can imagine the scene as he welcomed them. The younger ones shamelessly hugged his neck and crawled in his lap. The older ones sat at his feet, wide-eyed and curious. No wonder he said, ". . . for to such belongs the kingdom of heaven."

It is this real and living Jesus the Christian writer has to bring to the children of today. It is not an easy task. If you write for children in the religious market, make sure your products allow them the freedom to use their imaginations and to willingly respond to his call of "Come unto me . . ." The end results, we hope, will be a real acceptance of Christ as their savior and the application of the basic Christian principles throughout their lives.

CHAPTER FOURTEEN

WRITING FOR OTHER SPECIAL AUDIENCES

WRITING FOR WOMEN

by Lois N. Erickson

The author lives in Eugene, Oregon, and has written two books, curriculum material, and numerous articles on subjects of interest to women.

"I dozed . . . until abruptly I woke up. Without thinking, I ran out the door. A delivery truck was starting to back up—and Sharon was directly behind it! When the driver saw me, he hit the brakes. The truck stopped only inches from my little child.

"Was it good luck? Mother's instinct? Or did God wake me up to rush out the door?"

When I wrote how a truck almost hit two-year-old Sharon, I knew that any woman who had seen a child in danger would understand my panic. This identification holds the key to writing for the Christian women's market.

How can you help the woman reader to identify?

- *Write with emotion and feeling. Ask yourself, "What problems are universal?" Women—whether single or married, old or young—face sorrow and loneliness, fear and insecurity, discouragement and disappointment.*

  Take fear for example. In "Before I Knew I Had a Problem," published in *Purpose*, I express my fear. "In the darkness and rain I squinted at the traffic light and then turned onto the approach to the freeway. That's when the cable from the gas pedal to the engine broke. I felt completely helpless. My first thought was that my husband was out of town. Who would rescue me?"

  Virtue published "Abigail, a Woman of Wisdom and Beauty." In this fictionalized Bible story I bring out Abigail's reaction to danger. "Fear chilled Abigail like an icy wind. She clasped her hands tightly together to stop the trembling. She shut her eyes. She must think. 'Dear Lord, what shall I do? If David comes and kills all the men, what will his band of ruffians do to the women?' "

  Fear can also come from nonphysical causes. *Lutheran Church Women* published "Good News" in which I attempt to understand my feelings. "Why is it sometimes a struggle for me? I know the Good News. Why do I hesitate to tell others?"

- *Choose subjects that are life-related, everyday areas of concern. The messy house. The sick child. The too-busy husband. How do you cope with age forty? How do you meet the demands upon you as a single parent, or jug-*

gle two careers—home and away? In what ways can you help sons and daughters make decisions?

In a story about my foster son Jim, published in *Scope*, my concern is that he should be free of loneliness and rejection. The article starts with, " 'Mom, I have a problem.' Jim stood in the kitchen where I was scrubbing the potatoes before putting them into the oven. He held his books in one arm and his shoulders sagged."

The reader can picture herself in the same situation. As she prepares dinner, a son or daughter or friend brings a problem to her.

"I looked up into Jim's troubled eyes. I had been dreading the time when he would need to make a decision. Because I was frightened for him, I wanted him to refuse the invitation. Yet I couldn't let him know this. I had to let him decide. I put the potatoes in the oven—slowly, so I would have another moment to think."

Here I add a touch of fear to show the extent of my concern for my son.

Even a Bible study can be life-related. *Lutheran Church Women* invited me to write a series of devotional leaflets. In the Christmas selection Mary prepares for the journey to Bethlehem.

"What would she need in case the baby was born while they were traveling? Some pieces of linen cloth, old and soft, and a container of olive oil for cleaning the newborn infant. Long, linen swaddling clothes to wrap the baby soon after birth."

The era is different, but a mother's concern for her baby was just as real in Bible times as it remains today.

Remember also as you write that although most modern women spend a part of their day in the "homemaker" role, many also work outside the home and have other interests besides their families. In other words, don't be too stereotyped in the way you picture your reader. She is a many-faceted person and your writing should reflect this.

● *Bring out the five senses so the reader can experience them. Seeing, hearing, smelling, tasting, touching.*

Seeing.

In my book *Adventures in Solitude* (Review and Herald) I expect the reader to see with me.

"When I opened my eyes, I was aware that the partitions between the windowpanes formed crosses. 'Lord Jesus, thank You.' The philodendron plant on top of the television set was green and healthy. The painting that hung on the wall portrayed a mountain, serene and enduring, behind a forest of dark green trees."

Faith and Inspiration published "Kind Words Make Kind People." I describe the owner of a small hotel.

"The old man behind the desk had thick white hair and a neatly trimmed mustache. He was a tall, strongly-built man and I felt intimidated as he towered over me."

Hearing.

In *Adventures in Solitude* I ask the reader to listen. "I like the sound of moving water—the washing machine filling or water pouring into the bathtub. Good, clean sounds. I like the melody of river water tumbling over large rocks. I enjoy the percussion of ocean waves hitting sand. Good, natural sounds."

The Easter selection of the *Lutheran Church Women* devotional leaflets shows Mary Magdalene and the other women on the way to the tomb. "In the darkness of early morning, perhaps even before the first bird sang, they got up and ventured out. We can imagine the soft sound of their sandals along the quiet streets and the whisper of their voices."

Smelling and tasting.

I hope readers can smell and taste " . . . crusty, hot rolls . . . " while reading "Kind Words Make Kind People."

Or enjoy the pleasant scent in the Abigail story. "Abigail stood under a flowering almond tree. Sweet fragrance from its pink blossoms drifted to her."

Touching.

Faith and Inspiration printed "Never Throw a Seed Away." "I held the crumbling soil in my hand and let it fall back to the earth through my fingers . . . The spring sunshine was warm on my back . . . The seeds felt hard between the tips of my thumb and finger as I placed them one by one into the ground."

- *Weave in a message of hope.*

    As you write about life-related, everyday problem, let the reader know that solutions exist.

    Women could become discouraged if they compare themselves with the ideal woman in Proverbs 31. She got up before daylight and accomplished all her tasks. In one of the devotional leaflets, I address this dilemma. "We ask ourselves, 'How can I accomplish anything more than I'm doing now? The laundry is piled on top of the washer, I have to drop the children off at a basketball game before my 7:30 meeting, and I must go to work tomorrow morning."

    Women often find help in devotional thoughts and prayer.

The writer can meet this need by offering inspirational material. In *Adventures in Solitude* I have a conversation with God. I have been agonizing over the age-old question, "Why me, Lord? Why must I have so much pain?" Before long I realize that my thoughts are coming into order. " 'Lord, I'm learning something.' 'For example?' 'Maybe I should accept the benefits of solitude before I become sick.' 'Why do you wait so long?' 'I don't want to neglect my family.' 'Do you think you are indispensable?' 'Well, yes, I guess so. I've always thought they couldn't manage without me, but perhaps it's good for them to have some independence without my control.' 'Peace.' 'Thank you.' "

- *Tell how women can reach out to other persons.*

Many Christian women volunteer their time at church school and vacation Bible school. The writer can share teaching methods and new ideas. *Learning With*, a Christian education magazine, published this report on "Mini-Posters." "Soon the fellowship hall of the church was filled with voices as the amateur artists went to work. Grandpa Erickson helped little Sara with glue and scissors. Highschoolers Sonja, Heather, and Tony conferred about tissue paper and pieces of yarn while Christopher and Brenden weighed the advantages of plastic straws over cotton balls."

Women are concerned also about the needs of the world. *The Episcopalian* printed my piece about a Christian woman-activist. "Step two for social action comes when you learn facts. You think, 'I don't want to know how many children died of malnutrition today. That's a horrible thought.' You can't carry the burden alone. You must carry it in fellowship."

Opportunities for service sometimes arrive unexpectedly, and you can share them in writing. I tell of a wrong-number phone call in "I'm Glad I Listened" published in *Scope*. "I listened while he talked on and on. The clock by my phone showed 10 minutes, then 20, 25. He stopped talking and the phone was silent. 'You're spending a lot of money on this phone call,' I said. 'It's worth it. You're listening to me,' he answered.

" 'When there isn't anyone to listen, remember the verse, "The Lord hears when I call to him" ' (Ps.4:3). 'Is that from the Bible?' 'From a psalm. I forget which one.' 'I have a Bible somewhere here in my apartment. I'll look for the verse.' "

Identification—emotion-concern-action.

From your writing, the Christian woman reader will know that someone else has experienced challenges similar to hers. And as she learns how another woman has endured, she will find inspiration, hope, and courage.

WRITING FOR MEN
by Gary Warner

Gary Warner, of Overland, Kansas, is author/teacher, executive secretary of the Evangelical Press Association and former editor of the Association of Christian Athletes.

So you want to write for men. There are riskier ventures such as hunting sharks with your bare hands or trying to catch lightning bolts in a doggy bag.

If we're going to talk with each other about religious writing, we ought to be straight about it. So . . . a few facts. In this "information rich" age we are fast becoming a nation of video and computer watchers (and believers!) and print headline scanners. America has always been a nation of nonreaders. Reliable statistics claim that 98 percent of the U.S. population does not read books. Oh, Americans buy books—to give away as gifts to people who don't read them, either.

In the religious market, women are usually the target. It is the women, by and large, who read Christian family magazines. In the mushrooming Christian bookstores, more than 80 percent of the shoppers and browsers are women between the ages of twenty-five and forty-five.

OK, now that we've got some of the less encouraging facts of America's reading life on the table, let's get on with writing for men. It's needed. And if you do it well, it can be a tremendously important ministry.

You don't have to be a man to write for men, just as you certainly don't have to be a woman to write for women. Men read Meg Greenfield, Ellen Goodman, Jane Bryant Quinn, and others because they are contemporary, relevant, and write well. In Christian circles, such writers as Joyce Landorf and Catherine Marshall appeal to men as well as women because they are creative craftspersons with messages and stories men can buy into.

If you write for men it should be because you feel you have a particular message men should hear. This is basic in any reporter/researcher's feel for his trade and his gifts. But how can you get this message across to the men who are your potential readers? You must find out what men are interested in. What do men want today? What makes them laugh? What makes them cry? What do they fear? What counsel do they need? How can you put them in touch with God? Find out about men. Get in touch with them; know them. Don't write what you think men ought to read. Write to the deep parts of a man's life and experience to reach him where he really wants to be reached and understood and helped.

A lot of writing to men is more a matter of preparation than sitting down at the typewriter. If you know what men want to read, more than half of your writing battle is won.

That's not to say your success is therefore guaranteed. You may have the message and deliver it well. That doesn't mean it will get to your audience because religious publishing is generally geared up to reach women and not men.

But there are many things you can do as a writer:

1. You can reach a lot of men by writing material that is of interest to both men and women. And that's a pretty broad field: Write about the family, about parenting, about growing old, about sex, about divorce, about scores of things that affect men and women equally.

2. You can reach men by slanting your material about men to women. Jim Conway wrote *Men in Mid-Life Crisis*, a timely and needed book. But men did not stampede the Christian bookstores to scoop it off the shelves. No, women bought it. Bought it for themselves to better understand their husbands. Bought it as gifts for a husband or a brother or another woman. If you can write that article or book for men that has a strong appeal to women, you've found a formula that is every publisher's dream.

3. Find a man's "interest button" that once pressed will keep him sitting up in bed late at night to read. Many men have such a button. In some it's labeled "sport." If there were a Pat Jordan or Roger Angell or Roger Kahn in religious writing, men would be buying religious sport books. For others the "interest button" is labeled workaholism or sexuality or how to share and relate deeply. Study men. Find their "interest buttons." Write to them. The religious publishing establishment will take care of the rest.

4. Men need to see the real and human Jesus. If your spirituality averts its eyes and scuffs its feet in the dust and your Jesus is some sort of namby-pamby, men will turn you off. While men are learning the essential lesson that "macho" means compassion and sensitivity and caring as much as it does tattoos and biceps, men still want a Jesus who bleeds and hurts and has gravel in his sandals and sweat in his armpits. Give men the reality of the man Jesus and not a saccharin-sweet sissy hugging lambs on Sunday school walls.

5. Whereas most religious general and family publications slant the contents toward the woman reader, they are always on the lookout for those one or two exceptional articles for men. Most religious freelancers write for women. So become the exception. A magazine may receive 100 articles a month aimed at the seven or eight slots in the editorial well reserved for general or women-oriented pieces and get only a handful of articles, most of them poorly researched and focused, for the one or two "men on-

ly" openings. Let the editor know your interest. Tell him or her in your query letter that you have something different, something he needs—a well-thought-out, strong article for men.

Whether you're male or female, writing for men is tough. That's why not many writers are making the attempt. And that makes the odds better for you. Check the market guides; query editors. Check the local newspaper editor who may well be able to use that news story or feature profile about a male community member on his sports or feature or religious page. If you do your homework, you can be successful.

It's worth the effort. If you write a message from the Lord to the needs of men, you'll have a lot of grateful brothers (and sisters) in the kingdom.

WRITING THEOLOGICAL AND SCHOLARLY MATERIAL

by John Charles Cooper

John Cooper, of Findlay, Ohio, dean of academic affairs and professor of theology at Winebrenner Theological Seminary, is the author of twenty-six books in various fields of theology, psychology, and sociology.

Although not immediately inspiring, theological journal articles and theological books written in traditional scholarly style are the ultimate foundation of all religious writing. One may not feel directly uplifted reading an article on the origins of circumcision among the ancient Hebrews or on the textual problems of translating Luke, Chapter 22, but no popular "inspiring" work is possible without the time-consuming efforts of biblical scholars, historians, theologians, and language experts.

Just as the simple life saving techniques of first aid or CPR taught to lay people in Red Cross courses rest ultimately on serious, detailed investigation of the human body and its problems by physicians and academic researchers, so does religious writing of all kinds draw upon the research and understanding of academic religious scholars. Writing theological material is for the most part open only to professionally educated persons. One does not acquire the tools and insights needed in such a task on his own or even by exposure to undergraduate university courses. As in the writing of medical journal articles, only those who have obtained advanced degrees are qualified to write in this special field.

There are many persons with college and seminary educations (ministers, priests, Christian educators) who are *basically* equipped to enter the scholarly theological field, but even these professionals will need continued study to make written contributions to theological journals or attract the publishers of scholarly books. In the main, a minimum of a master's degree (MA or STM or ThM) beyond the first professional degree (M Div) is desirable for theological writing. Most people writing in this area will have a Ph.D. degree in one of the major theological disciplines. They also will generally be limited to a specific theological discipline (Old Testament, New Testament, church history, systematic theology, history of religions, practical theology, and religion and literature) pursued in graduate studies.

One thing that may deter the freelance writer from trying the scholarly journals is that they pay little or nothing for the material they use. This is understandable since they are usually subsidized publications without advertising that have difficulty even covering their production and printing costs. In spite of this fact, if you have the qualifications and can handle the subjects, you may well want to try to write for this market. And, who knows, perhaps having your article appear in one of these journals will eventually lead to other writing and even book contracts for which there is good payment.

SUBJECTS AND APPROACHES

The how of writing scholarly theological articles is very flexible. Journal articles and books run the spectrum from historical studies of ancient Judea to word studies of New Testament Greek to the teachings of fourth-century church fathers to the trickster figure in West African religions to new techniques in pastoral counseling. The subjects available for research that can be turned into articles and books are as broad as the sixty-six books of the Bible (plus the Apocryphal books), the decisions of the ecumenical councils, the writings of the fathers, the saints, the theologians, the mystics, the Reformers and modern Christian interpreters of the faith. The chronological history of the past 5,000 years and the geography of the entire globe are open to investigation and the writing of new material by qualified people. The approaches that may be taken are as varied as the subjects: description, measurement, statistics, translation, interpretation, analysis, criticism, and appreciation, among them.

Since this is a precisely academic area of work, all theological writing must be accurate, factual, and logically developed. One must also look for the new insight, the effect of new linguistic or archeological discoveries, for example, on traditional understandings of texts, events, or doctrines. The discovery of the Dead Sea Scrolls, for example, revolutionized articles and books on biblical subjects. New information on the meaning of Hebrew, Aramaic, and Greek words used in scripture has the same revitalizing effect—and is the source for many articles and books. The audience for such material is highly educated and well acquainted with whatever theological discipline is being addressed, so the prospective writer must not recount knowledge known to all; he must analyze or criticize the generally accepted knowledge in a new and fresh way.

There are many opportunities to publish responsible, well-researched, clearly written scholarly theological material. Beginning with the most general, religious magazines reporting news and opinions such as *The Christian Century, Christianity and Crisis,* and *Christianity Today* come to mind. Beyond these magazines lie many journals devoted to individual theological disciplines, such as *Theology Today, The Expositor, The Biblical Archeologist,* and *Novum Testamentum.* A visit to a seminary library will acquaint the writer with the many journal possibilities. For longer works, publishing houses operated by various orders and interests in the Roman Catholic and Eastern Orthodox churches and by the Protestant denominations and religiously oriented universities are open to new book ideas on scholarly theological themes.

218   I have published in a number of theological journals and have written books for several of the more scholarly religious presses. I find that such writing can be religious, even pastoral. Such works help people make sense of their faith and give them the resources to grow in their understanding of God, the holy scriptures, and the implications of the faith in a difficult time. Finally, as in medical research, scholarly theological investigation ultimately serves the person in the pew who thirsts to know God and find solutions to personal and social problems.

WRITING FOR CHURCH LEADERS
by Phyllis Mather Rice

The author, of King of Prussia, Pennyslvania, is editor of Your Church magazine, an interdenominational journal for clergy and other professional church staff.

In order to write successfully for church leaders, you must have both background and experience in the work of the church. Many articles used in such magazines as the one I edit are written by the clergy or other career church workers. Many other articles are written by the laity. But in all cases the material comes from those who have ideas they want to share with fellow workers.

For example, an article written by a pastor about how to deal with conflict in the church was very effective and eagerly read because the writer had lived through such an experience and found ways to resolve conflict successfully without disturbing the ongoing program of the church. Another recent article that met with good response was written by a lay person who is an alcoholic. She wrote about her struggles with the disease and how with the help of Alcoholics Anonymous she overcame her difficulties and learned to live with herself. This was of interest to our readers because many churches sponsor AA groups and almost all of our readers at one time or another meet the problem of alcoholism in counseling sessions. These articles contained two elements that are essential in writing for church professionals: help and inspiration.

WHAT SUBJECTS ARE OF INTEREST?

The most important ingredient in writing aimed at church leaders is content. Such articles should deal with something of importance in the work these people are doing; there is a great stress on "how to" in this material. The information given should enable church leaders to do their ministry better and more effectively.

Have you had an experience connected with the ministry of the church that has made a profound impact on your life? If you shared this experience in writing, could the work of a church leader be enriched? For example, your Christian faith has grown through your participation in a home study group in your congregation. In an article for church leaders you would describe this experience, what happened in the group, how the study was organized, and what key factors made the project a success for you.

There are many subjects that interest church leaders. If they are in the pastorate, their major concerns are the church and its program, ministering to people, and overseeing church property. Some specific subjects would be church administration, time management, dealing with church personnel, administering a church office, managing a building, energy conservation, fund raising, counseling procedures, working with committees, dealing with conflict, visiting the sick, Christian education, evangelism, missions, teacher training, camping, youth programs, reaching different age groups, worship, preaching, music, the choir.

The physical church structure itself is important to church leaders. Building a new church, remodeling, insulating, maintenance, choosing an architect, stained glass windows, and interior furnishings are just a few ideas for articles that appeal to this group.

Another topic of great concern to church leaders is management of their own personal lives: personal devotions, dealing with ministerial burnout, family relationships, marriage, divorce, parenting, retirement, money management, friendships, physical fitness, hobbies, and free time. Writers should remember that church leaders are also human beings with all of the interests and needs of any adult group.

HOW TO WRITE

The most important thing to keep in mind when you are submitting an article for church leaders is to fit your material to the group that reads the publication. For example, an interdenominational publication is read by leaders with varied theological backgrounds. An author writing for this type of periodical would need to use language that people with differing theological backgrounds could understand. It would not be wise to write a charismatic article in the assumption that all readers are charismatics and submit the article to an interdenominational publication. If you are planning to submit an article to an evangelical publication, write from the point of view that most evangelicals accept and understand.

Most publications for church leaders do not use fiction or sermons. Some publications print sermon outlines, and many feature articles on preaching, but actual sermons are rare. Most publications want serious, nonfiction articles designed to aid religious leaders. They should be practical how-to articles or inspirational thought pieces.

Discover the style of a publication before writing an article for it. Find out the average length of the articles. You would insure rejection if you submitted a twenty-page article featuring six-syllable words to a publication that features short, easy-to-read articles.

The best way to write for church leaders is to be straightforward. The dissemination of information—experience, knowledge—should be the main goal; a little humor now and then is also helpful. The more concise, understandable, and interesting your information is, the more likely your piece will be published.

OPPORTUNITIES FOR PUBLICATION

There are many publications planned specifically for church leaders. Some are interdenominational; others are published by denominations or special interest groups—there is a great variety among them. In addition, church leaders are avid readers of the more general religious publications; therefore, many of these will use an occasional article aimed at this group. Don't pass these up as you look for an outlet for your writing. Any of the market guides will give you ideas for finding the right publication for your material.

Writing for church leaders can be very rewarding. When you write for these people you reach a vast audience through them. If you can help a leader to do his job better, to be more effective in spreading the truths of scripture, you are engaged in an ever-widening ministry that is endless in its effect.

WRITING FOR PEOPLE WITH SPECIAL NEEDS

by Patricia C. McKissack

The author lives in St. Louis and is Children's Book Developer for Concordia Publishing House. She is also guest lecturer for the Learning Institute, Palo Alto, California.

Until recently, only a few churches were equipped to handle the needs of members with special problems. But it's not uncommon today to see a church building with a ramp to accommodate people in wheelchairs. Church librarians are ordering books in Braille and large-print editions as fast as they become available; volunteers tape books on cassettes for those with sight impairment. In both urban and rural areas people skilled in sign language (manual communication) convey sermons to the deaf and hard of hearing. Special telephone hook-ups have made it possible for the bedridden, sick, and elderly to share in the fellowship of worship with their own congregations, and college graduates trained in special education are developing programs and curriculum for children and adults who are physically or mentally handicapped.

Although there is a greater awareness among the general public of the plight of those with special needs, many old myths and stereotypes still exist. Unfortunately, many of these false ideas were perpetuated by the Christian church; for example, Medieval clergy often taught that the mentally retarded or physically disabled were possessed by demons or suffering from God's punishment for some wrongdoing. These assumptions were not totally abandoned by the church until the mid-twentieth century when a more enlightened clergy and a more informed laity took the initiative in helping to change attitudes. In a complete turnabout, the modern church became a leader in the fight to get rid of the fear and guilt that surrounded the handicapped. Pastors, Christian educators, and others have been constantly involved in the struggle for human rights; because each individual has the right to serve God and celebrate with dignity the life he has given, and not to be excluded because of a handicap. But despite all the efforts that have been made, old ideas die hard.

Christian publishers have supported the work of the churches by providing the clergy and laity with products to use in their work with the handicapped, and they are always seeking good writers.

Writers often have a special sense of empathy which leads them to write for this field; they must be dedicated to helping the less fortunate. Also, writers often need to have special training or experience working with the handicapped before they can understand and meet the needs of this market.

Publishers are interested in writers who are accurate and honest in their representation of handicapped persons; they are not interested in sensationalism or emotionally biased materials intended to exploit the handicapped or present them as stereotypes. Publishers want writing that shows compassion without being trite or predictable; sensitivity without pity. Writing for this "highly specialized market" is really no different from any other form of writing. Publishers seek creative writers who know their subject matter and present the material in a fresh, appealing way.

Some publishers have an editor who is responsible for developing special products for this particular market. The editor or "project developer" is looking for new ideas; this editor is usually the person who follows the book through the development stages. Therefore, if you have an idea for a book or a project, and it has a large enough potential interest group to merit the expense of the publishing venture, an editor will be willing to review your proposal.

Christian publishers who produce materials in the "special needs" area usually divide them into two categories: professional and general.

The *professional products* include a wide variety of subjects and formats; e.g., bulletin board ideas, how-to books, craft and game books, Bible study books, vacation Bible school, curriculum, counseling manuals, etc. These products are used by pastors, Sunday school teachers, Church school teachers, librarians, and other professionals and paraprofessionals who work with disabled persons, their families, and friends.

Because of the technical nature of these products, publishers usually assign the writing to an experienced person with either academic credentials or years of on-the-job training in counseling or teaching in special education.

So, if you are qualified to write materials for professionals who work with the handicapped or special education curriculum for the classroom, query the publisher with your idea; send a sample of your writing and state your qualifications and experience. The topic you suggest may not be accepted immediately, but by using this approach you will make an impression on the editor and he or she may assign you something later on.

General products are those that are presented to the general public and include fiction, nonfiction, short stories, children's books, documentaries, plays, poetry, devotionals, and others. For these, an author is free to use any literary form that best suits his purposes. The writer doesn't necessarily have to be a trained professional in special education, counseling, etc. However, publishers expect a writer to be familiar with the subject and treat it with the same care and integrity he would give any other special topic. A publisher will consider a proposal submitted by an inexperienced writer who clearly shows that he is knowledgeable of the subject and can write with credibility.

General products can be divided into three subcategories: (1) materials *for* the handicapped, (2) materials *by* the handicapped, and (3) materials *about* the handicapped.

Books for the physically or mentally handicapped

A physical handicap may be present at birth, but often it is the result of an accident or disease that happens late in a person's life. A recently stricken person sees his handicap as totally disabling, and often the effects are more psychological than physical. The fear, anger, and frustration can be devastating.

Publishers regard this as a "special need," and produce products especially designed for those who are in this extremely difficult period in their lives. Often these products are written by handicapped persons, their family members, or friends.

Our attitudes about the physically and the mentally handicapped are important, for they can be harmful rather than helpful if we are not careful. I once heard a woman in a wheelchair snap at her oversolicitous nephew, "I'm in a wheelchair, but I'm not helpless!" Although great strides have been made in educating the general public in the distinction between handicapped (a disadvantage that makes achievement unusually difficult) and disabled (unable to pursue an occupation or lifestyle because of physical or mental impairment), people still use the two interchangeably.

This woman's protest is regrettably common among the millions of people who find themselves coping with the attitudes of those who will not accept their ability to lead "normal" lives. Living with society's prevailing currents is not easy, and publishers are always seeking materials that will help handicapped persons adjust to the benign ignorance of the public.

Products written for the mentally handicapped themselves are few. There are three types of retardation: dependent, trainable, and educable. Only the educable can be taught to read, but there are a number of products written for the parents and families of all three types. Young parents, for example, who learn that their newborn is mentally (or physically) handicapped are often filled with anger and guilt—yet some parents choose to adopt children who are less than perfect. Publishers are interested in products that will help these people, guide and encourage them in coping with the frustrations and the joys associated with parenting a child with a physical or mental handicap.

Materials written by the handicapped

Stories written by the handicapped can be inspirational to those who are trying to overcome a debilitating illness, a serious injury, or who are adjusting to permanent disability. The general public is usually interested if the writer is a well-known celebrity, and some people believe an article about the handicapped is more credible if it is written by a handicapped person. However, most handicapped writers find it difficult and unrewarding to write about their own personal experiences. Their writing is against this background but comes "out" of their experience, which they use as a springboard.

Handicapped writers should be encouraged to write because they can bring to the art a special sensitivity that can enrich the lives of their readers. If *you* are a handicapped writer, or know of one who has a story to tell, a poem to share, a project that works, a piece of criticism or a review that is worthy of publication, encourage that person to submit a query and a sample to a publisher. We could all be richer for it.

For example, a blind author writes about "seeing" the daffodils of spring and helps a sighted person experience daffodils in a new and wonderful way. A man who has never walked can make a significant contribution to those who are rendered helpless by fear, anger, and frustration. He knows about those subjects well. A mother who has no arms can speak to us about the value of touching in a nonphysical way, reaching out to our children with love and understanding.

Materials about the handicapped

Who hasn't been inspired by the wonderful stories of Helen Keller, the delightful Joni Erikson, or Roy Campanella? Books about people like these have helped the handicapped overcome "being different." (The term *different* has become synonymous with *wrong*—therein lies the problem.) Writers who have told the stories of the handicapped in fiction and nonfiction have built a better understanding and made an important contribution to the Christian church and society in general. More of these stories need to be told.

More Special Needs

A large number of people in this country can't read, or read below their ability. The terms used are *slow learners* and *learning disabilities.*

A slow learner may be mildly retarded, or he may just never have had the benefit of an adequate education. A learning disability might be caused by a physical problem such as poor eyesight, poor hearing or an undiagnosed hearing problem, or dyslexia. Some people have problems reading because they are just learning to read and write English as a second language.

The "Adult Reader" is a recently developed product for adults who are having reading problems. The subjects are adult but written on the second- or third-grade level. In no way do these books look like a children's book. But they are usually limited to 3,000 to 7,500 words and most publishers have strict guidelines and a vocabulary list. Only a few religious publishers are producing them now.

Hi-lo (high interest/low reading level) books are designed for teenagers who have the same problems—lack of education or a learning disability. The reading level of hi-los ranges from second to sixth grade. These books deal with subjects that would interest a teen and average 5,000 to 7,500 words with a restricted vocabulary. There is a great need for these products in the religious market, although only a few publishers have actually produced them.

If you think you would be interested in writing for a "special needs" audience, first you must identify that group and review what's already been written. Then approach a publisher with a query, state your qualifications, and make a general statement about why this book is needed. Include an outline and a sample of your writing.

There are as many needs as there are people in the world. If you don't feel adequate to write for the physically or mentally handicapped, or those with learning disabilities, you might want to consider writing for others who need help coping with their situations—the elderly, or those undergoing cult deprogramming, for example.

The better you can present evidence that there is a sizable market for what you are proposing, the better chance you have of finding a publisher, whether for professionals or for the general public.

If you want a guide for writing for people with special needs, read Matthew 25:31-46, the scene in which people from all nations are gathered in front of Christ. Those who are praised by him are those who have ministered to the unfortunate, the hungry, the poor, the prisoners. Writing for the handicapped or people with special needs is just such a ministry.

CHAPTER FIFTEEN

WRITING CHRISTIAN CURRICULUM

by Herb Montgomery

Herb Montgomery of Edina, Minnesota, a former editor with Winston Press, is a prolific Christian writer. He and his wife Mary have collaborated on several curriculum projects. They are the authors of two preschool programs: The Jesus Story *and* The Bible Story. *Their books include* Beyond Sorrow *and* The Splendor of the Psalms. *They have also written various reading programs.*

THERE'S AN IMAGINARY ladder stand-

ing beside my desk. I've climbed its steps many times. Unless you're already a curriculum writer, you probably don't know about the ladder. With a little help you too can see it, climb it, and test ideas on every step until you discover one just right for you.

The ladder is my way of visualizing a basic curriculum, or course of study, used in Sunday school and other religious education classes. The ladder's steps—beginning at the bottom with preschool children and ending at the top with adults—are the grade or age levels of the people for whom educational materials are to be developed. The ladder's side rails are the supporting theology, subject matter, and themes that will be incorporated in keeping with the age of the group. Although Baptists, Catholics, Lutherans, Methodists, and others have their own basic curriculums, each follows the step-by-step structure of the ladder.

CONSIDER THE FIELD

Maybe you've overlooked curriculum writing, thinking it was too complex or open only to a select few. I used to feel that way but now know that the door to this field is either ajar or wide open. It all depends on the publisher.

The creation of a basic curriculum is an enormous task because it deals with such a wide range of age levels. Preparing materials for toddlers is quite different from developing a program for the elementary grades or a course of study for high schoolers. Yet each level has to be conceived, outlined, researched, and written. The editorial work involved is rather like the assembling of a thousand-piece jigsaw puzzle. Everything interlocks horizontally and vertically. That is, the year-long sixth-grade program with its series of thematically related lessons must flow smoothly out of the fifth-grade and into the seventh-grade program.

Once the publisher's outlines are complete, who creates all the materials? Christian writers. Many are members of editorial staffs. Others freelance as professional writers the way my wife Mary and I do.

We began our collaborative writing career with stories and articles. Christian magazines turned out to be a ready market for much of what we did. When a growing family demanded more income, a portfolio of our published works helped me locate a job as an editor. That started me in the curriculum field. For nearly ten years I was involved in all phases of program research and development at Winston Press and ended up working as an administrative editor responsible for long-range planning. In 1973, I left management to return to the freelance life. So what I say about curriculum writing is based on personal experience from both sides of the editor's desk.

Despite their many differences, the Christian churches all have a common interest in education. That makes each denomination a potential user of materials that you might have a part in creating. Your contribution could be to a basic curriculum, which I've likened to a ladder with many steps. Or it could be to a curriculum that you might think of as part of a shorter ladder. On this one there is no grade-level progression. Instead the steps are made up of specialized curriculums that fewer people follow. For example, not all members of a denomination need a marriage preparation course, but some will. A church's basic curriculum may not call for a detailed study of world hunger or Luke's Gospel, but some people will be interested in these subjects and want to follow a course of study.

By now you may be thinking that to write for either a basic or a specialized curriculum it's necessary to be a Bible scholar with a Ph.D. Not true. Higher education certainly helps, but a degree is no guarantee that one can communicate effectively or has a corner on ideas. You may well have an idea whose time has come. Even high school dropouts with a flair for writing have contributed to published programs and the take-home papers that accompany them. Such contributions can be accepted because every publisher has staff members or consultants to insure that content is theologically and psychologically sound. What may be submitted by an individual writer is reviewed by a team made up of theologians and religious educators.

My experience has shown me that one basic ingredient plays a crucial part in writing curriculum: a personal belief in the importance of Christian education. For a long time that belief wasn't part of me. I grew up with an intense dislike for Sunday school and considered the memorization of catechism answers for Confirmation equal to having a tooth pulled. Other unfortunate experiences left me feeling that God was a grumpy, spying grandpa in the sky. Later in life I came to realize that my "right to religion" had been violated by people who had the best of intentions. I'd been turned off to what could have been an enriching journey in faith. My comeback left me believing in a religious education that nurtures children's sense of the sacred so that they might grow in love rather than shrivel in fear as I felt I had. While a teen, I vowed that if I ever had children they would be educated quite differently from the way I was. Later, when I did become a parent, the curriculum my children grew up on was called *Joy*, and I had a part in creating it.

FOLLOW A PLAN

Do you have a personal belief in the importance of religious education? If so, writing curriculum materials could play a role in your writing future. The following five steps will help you decide how seriously you might want to pursue the field:

1. *Assess your background.* Look for clues that suggest a more-than-average interest in religion and education. Are you active in your church? Have you taught a Sunday school or Confraternity of Christian Doctrine (CCD) religion class? Do you like people? Have you participated in prayer groups or other Christian organizations devoted to education? Are you familiar with, or a student of, the Bible? Do you have any formal training in teaching, psychology, writing, or theology? Can you organize and outline ideas?

Positive response to two or three of these questions are a hint that you should investigate further. If the interest is there, you can develop many of the skills necessary for curriculum writing.

2. *Familiarize yourself with the publishers and their materials.* Your public library may have files of catalogs from the religious press that you can look through. Or send for church school catalogs and curriculum brochures from those publishers most likely to serve the denomination you'd be interested in writing for. (You'll find the names and addresses in *Writer's Market.* When you write for catalogs, remember to include postage.) If you're a Christian without a church preference, you can locate a publisher compatible with your background. There are both progressive and conservative presses.

Enlist the help of the secretary or pastor in your local church. Either one may point the way to curriculum catalogs on file, the resource center (which could be a gold mine filled with sample materials from various publishers), the library, or a teacher most likely to have curriculum items to review.

What you're looking for is general information to enable you to think and talk intelligently about curriculum. You'll become aware that every program has many possible parts (student and teacher materials, workbooks, handouts, records, filmstrips). A vacation Bible school program may even include puppets, balloons, nametags, and announcement posters.

Every publisher's approach to basic curriculum includes a grade level breakdown, at least from kindergarten through high school (K-12). Be alert to the ways in which publishers approach specialized curriculums. (Remember the shorter ladder whose steps are made up of special-interest courses focusing on one topic, such as marriage preparation, Lent, or grief. Some publishers provide single-book mini-courses. Others develop workbooks with study guides, filmstrip kits, and elaborate cassette tape programs.)

Extend your research by going into churches to see where classes are held. Some teachers have large classrooms as well equipped as those in public schools whereas others meet in a corner of the basement and pull curtains to form bare cubicles. When compiling or editing guides, writers must have a knowledge of the teaching environment and provide alternative activities so lesson plans can be carried out anywhere.

3. *Narrow your field of interest.* None of us can do everything with equal skill, but all of us can do something well when we give it our full attention. A consideration of your background plus a look at published materials and the place in which they are likely to be used will help you determine the audience you'd like to write for.

When I first evaluated the field, I found myself drawn to preschool programs. I had written some read-aloud stories and read extensively about child psychology. My wife was a trained teacher, and our growing family gave us a mutual interest in early childhood education. All the clues in my life pointed the way. Since then I have written for people of every age, but my most rewarding work has been for young children.

Have you wasted your time if you decide that curriculum writing doesn't interest you? Not at all. You can apply this same process to another kind of writing. Flexibility is an author's greatest ally. Even those who've had considerable success in one area never know when they may have to switch fields because of a change in editorial needs.

4. *Educate yourself for a specialty.* Writers should be knowledgeable about many subjects, but those who make the effort to specialize often have the edge when it comes to making a sale. These two approaches can be compared to a view through a funnel. The generalist looks through from the small end and sees a big picture. The specialist looks through the large end and has a more focused view. Develop a specialty and you'll have the confidence to write boldly and optimistically even when the odds seem to be against you.

Suppose for a moment that you have narrowed your field of interest to teens. Of course you'll want to know all you can about this age group, but what will the content of your writing be? Interpersonal relationships? Sexuality? Spirituality?

Your answer should come from your personal interests. Let's say you decide on "teens and prayer." Begin by focusing your self-education. Take courses in prayer, read books, investigate meditation, keep a journal, begin a clipping and article file on the subject. Find out when and why teens pray. Discover the forms their prayers take. Do whatever you can to increase your personal knowledge of both teens and prayer. All this ingathering will be rewarded when you begin writing. Then you'll have quotations, anecdotes, and the words of experts within reach.

5. *Seek an editorial connection.* Curriculum writing is a tightly controlled, highly organized process. The stories and articles you might sell to a denominational magazine would probably be rejected by the curriculum department of the same publisher. Why? Because your writings don't match the openings in the curriculum jigsaw puzzle. The editors may need profiles on Christian women at a time when you're writing about Christian men. They may be in need of material on missionaries for ten different levels when you're concentrating on family and forgiveness. You won't know these things without the guidance that only the editorial staff can supply.

The best way to seek an editorial connection is by letter. Phone calls and drop-in visits disrupt editorial routine. However, if you're determined to meet face-to-face, at least set up an appointment.

Letters to editors are your sales pitch and should be carefully written. Write to a specific editor whose name appears in the curriculum materials. I prefer the project or coordinating editor because this person leads a team and is apt to be most familiar with the range of needs.

Your letter should sell the editor on what you can do to help her or him do a better job. Don't write a "what-have-you-got-I-could-do?" letter. Always be specific about what you can do and try to limit yourself to one page, two at most. Cover points such as:

1. Sales you've made, especially those of a religious or educational nature.
2. Your special area of interest or concern.
3. Pertinent training or experience.

Here is a sample that might be written by a woman who is familiar with teens and has done some innovative teaching. Notice how the writer capitalizes on her experience and talent. Of course your letter will focus on your skills.

Dear Mr. Smith:

As a writer I have a special interest in curriculum development. Although I haven't yet contributed material to a formal course of study, I have been writing for the Christian press for some time. Recently I've contributed articles and stories to [name the papers or magazines].

Having a teenage son provides me with everyday information about this age group. I'm very concerned about young people and the moral and ethical problems they face in society today. Because of this concern, I've led prayer groups for troubled teens for the past three years. Our pastor considers my work especially successful, and teachers from other churches come to us to learn more about the methods I've developed.

What I call "Prayer Starters" help young people open up to God in an unusual way. I believe these icebreakers and other strategies I've refined would be useful to a much wider audience.

Since prayer is always a big part of our curriculum, I would like the opportunity to contribute some of my ideas to a future program. Would you be interested in knowing more about my approach?

Enclosed are sample "Prayer Starters" and a stamped, self-addressed return envelope. Thank you for your consideration.

Sincerely,
Sally Writer

If the writer gets a negative response to this first letter, what should she do? Follow it *immediately* with a second letter in which she reaffirms her interest and offers a related but different idea or service.

Dear Mr. Smith:

Thank you for your prompt return of my sample "Prayer Starters." I was pleased to hear from you, but was disappointed that my material didn't meet any current needs.

I know your curriculum is planned far in advance, so I would appreciate it if you would keep my name on file for future needs. I'm a dependable writer who meets deadlines and is willing to work on speculation. There are three specific things I believe I could do for any project you—or a co-worker—might be planning that involves teens and prayer:

1. I can write open-ended prayers for teens that encourage participation.
2. I can write background material on prayer for teachers. Since I am a volunteer teacher, I know the problems well. Practical teacher helps are my specialty.
3. I can arrange with our pastor for field-testing of lesson plans and return them quickly with constructive criticism.

Again, thank you for your response. I'm still teaching and hope to assist in curriculum development in the future. Please keep my name on file as a possible contributor. I'd appreciate having this letter passed along to any other editor who might need material on teens and prayer.

Sincerely,
Sally Writer

Short, factual letters such as these are like seeds cast out; some wither and die while others produce abundantly. Good editors are always on the alert for potential contributors, but they are wary about committing themselves. They know that many beginners exaggerate their skills and others get discouraged by criticism and the need to rewrite. Writers who keep knocking on the door with helpful ideas and friendly letters eventually make worthwhile editorial contacts. The response you get, however, may not be what you asked for. Instead of contributing to a curriculum, you might be asked to submit ideas to a magazine. If so, follow through. Every additional sale will add to your professional status.

While I was an editor, one unpublished writer sent me at least a dozen letters during a period of two years. An idea finally clicked just as we were beginning plans for a new program. I offered her work on speculation. She completed the assignment on time and made her first periodical sale. Other work followed and was published in curriculum form. As a result of her persistence, this woman launched a writing career that has since earned her many checks.

KNOW THE BUSINESS

Producing basic and specialized curriculums for religious education is big business. There are two distinct publishing groups: the church-related houses and the independent publishers. Church-related firms include such publishers as Augsburg (American Lutheran Church), Beacon Hill Press (Church of the Nazarene), and Sunday School Board of the Southern Baptist Convention (Southern Baptist Church). These are houses whose main concern is the education of members of their individual denominations. Most of the large denominations have an official, church-related press that produces an all-encompassing Sunday school curriculum. The Roman Catholics are an exception. Although many Catholic religious orders do considerable publishing, there is no central publisher comparable to the Protestant church-related houses.

Publishers who produce religious education curriculums but are independent of church affiliation include such companies as David C. Cook, Gospel Light, and Winston Press. They market their materials across denominational lines; however, some independents produce special programs for specific denominations. For example, aside from its Christian curriculum, Winston Press offers exclusive denominational materials for Roman Catholic, Episcopal, and Lutheran audiences.

Many publishers prepare programs for Catholic parochial schools and offer variations for use in CCD or Sunday school-type classes.

Publishers generally operate on a three-to-five-year plan but may be making projections for as long as ten years. If a publisher is developing curriculum, it's probably the backbone of the company. Even though curriculum plans aren't stamped Top Secret, they are closely kept because there is stiff competition in the marketplace. Church-related presses have loyal users from their denominations, but independent publishers compete for a share of the church dollar. They wage intense direct-mail campaigns, conduct teacher workshops, and display their products at various conventions.

In producing a basic curriculum, different publishers work from different outlines, but even those who use the same outlines produce differing materials. Basic curriculum outlines are available to publishers from various sources, including the National Council of Churches. It has a curriculum committee that prepares outlines for sale. Another series, the Aldersgate Graded Curriculum, is developed jointly by nine small-to-medium denominations. Some publishers, however, create their own outlines. Thus it's evident why editor contact is crucial for a writer hoping to contribute to a basic curriculum.

Outlines are commonly referred to as having "spiral" development. This means that a theme such as "forgiveness" (think of it as the side rail on the ladder) will be studied during a certain day of the year by everyone from toddlers to adults. The approach to the theme will, of course, differ from level to level. Staff writers take on a portion of the writing, but it's a big job that calls for many ideas. This is when editors appreciate having reliable freelancers available.

WATCH FOR NEW IDEAS

Many local churches have teachers and pastors who don't like the prepackaged programs available to them. So what do they do? They develop their own courses of study. The programs these people create may be a hodgepodge of notes, lesson plans, and work sheets. Such a collection offers both the originator and the freelance writer an opportunity to collaborate. The program has probably been tested and revised until it works well, but it still needs a writer's touch to pull all the elements together and get a manuscript ready for submission to an editor.

Independent presses give such programs careful consideration. And the giant, church-related presses are inclined to consider them as well because they can't afford to overlook what's going on at the grass roots level. No publisher—secular or religious—will succeed for long if it ignores what's happening in the total society.

A look back at the clamorous '60s and early '70s reminds us that political and social events shape curriculums. Those programs lacking racially integrated illustrations and showing Mom as always wearing an apron were severely criticized. So too were programs that didn't tackle the moral issue of war. Vatican II polarized Roman Catholics into liberal and conservative camps that required some parishes to offer two courses of study for the same age group! Some publishers responded quickly with specialized programs that hadn't been part of their long-range plans. They recognized the influence of Vietnam, assassination, drugs, and "Jesus freaks" and tried to create programs that related religious teachings to contemporary concerns. Liberalism left its mark and in time such things as psychedelic colors and articles about TM appeared even in conservative publications.

Aware writers know that events such as Watergate and groups such as the Moral Majority influence thought and bring about change in emphasis and direction. This is true in our national life and it's true in religious curriculums as well.

PROCEED WITH A PROJECT

Let's say that you find a pastor, teacher, or church using an original curriculum that reflects new thinking. As a writer, how do you proceed?

The first step is to discuss the program in detail with the originators to discover its unique qualities. How, why, and in what way is it superior to, or different from, existing curriculum materials? Does it recognize a new trend? Does it fill a need as yet unseen by the major denominations and their curriculum developers? Will the materials have more than a regional application?

If the program appears to be worthwhile, it's up to you, the writer, to take step two and suggest that you collaborate in bringing the program to the attention of a publisher. Getting a program in print is usually not a get-rich venture, so be aware that you might have to write off your contribution as missionary effort. On the other hand, your work may pay off extremely well. Find out early on what the originators expect in the way of return. Many people have outrageously unrealistic ideas about the financial rewards of published material. If the originators appear to have mercenary motives, move on and look for another innovative program.

A program is not sent in its entirety. A promising idea requires the writing of a project proposal, preparation of one to three sample lesson plans (including student and teacher materials), and a sample of any other components. To the originator, all of this may seem like "minor detail." It's not; it's time-consuming, so proceed cautiously.

A project proposal is really a query in disguise, but it is more detailed and sounds more official. Either a letter or memo form may be used, and your proposal should include the following:

1. Brief background on the originators and you.
2. The program's title and a listing of all components.
3. Audience for whom it is intended.
4. Number of sessions/lessons the originator believes are required to complete the program.
5. Listing in outline or chart form of the subject matter and/or theme of each lesson.
6. A tightly written description of the program that includes the goals and summarizes the content.
7. Samples of the lessons and accompanying guide material.

Editors don't receive many well-prepared project proposals. Your proposal will get attention if it's presented clearly enough so that strangers to your program can work their way through it. Even though the idea may be rejected, a proposal can begin your editor contact which you follow up on.

What about payment? Whenever I collaborate, I talk about money up front, making it clear that the presentation may come to nothing and our time investment will never be repaid. With this understood, the persons I'm collaborating with can decide whether to proceed.

Publishers buy programs on either a royalty or an outright purchase basis. I always prefer royalty contracts because they involve me in taking a risk along with the publisher. I tend to put forth a little more effort in writing and rewriting when I know that by creating a better product I can hope for more sales and more money.

On an outright basis, a simple, specialized curriculum consisting of no more than a workbook or a filmstrip kit with a limited audience may sell for no more than $500. On the other hand, a really well-developed program with many components might return more than $100,000 in royalties. Writing will always be a risky adventure!

In a collaborative effort, percentages range from an even split to 40 percent to the writer and 60 percent to the originator on a small project. This is true of outright payment, advance payment against royalties, and royalties themselves. On a large curriculum with many developers and several levels you'll have to accept less. Anything below 25 percent for the writer brings you close to an agent's fee (10 to 15 percent). As a writer you will do more to earn your money than an agent would, so be cautious about accepting a very low percentage.

DISCOVER FRINGE BENEFITS

As curriculum writers we can't always pin neat labels on what we do. Besides basic and specialized curriculums, there are "supplementary" or "enrichment" materials. I think of them as fringe benefits, and a beginning curriculum writer is just as likely to discover one as is the experienced writer. My own recent collaboration on a single book illustrates this.

Father Ron DelBene, an Episcopal priest, is a well-known spiritual director who teaches a personal form of prayer in workshops across the country. As a teacher and speaker, he had reams of material but had never written a book on the subject and wasn't sure when he might do so. With my help, he prepared an outline and wrote a first draft. I worked out a project proposal, helped with the rewriting, did the final typing and manuscript submission, and obtained all the necessary letters of permission to reprint copyrighted material quoted in the book. This involved correspondence with both U.S. and British publishers. Winston Press took the book on a royalty contract and released *The Breath of Life: A Simple Way to Pray* in 1981. Father DelBene now uses it in his teaching.

Labels can be limiting. By expanding our thinking of curriculum as "any course of study," we're ready to take on all promising writing jobs. A regular review of every religious publisher's offerings helps us maintain a broad view of the field.

What happens after you get an assignment or a go-ahead on a project proposal? How you follow through will determine your success. Rule one is: meet your deadline. Then follow all editorial suggestions. If you're assigned to write 750 to 1,000 words, aim for the middle ground and don't submit a 2,000-word piece. When you're asked to take all scripture from the RSV, don't quote the KJV. If you're to avoid talking down to children, leave off the moralizing at the end. Disregarding directions always makes an editor's work more difficult. Once you've sold an editor on what you can do, follow through and collect your check. More work is sure to follow.

Dry spells and rejections happen to all of us. Whenever they hit you, remember those two curriculum ladders—basic and specialized. One or the other is sure to help you climb to success as a Christian writer.

CHAPTER SIXTEEN

WRITING IN
OTHER SPECIAL
FORMATS

WRITING A COLUMN
by Edith Flowers Kilgo

The author resides in Forest Park, Georgia, and has written two books and many articles for religious magazines. She writes the column "What Every Woman Should Know" for Today's Christian Woman.

Back in the days before I had a column in either of the two magazines which now carry my by-line regularly, it seemed to me that writing a column must be one of the easiest tasks a writer could take on. After all, what could be more pleasant than choosing any subject you like to write about and then writing with the assurance that your recompense would be a regular paycheck. It sounds simple, doesn't it?

Actually, it isn't simple at all.

Being a columnist does offer a writer certain advantages. It means your manuscript bypasses the slush pile. It means seeing your name in print on a regular basis. It even means getting a paycheck at decent intervals, thus eliminating one of the insecurities involved in freelancing. In addition to these niceties, your credit line for the column can also carry a free plug for any books you've authored. Even better, if you haven't yet written a book, a collection of columns could be just the toe in the door you've needed for your approach to a book publisher. Columns are not as common in religious periodicals as in secular ones. However, a number of religious magazines do have them, and others might consider a column if you have a good idea for one. Most columns are designed to reach readers with a specific interest (such as teachers, parents, or musicians) or specific age groups (such as children, youth, or senior citizens).

How then does an aspiring writer become a columnist and acquire some of these advantages?

Basically, it amounts to discovering a way to build credits upon which a column idea might logically and ultimately develop. While it is not impossible to become a columnist without having first established yourself in other journalistic endeavors, it is unlikely. Do your own survey of columns in the magazines you read regularly and you'll see that most of the writers have credentials that they established prior to becoming a columnist. You need not necessarily be the author of books—although it can be a plus factor if you are—but you should have had at least enough experience with magazine writing to understand how things are done. When an editor is persuaded to make a commitment toward publishing your column on a continuing basis, she has to feel that she will be working with a writer who can meet deadlines and who can revise when necessary and who has the personality to become an asset and not a migraine headache.

Magazine columns usually develop as either the idea of the editorial staff or the idea of some freelancer who follows the selling rule of "Find a need and fill it." If an editor originates the column idea she's likely to turn first to her stable of dependable writers who have already shown her they can work in a professional manner. Consequently, if you've already established a good working relationship with a magazine editor she may call on you for a column, particularly if you have developed a specialization in a certain field.

USE YOUR INGENUITY

However, if you yearn for a column, it's more likely to become a reality if, instead of waiting for it to come to you, your ingenuity devises a column idea that's too good to refuse. To help you ascertain what an editor needs *before* she finds out she needs it and subsequently assigns the column to somebody else, try imagining yourself in her position. Each issue of the magazine requires a certain number of pages to be filled and the features she chooses must appeal to most of the readers. She has to stay within a specific range of subjects, depending on the preference of the majority of her readers. Therefore, it is to the advantage of the would-be columnist to determine exactly what characteristics a typical reader of the magazine might have. Try making an intensive study of the magazine you have targeted for a column. Make a composite—based on the features, current columns, editorials, and even the ads—of the kind of person you visualize as the average subscriber. You'll need to know such things as age, income, sex, education, and religious viewpoint. You might even write the magazine and ask if they have made a study of their readership that would give you this information. Then, ask yourself: What interest, within the framework of topics normally covered by this magazine, would this typical reader have on a continuing basis? Remember, for a column to maintain reader interest, it has to appeal to a large portion of the readership on an issue-after-issue basis for perhaps a number of years.

However, before you mail your column proposal, give some thought to what you'll be getting into if your idea is accepted. First, writing a column does *not* always mean you can choose your own subject. Not only are you limited by the confines of the magazine's particular style and your own area of expertise, you must also conform to the editor's concept for the overall context. Sometimes an editor might ask all her columnists to follow a particular theme that is planned for an entire issue. Christmas topics are an example of this. At other times, you may have a perfectly wonderful idea that simply won't work because your editor has already contracted to use a book excerpt on a similar subject or another columnist did his column along related lines.

A number of factors go into the editor's decision to add a column, but undoubtedly one factor may be that editor's desire to know that a certain portion of the magazine is taken care of without necessitating a last-minute flurry to fill that spot. Consequently, a columnist has an obligation to her editor to see that the column is in on time and that revisions are handled in a professional manner.

Yet, writing a regular column is much more than just a matter of doing a professional job and cashing a regular paycheck. It's also an outlet for your Christian service. You are influencing the lives of your readers with each issue, in much the same way as the pastor of a church does with his sermons each week or a Sunday school teacher with the weekly lesson. After a while, too, readers begin to realize you are there on a regular basis, and they come to feel that they know you. As a result, writing a column may mean you'll become involved in answering a great deal of mail. This takes up hours and hours of your time—and the magazine doesn't pay you for this because it isn't required of you. So, before you agree to write a column you might want to consider how you feel about dealing with readers' letters. If you are writing a column with a religious message and especially one for a religious publication, you must be ready to answer the questions and back up the statements you have made in your column with good sound religious teaching and reasoning.

Writing a column can be one of the most satisfying writing tasks you'll ever undertake. It's rewarding, challenging, fascinating—and hard work. It *isn't* quite as simple as I thought it to be before I experienced it—but I love it anyway, and I think you will, too.

WRITING NEWS OF RELIGION

by Gary Warner

Gary Warner, of Overland, Kansas, is author-teacher, executive secretary of the Evangelical Press Association and director, EP News Service.

There's a problem with news writing among religious writers: it's had, paradoxically, a bad press.

To most fledgling writers, news writing has all the appeal of leftover hash. Why should one write seemingly mundane news copy when The Great American Novel waits to be unleashed from the typewriter and the resultant treasure chest of royalties and movie rights is there for the taking?

Let me assure you, whether you are a beginner or a starving-to-semisuccessful writer, there's a far more realistic opportunity in news writing.

As executive secretary of the Evangelical Press Association, I've seen a perceptible increase in two primary areas of publishing over the past several years—specialty magazines and community religious newspapers. Christian newspapers are springing up all over the country. And these publications are anxious for contributions from writers willing to write hard news and news features.

Writing news about religion is not that different from writing news on any other subject—in this case, the subjects just happen to be religious. The people involved in the news are professionals in the religious field, or the event is sponsored or taking place in a church or religious community, or what has happened or is about to happen will affect the religious life of many people. In religious news, as in all news, the important thing is the significance of the event in relation to people. Is it unusual? Is it happening to important people? Does it change the lives of others? Will it interest the reader? Is is exciting? A religious event will not be of interest even to religious readers unless the answer is yes.

You should consider writing news because there is more and more opportunity to have your work published both in the secular and the religious arenas and because, like those cold peas that we rolled around on our plates when we were kids, "it's good for you."

First, the "it's good for you" aspect. If I had my d'ruthers, I would take every Christian journalism student and all others bitten by the writing bug and sentence them to a mandatory one-year stretch on a weekly or daily newspaper.

There is no better discipline than that of writing straight news. Of writing concise, lean copy. Of making every word count. Of getting the five W's and the H into the first several graphs. Of writing against an inflexible deadline and learning you can write solid copy when you don't think you can. (Just try telling your editor that he'll have to leave a hole on page one because you don't feel "inspired"!)

News writing is the prerequisite to every other kind of writing. Many of our greatest writers began their pilgrimage on a newspaper. If rung one on the ladder was good enough for Hemingway, it's good enough for you and me.

Another reason for writing news is that you will get published. In fact, you'll get published in the secular world far more quickly than if you're engaged in any other form of religious writing.

You can walk out your front door, take a long stick and almost touch a half dozen sources that will be happy to have you write for them: your church, your club or special organization, your school, your favorite charity, your company newsletter, your local "shopper," or your weekly or daily newspaper.

Want to see your by-line in print? Want to make a solid and needed writing contribution? Want to see your writing career blossom? Want to learn how to gather information and do research and sort fact from fancy and put together a definitive story, the kind of research/writing that will aid you in anything else you attempt to write? Want to let a little light into that seemingly darkened and stagnated writing career? Try writing news.

The writer who is first capable of gathering accurate and detailed information and then can set it out in an interesting manner is a writer who will be in demand. However, don't expect to make a financial killing. But then, folks, let's be serious about this religious writing avocation—if you're in it for the money you'd better start hawking Amway.

SOME INITIAL STEPS

Here's how to get started in news writing. Pick your local news writing opportunity, such as a community religious newspaper or the church page in your local paper, or visit the editor. Tell him or her about your interest. See what assistance he needs; take an assignment. Give the editor the copy he wants in the way he wants it by the time he wants it. Remember—what *he* wants, not *your* attempt to witness in disguise. If you have the gift of news writing and the Lord has a further place for you in this sector of the writing world, further opportunities will materialize. I know several beginning writers who started as "stringers" or by producing periodic pieces for a local paper and, because they had the talent, soon were writing weekly columns under their by-line and photo.

There are many opportunities for the writers of religious news to be published on a national scale. Most denominational magazines, for example, have news columns. They subscirbe to news services, but these often do not serve them directly. If you can furnish news that has a special interest to a magazine (news of people and events of its own denomination, for example) the columns are open to your material.

How do you know if you can write news? Well, everyone *can* do it. And every aspiring writer *should* learn to do it. So the better question is, how do I know if writing news is my particular writing gift?

Here are a few clues: 1) Do you have a "nose for news"? That is, can you smell out and develop a story? 2) Do you have an incessant curiosity? Are you always asking "why?" Do you carry on interviews in your conversation? If so, you have a reporter's instincts. 3) Do you enjoy researching, digging, probing, unearthing, and developing a story? 4) Do you like to be informed and to inform others? 5) Do you enjoy people, enjoy interviewing? 6) Do you like to see what you write in print *now*, not six months or a year from now?

If so, for these and other reasons, news writing is for you.

Kipling wrote:

> I keep six honest serving-men
> (They taught me all I knew);
> Their names are What and Why and When
> And How and Where and Who.

Serve these servingmen and they'll serve you.

INSPIRATIONAL GREETING CARDS

by John McCollister

John McCollister is consultant to the president of Embry-Riddle Aeronautical University in Bunnell, Florida, author of several books and articles and a prolific writer of greeting cards.

In days past the art of condensing eternal truths into pithy expressions was reserved for the seer who sat at the village gate keeping his audiences spellbound with his wisdom. Today, many of these same kinds of thoughts enlighten, comfort, and inspire people through a more contemporary form—greeting cards.

People send greeting cards for many reasons, chiefly because the verses express emotions and sentiments in beautiful ways. And, of course, in the realm of religion, these words keep our spirits tuned to an even higher dimension. Here is where you fit in.

If you can put your thoughts into verse (rhyming or free) in a way that relates Christian truths to modern times, you can provide greatly appreciated insights for important moments in people's lives.

The tradition of sending greeting cards began in London when a printer introduced this form of yuletide cheer in 1843. The idea caught on. Since that time, a large number of publishing companies have solicited writers who can create religiously oriented verses for practically every occasion. In addition to Christmas, cards are wanted for Easter, Thanksgiving, weddings, anniversaries, baptisms, confirmations, funerals, Mother's Day, Father's Day, birthdays, get-well, and many more.

Visit your neighborhood card shop and study the cards on display. That's the best way to discover for yourself what publishers are looking for. (Notice that many of these cards have biblical themes and quotations for that special occasion.) Make a list of companies that publish inspirational cards. You'll want this information when you're ready to submit your ideas.

FOUR BASIC RULES

Successful authors follow four basic rules when submitting their verses for publication:

1. *Be simple.* Keep your thoughts big but your words small. Greeting

cards are designed to touch the heart, not challenge the intellect.

2. *Be positive.* You will never find religiously oriented verses shouting: "Thou shalt not!" Instead, the positive thrust—the Gospel, if you will—rings forth loud and clear.

3. *Be personal.* It's a one-to-one relationship. Write your verses as though you were jotting a note to a close friend. Although you're writing for a large audience, always imply the personal relationship.

4. *Be imaginative.* There may be, as Ecclesiastes claims, "no new thing under the sun," but this does not prohibit you from using your skills to express an age-old truth in a unique package.

One of the verses recently sold to Gibson was a Christmas message centered upon the Star of Bethlehem. It was simple, positive, personal, and, I think, showed a bit of imagination. It offered an invitation:

> Let us follow the Christmas Star . . .
> forever . . .
> together. . . .

You're probably thinking to yourself: "That's easy. I can write something like that."

Perhaps you can, indeed. Yet *thinking* about it is not enough. You must get the messages on paper and send them to a publisher. It's a good idea to check the market before submitting your ideas, however. You'd look pretty foolish if you sent inspirational material to a company that handles only novelty cards. You've already done some market research, browsing in the card shop. You might also want to write to editors and ask if they need inspirational material for any particular occasions, or if they're overstocked with certain kinds of cards. They'll also tell you if they even accept outside material; some companies have in-house writers and don't use freelancers.

When you have several verse ideas that you feel have merit and want to submit them for publication, follow the advice of the pros. Send your ideas in groups of ten to fifteen along with a self-addressed, stamped envelope. Type each verse on a 4x6-inch file card. On the back of each card put your name and address along with a code number. The number helps with your record keeping. For instance, if you're submitting ten verses to the American Greeting Card Company for the Christmas season, you could label them: C-AM-1, 2, 3, etc.

Categorize your ideas by season or occasion in a file box. Be sure to indicate on each card to whom and when you sent your idea. Remember, too, that card companies work far ahead in schedule. "We work eighteen months ahead," counsels Bernice Gourse, editor of the Paramount Line Card Company. "Therefore," she says, "submit Christmas ideas in May and Easter verses in October."

One warning: *Never, never* submit a verse idea to more than one publisher at a time. This mistake will catch up with you sooner or later, when two companies both want the same card. Once a greeting card company discovers you did this—just one time—the word quickly spreads around the industry, and your chances of ever selling another verse are mighty slim.

What sort of money can you expect? Ask any seasoned writer and he'll tell you—the religious market, in general, will not guarantee you financial security. Nonetheless, those who create verses of inspiration and comfort for greeting cards can earn top dollar. Authors for major card companies average $25 for as little as a twelve-word verse. That's more than $2 a word!

The book of Proverbs says it well: "A word fitly spoken is like apples of gold in a setting of silver." May your verses bear fruit, and may your sales bring enough gold and silver to make it all worthwhile.

GAMES AND PUZZLES
by Carol Schmelzel

Carol Schmelzel, of Lakewood, Colorado, is a home economics consultant/writer, specialist in educational materials development, Sunday school teacher, and author of several religious articles and books plus religious games and activities.

If you like to play games such as Scrabble, Monopoly, or Old Maid, and can't resist grabbing a pencil and working every puzzle you run across, you are probably a natural game and puzzle designer. But I can't say for sure. Because, to tell you the truth, although I've published numerous games and puzzles, I am not and never have been what you'd call a game or puzzle buff. I played card games as a child, participated in spell downs, but I was not especially intrigued by puzzles.

How did I get into the game and puzzle business? Quite by accident. I was given an assignment in a teacher-training class: design an educational game related to your field. Mine happens to be home economics. To my amazement this assignment was neither a drag nor a chore. It was challenging, exciting, and rewarding. I have since published many, many games and puzzles both for home economics education and religious education. I like designing games and puzzles more than I ever liked playing or working them! The moral of this little story is that even if you are not fond of playing games or working puzzles, you just might thoroughly enjoy and be good at designing them for publication.

OPPORTUNITIES FOR PUBLICATION

Games and puzzles are often found in church school curriculum materials and in publications for church school teachers and leaders.

Entire books on games with religious themes for use as a resource in religious education or recreation have been published by book publishers as well as entire books of puzzles on religious topics for children and adults.

Game and puzzle activities may be used in magazines for children, teenagers, and young adults that are produced by various religious groups. You may also be able to market games and puzzles to religious family magazines that feature a special page for children or family fun activities.

Another marketing possibility is to design a commercial game on a religious theme to be produced and sold to families or church schools. Some religious book publishers produce board games, card games, and other games of this type. Look for them in church supply stores or church supply catalogs.

TIPS ON CREATING AND PREPARING GAMES

1. To get started, clip, save, and study games of all kinds that you find in newspapers, magazines, anywhere—religious and secular. Set up a game file in standard file folders categorized as to format: board games, bingo-type games, word games, action games, card games, relays, memory games, and others. This will make you aware of many varieties of games, and you will have a ready reference when you start developing your own game.

2. Start another file system on index cards called "My Game Ideas." Headings might be Title Ideas, Game Topics, and Game Components. Jot down game ideas as they pop into your head (and they will!) or you may forget them.

3. Here is a checklist of important elements you should consider in developing and organizing your game:

- *Title.* A catchy title is important. "Bible Safari" is more interesting than "Animals of the Bible."

- *Format.* Plan the total game in such a manner that it can be easily produced by a manufacturer or easily assembled by the user.

- *Age Level.* Make a study of games on the market concerning their difficulty for the age level for which they are suggested. Be sure that what you are planning fits the age you are aiming at. Be sure that materials used are not dangerous for the young child if that is your market. Try your game out on a person of the age you have in mind.

- *Subject Matter and Teaching Objectives.* Focus on a specific topic or deal with only one or two ideas to be conveyed by the game such as "unselfishness" and "willingness to share."

- *Time Required to Play.* Keep the age and attention span of the players in mind. Also keep the game short if it is to be used as supplementary material in a Sunday school lesson.

- *List of Materials Needed.* Always include this at the beginning; also give directions on how to construct or put together the materials. Keep these directions simple and direct.

- *Step-by-Step Playing Directions.* State the object of the game, the rules, and the scoring. Keep the rules and the scoring method simple.

- *Answer Key.* For some games, such as guessing the names of Bible animals or characters, you may want to provide an answer key in a form that the teacher or leader can have without giving the answers ahead of time to the players.

4. In some games, the topic is merely suggested for the teacher to develop. In others the writer supplies the game questions or subject matter text.

5. A mixture of luck and knowledge required in a game makes it more interesting and works well for students of varying abilities, because winning depends partly on knowledge and partly on luck. Make the knowledge-luck ratio fair and reasonable.

6. Experiment with different methods of play, rules, or equipment to improve the game.

7. Test the finished game with "live," objective players. Observe their reactions. Make adjustments as necessary. *Testing is important!*

8. Evaluate the finished game. Do the teaching objectives come through? Might the game be used incorrectly and give wrong emphasis unintentionally?

TIPS ON CREATING AND PREPARING PUZZLES

1. Set up a puzzle file as suggested in the preceding section. There are many puzzle formats: crosswords, word-search puzzles, scrambles, certain types of quizzes, mirror messages, picture puzzles, mazes, code puzzles, and variations of these. Your puzzle file will be important to you in learning how to number crosswords, how to write puzzle clues, construct diagrams, and other "puzzling" problems.

2. Start another file system of "My Puzzle Ideas" on index cards. Headings might be Title Ideas, Puzzle Topics, Word Lists—especially for crosswords and word-search puzzles. Example: words related to faith.

3. Here is a checklist of important elements you should consider in organizing and developing a puzzle.

- *Title*

- *Format*

- *Age level.*

- *Subject matter and teaching objectives.* Focus on a *specific* theme or topic.

- *Directions for working the puzzle.*

- *Type of clues* (if clues are part of your puzzle).

- *Graphics.* Puzzles often are made more appealing with a sketch or some type of graphics related to the subject. Example: In a word search about Noah, enclose the block of letters in an ark.

- *Answer key.*

4. Have a supply of quadrille paper with different-size printed squares for word-search and crossword puzzles.
5. Have someone test the finished puzzle if possible. Check text and puzzle diagrams carefully for accuracy.
6. Evaluate the finished puzzle as in No. 7 in the previous section.

MISCELLANEOUS SUGGESTIONS ON GAMES AND PUZZLES

- Study the style of the games or puzzles in the publication you are submitting to. Or write the magazine or publisher for a specification sheet on how they want them set up.

- Teachers use games and puzzles in various ways such as to review or reinforce concepts, to help students categorize information, to improve vocabulary, to promote understanding and to apply the concepts learned. Some games are designed to simulate real life situations. Keep these uses in mind.

- Be sure the game is fun! That's the main reason students like games so well. Insert humor whenever possible and appropriate. Keep the game lively and timely. Games involving some physical action are good for students with pent-up energy in the classroom.

- Be aware of differences of opinion regarding types of games that are acceptable. Some denominations do not approve of using regular playing cards, for example.

- Recycle old tests or refer to chapter study questions or chapter summaries for ideas on game questions or puzzle clues.

- Some games are quite complex; others are very simple. Both can be useful. A game idea for a quick, no-preparation game (sometimes called an instant game) might make a good filler item.

Developing a game or a puzzle may appear to be a simple job that you could whip out in an hour or two. Don't be fooled. This type of writing takes a lot of time, energy, and creative effort. But I find it satisfying and think it's worthwhile because games and puzzles make learning more fun.

WRITING SONGS AND HYMNS

by Jaroslav Vajda

The author is a resident of St. Louis, and is book editor at Concordia Publishing House; he is also a hymn writer, who has taught this subject at writers' conferences.

If, as has been observed, "true theology is doxology," it is not surprising that Christian poets often feel inspired to express their adoration of God in hymns and sacred songs.

Not all poetry, however, is suited for hymn singing. Nor are all sacred songs sung by Christians true hymns. Yet there is a use for both, and Christian poets should know their definitions before they attempt to produce either hymns or sacred songs.

A hymn has been defined in many ways, but most scholars agree that a hymn is metrical verse that consists of two or more stanzas with the same number of lines and accents per line. It is usually set to music and may be written before or after the melody is composed.

In content, a hymn is usually objective, dwelling primarily on God, his attributes and acts, and expressed in language with which worshippers gathered in a body can honestly agree. Hence the feelings expressed by the author should be universal and befitting formal group worship. In Christian hymnody, God's grace and love in Christ are preeminent. The hymn gives voice to the worshipper's awe, gratitude, trust, hope, and love. Some hymns dwell entirely or chiefly on the nature and majesty of God (e.g., "Holy, holy, holy," "Crown him with many crowns," "Lift high the cross," etc.) and on the work of redemption wrought by Christ. Such hymns can be sung without reservation by any believer.

From such exclusive concentration on God and his majesty, preluding the Hallelujah Chorus of the angels and saints in glory, hymnody approaches God from another direction: It takes the form of prayer in confession, thanksgiving, and supplication. Such hymns are subjective only in the sense that they place the worshipper in relation to God and express universally held truths about life in the kingdom of God; they are still God- and Christ-oriented.

Gospel songs, on the other hand, tend to be quite subjective, focusing on the worshipper and his or her needs and feelings, sometimes becoming so personal that few others can identify with them. Seldom in formal group worship can an entire congregation sing Gospel songs with one accord. This is not to say they do not have a proper place in Christian worship; but that place is in worship that is informal, private, or with a like-minded group of people.

THE CURRENT TREND

Most recently the trend in Christian songwriting has been toward scripture songs based entirely on verses from the Bible or slight paraphrases to fit a melody line. These songs, like Gospel songs, tend to follow a ballad pattern, with repeated refrains and a simple thought, whereas the congregational hymn ranges more widely and plumbs deeper into the expanses and depths of theological concepts. The true hymn works at several levels and is therefore more enduring than the more emotional sacred song.

If you are inspired to write texts for singing, you have several choices: hymns, sacred songs, Gospel songs, scripture songs—or if you dare to be creative, you can launch new forms and modes, as Isaac Watts did when he found the Psalm paraphrases of his day boring and unsatisfying. But you must know the parameters of the form you are pouring your inspiration into and fulfill its poetic requirements. Doggerel set to music is still doggerel— not a sacred song.

Why should you write sacred texts for singing? Because you have to, for one reason. Reason enough for a poet. You are awestruck by some aspect of God or of faith, and you are moved to give voice to it in verse. Let it flow naturally into the most fitting of the forms cited—or create a new one.

If you are writing for a special purpose, your composition must suit the need. Often a hymn or song is written to commemorate some special occasion: an anniversary, a wedding, a baptism, a confirmation, a funeral. The form of the hymn should match the occasion—or should fit an appropriate melody.

You should note several checkpoints when writing a hymn or sacred song: Is the theology sound and scriptural? Is it poetry rather than rhymed prose? Does it present a unified thought? Is it original in concept and expression, or does it imitate familiar classics? Are the words contemporary yet reverent? Does it scan strictly so as to fit a repeatable melodic line? Do the accents fall on the right syllables? Have you avoided tongue-twisters? Are the vowels singable on high notes? Have you chosen an overused meter or a tune that is wedded to a traditional text?

When writing hymns you must be extremely careful about plagiarism. The copyright laws are very strict about music and poetry and the writer must make absolutely sure that nothing under copyright is used without permission, however unintentionally. Could the words and phrases that are coming into your head be from recesses of the mind that hold earlier associations with a written (and copyrighted) hymn? Be sure to check everything out carefully before submitting any piece of poetry for hymn use.

Where do you go to have a hymn or song text published? Is your church body preparing a new hymnal or publishing smaller collections of new hymns? Write to the hymnal commission of your denomination, asking what gaps need to be filled, e.g., hymns on the centrality of Baptism, mutual forgiveness, social concerns, hunger, sickness, work, marriage, etc. Join the Hymn Society of America and get their quarterly, *The Hymn*, which announces contests and prints new hymns. Submit potential hymn texts to your church periodicals, especially on seasonal themes. Find out from publishers of hymn or song collections what they are looking for. Check the most recent *Music Market* reference book listing religious music publishers. Collaborate with a recognized composer who is looking for suitable texts to set to music. Attend hymn- or song-writing workshops or seminars for further training in skills and listings of new markets.

The writer of religious hymns or songs is not likely to be paid a great deal for the effort. Most hymns become part of a hymnal and are bought on a one-time payment basis. However, if the writer retains copyright of the words after the hymn is printed in the hymnal, any other printed or commercial use of the words will guarantee additional payment. This process usually goes on for many years, sometimes for generations, as hymns that "catch on" are reprinted in new collections. Occasionally a hymn that appears in a collection will be picked up for a more commercial use, become a popular "hit" and thus bring a greater return to the author.

The hymn writer's modest financial rewards are offset by the satisfaction of knowing that he is influencing the lives of many people. The singing of hymns is an important part of the worship of all denominations, and the words on the page take on life as they help the worshipper feel a little less earthbound and self-preoccupied—at least for a time. The writer of hymns can also be encouraged by the fact that once a hymn is in a hymnbook it endures for a much longer time than an article printed in a periodical or even the ordinary book that sometimes very quickly goes out of print and out of date.

Finally, don't overlook translation as a way to use your poetic skills and to enrich American/English hymnody with the treasures of other languages and cultures. You may be another John Mason Neale or Catherine Winkworth whose lasting contribution is made by way of masterful translation.

One way of assuring oneself of immortality is to write an immortal hymn. Some poets are remembered for just one outstanding text. But the higher goal is to dedicate one's poetic talents to the giver of all good gifts and to strive for the loftiest writing: that which glorifies God. I leave you with the motto of Oswald Chambers: "My utmost for His highest!"

❧ *CHAPTER SEVENTEEN*

WRITING FOR RELIGIOUS TELEVISION AND FILM

by Donald Davenport

Donald Davenport of Newbury Park, California, is the principal writer of eight films, documentaries, and TV programs. His first film, Doomsday Ward, won the gold medal at the Houston International Film Festival in 1979. For four years he has been a staff writer for the nationally syndicated Westbrook Hospital series, serving as associate producer and second unit director. His major work to date, The Third Cry, will be released nationally in 1982. His films have won awards in seven competitions and film festivals.

FOR THE WRITER of inspirational films and television, it is, to steal another's lead, the best of times and the worst of times. With the emergence of Christian-owned and -operated stations and cable outlets, the television marketplace is hungry for quality religious products. Movies. Documentaries. Series ideas.

The church film-rental business has continued to grow during the past decade, and producers are eager to generate new films for that market. Good films for kids are always in demand. In addition, Christian films are now being shown in neighborhood theaters. Christ may now be on the marquee where once Godzilla reigned! The Christian visual media have indeed come into their own.

At the same time, however, the cost of quality film production is higher than ever, making the financial risk for investors greater than before. With money tight, the lure of a successful investment or even a tax shelter isn't always enough to generate funding. Nevertheless, when a film is successful, the rewards for the writer—financial and otherwise—can be substantial.

On commercial television, the climate for "inspirational drama" has improved significantly. Historically, if a religious show was to air on commercial television, it had to be diluted in terms of message to the point of being rendered only vaguely spiritual, or else it was relegated to the "Sunday morning ghetto" when the station schedules religious programs, often to fulfill the FCC's requirement for public service programming.

But with the emergence of Christian television—PTL Network, CBN, and others—the ability to air inspirational programming on television in prime time periods has never been better.

The film-rental market offers other alternatives for selling ideas and materials. Religious film companies such as Gospel Films, Gateway Films, Cathedral Films, and others are looking for stories and ideas that can be adapted to film and produced for church rental. There is a sweeping market for quality films of an inspirational nature, and some of the best ones over the years have become classics. Films such as *The Ant Keeper*, *The Parable*, and more recently, *The Train*, are booked thousands of times annually and seem to have an unlimited life. Many are dubbed into foreign languages for overseas rentals.

Historical films about religious champions have also been quite successful in the rental market. For example, *The Life of Paul* series, produced many years ago, is still widely shown. More recently, Michael Economou's drama on the life of reformer John Hus, originally planned as a television special but never released in the United States, has done extremely well in the rental market and won the Christian "Oscar" for the best dramatic film of 1980.

Obviously there is a market for ideas and scripts, but there are some special skills that have to be acquired if those ideas are going to be successfully developed.

PREREQUISITE SKILLS

The Christian writer needs to continually remind himself of several things that are germane to any kind of script writing.

Foremost is the tenet that a successful script must work *visually*. Film is too "concentrated" a medium to carry any extra verbiage, characters, or plots. Wordiness is fatal to a script. Creating visual scenes often means shorter scenes. Anything that can be *shown* rather than discussed is preferred. The proper glance or even a grunt can often communicate more effectively than a page of dialogue. Transitions must work tightly and visually. If you are moving from an outdoor to an indoor scene, for example, showing the doorway to the house will indicate to the viewer that you are going inside. Conversation can also tie in with the previous scene and help the viewer realize what has happened. A change of scenery must seem logical to the *eye* and should not set up extraneous thoughts in the mind of the viewer.

In general, successful script writers have a certain "filmic sense," an almost mystical instinct for drama. Writing fresh and interesting characters and dialogue, creating subplots that act as effective foils for the main plot, compressing years of "real" time into minutes of screen time—all these elements must be mastered.

What skills does a writer need to develop to successfully write for film and television? To start with, a clear conception of the mechanics of "story" and a general understanding of the technical aspects of filmmaking are needed.

"Story" is not an unknown quantity that one stumbles on like the "pearl of great price." "Story" is an orderly assemblage of events and characters, with a beginning, one or more conflicts or crises (one of them a major crisis), and a denouement.

The "payoff" is a story editor's favorite diagnostic tool for analyzing a story. A subplot that doesn't reinforce the main plot, for example, doesn't pay off. A character who remains undeveloped and doesn't advance the story doesn't pay off. A scene without a *specific* purpose won't pay off. In an effective "story," there is no room for loose ends. *Everything* must pay off. If you think that *perhaps* the story will work without a certain story element, you can almost be sure that it isn't needed.

A script is rarely seen by its audience in the form that the writer has completed; it is merely a blueprint, subject to the interpretation of producers, directors, actors, film editors, and whoever else has the opportunity to put his thumb in the creative pie. If we accept the notion that the screenwriter is actually drawing blueprints, then we see why he must understand a little about the "building" process itself.

Simply put, a screenwriter must grasp enough technical information to describe "filmically" what he sees in his mind's eye. A knowledge of photography is helpful so that optical effects, desired lenses, and the general "look" of a scene can be described in the script. This technical description of camera moves, sound effects, and visual transitions requires a new lexicon of terms, equipment, and technique—the language of film.

The best way to learn this language is to sit at the feet of the masters—acquire and read some good scripts. Libraries often have books that contain script excerpts. Bookstores have whole sections devoted to screenplays. If you live in an area of major film production such as Los Angeles or New York, you can visit complete libraries that contain the screenplays of most major films and many television shows. The American Film Institute in Los Angeles is a rich resource for scripts.

There are also good books on the market specifically dealing with scriptwriting. They include sample formats and the technical information necessary to help a writer adapt a good story into a nicely crafted screenplay, complete with camera blocking and other technical descriptions.

Let's pause for a word of comfort, however. Most religious film producers don't require a writer to block out scenes in the script by describing *every* camera shot and move. A practical rule of thumb is to use only the technical information you *need* to adequately convey a scene. If a specific lens or optical effect is essential to the story line, include it.

The following is an excerpt from "One Sunday in Searchlight," an award-winning episode of the *Westbrook Hospital* series. Notice how a balance is maintained between describing the scene visually while including sufficient technical information to convey the concept to the director.

EXT—COUNTRY ROAD—NOON

MATT quickly exits the cab of the truck. He opens the hood and is briefly enveloped by the escaping steam. He returns to the cab and tries to restart the engine, but it doesn't fire. He grabs his medical bag, stuffs the Styrofoam container that contains the serum into the bag, and exits the truck.

We SEE Matt begin to run down the road. The SHOT is TELEPHOTO, creating the illusion that he is making no progress. The abandoned truck in the b.g. (background) is still visible, hood still up, venting steam like a burned-out

tank on a battlefield.
MEDIUM SHOT—MATT

As he runs out of FRAME, the camera PANS UP, catching a
flare from the blazing sun . . ."

In this example, notice how the technical form *does* affect the narrative itself, and the writer was able to convey the images he wanted. The scene *was* directed as written (a rare occurrence, but not without precedent).

A final word on screenwriting skills: Become immersed in the media. Consume a steady diet of well-produced film and television shows. Pay attention to where the plot will lead, how the characters are developed, and how the writer was able to effectively convey information, advancing the story line, making the story live. Imitation is still the most effective way to learn writing, and after a while the things that successful writers do well will become quite apparent, and the "story" will become second nature.

TYPES OF STORY

Stories that adapt successfully to film usually have certain elements that make them marketable. Many good stories may not be suitable for a film treatment for a variety of reasons, not only the particulars of the story itself, but the constantly changing attitudes of the film marketplace. In 1981 the market was glutted with tragic illness stories. (That didn't mean a tragic illness story couldn't be sold. It just meant it had to be a *very* good tragic illness story.) The public taste changes and what may be in vogue one year can't be sold the next. Thankfully, this is less a consideration in the religious film market, but general trends still apply.

Christian audiences tend to judge a Christian film not only on whether it is good or bad artistically, but also on whether it is doctrinally sound. Whereas a secular audience may simply be bored by a poorly written film, a poorly executed religious film may end up chipping away at someone's belief structure. A Christian film may be artistically well done and present a story with power, but if it is teaching a lesson which is theologically unsound, it will be judged negatively by the audience. It is safe to say that Christian media audiences generally use films less as entertainment or as means for examining diverse points of view, and more as a way to be evangelized and inspired. This means that stories must be chosen with care and must represent models of Christianity that portray universally accepted themes and beliefs.

True life stories are much more likely to succeed in the Christian marketplace. Stories of personal trial and victory that in some way typify Everyman's experience will be an easier sell than fiction. Stories of conversion. Stories of triumph. Stories of incredible faith. "Small" stories are an easier sell than epics. Small stories usually have only a few characters and often have contemporary settings that do not require elaborate sets and costuming. These kinds of stories will be much more appealing to a filmmaker's budget. A love story is usually cheaper to film than the battle of Armageddon. Likewise, upbeat stories with happy endings are generally more in demand than ponderous or philosophical stories that conclude on a less hopeful note.

But big story or small, the most important thing for the screenwriter to remember is that the viewer must grow to *care* about the characters he sees on the screen. Many scripts fail because the writer was unable, for whatever reason, to generate sympathy for the protagonist. If the viewer doesn't care about the character in a story, whatever happens to him along the way will not produce the sense of fear and pathos that the Greeks declared were vital to successful drama.

Books are one significant source of good story material. Adaptations of existing books into screenplay form are often successful because, with a book, the audience is already established. If the book was successful, the odds for a successful film improve greatly. The "pre-sale" factor of a book is very important in the minds of producers. It says to them that there may be less risk involved in an adaptation because it was the publisher who first tested the water by taking the initial risk. But that privilege must be purchased.

The legal considerations involved in optioning material are beyond the scope of our discussion here, but a query letter to the writer or publisher inquiring about the status of the movie rights for a particular book is the basic starting point. Many authors will be willing to allow a writer to take an option on a book with a minimal investment, with the full remuneration coming when the film goes into production. This agreement, however, must be properly contracted and documented. (Never send out anything to be read by anyone unless it is copyrighted. Undocumented scripts, story ideas—even concepts—are fair game in the minds of some.)

Copyrighting can take several forms, official and unofficial. It can be as official as filling out forms and submitting a fee to the government, or even mailing yourself the manuscript and keeping the sealed letter (with its postage date) to verify when the manuscript was completed. Perhaps the easiest method of protecting one's work is to register the manuscript with the Writers Guild of America. For $10 to nonmembers, the WGA will microfilm and document your script or idea and will also offer guidance if a dispute over authorship should arise. An inquiry to the WGA office at 8955 Beverly Blvd., Los Angeles, CA 90048 will yield further details about manuscript protection.

THE TREATMENT

Once a story is clearly in mind, the most easily written and read form of a film idea is the "treatment." Most producers prefer to see a treatment before they will seriously talk to a writer about the merits of an idea.

A treatment is usually a ten-page version of the story, complete with brief scene description and action, and often with some sample dialogue. Some writers think of a treatment as a pithy, present-tense short story, but most important is that it capture the spirit of the story. Since the treatment is an important selling tool, it should be a best effort.

Doing a treatment on a story idea is also very good discipline because when you're forced to boil down the action to just a few pages it often helps you reveal the essence of the story more clearly. Literary agents will tell you that every great film can be sold in a sentence. Ten pages of diamond-hard narrative is even better.

GETTING IT READ

Despite its rapid expansion in recent years, the Christian media marketplace is still relatively small. That is an advantage for several reasons. First, there are more than a thousand production companies listed in the Los Angeles Studio Directory alone. Ferreting out which company might find your idea suitable for production is a monumental task in itself. The larger Christian film producers number in the dozens nationwide. At a broadcast convention such as the National Religious Broadcasters, one can meet representatives from most of them.

Another advantage of the Christian marketplace is the openness of most producers to ideas. In the commercial marketplace, a major studio will not even read a manuscript unless it has been submitted by a reputable agent. My experience with Christian producers has been that, almost without exception, my material has been read and often read promptly. That alone is encouraging.

Pick five of the most active Christian production companies and send each a treatment, accompanied by a letter giving some background on the story—who the projected audience is, what is the message to that audience, and what needs are filled by the film. Convince the producer that the audience exists, the need exists, and the story will fill that need.

FOLLOWING THROUGH

No matter how much interest may be generated by a treatment, it is doubtful that your idea will be sold in that form. That is the *disadvantage* of the Christian marketplace. In the commercial marketplace, a writer with a track record can often sell ideas verbally, and unless he is very hungry, will not consider writing a full-length screenplay on "spec."

Most Christian producers will want to see a completed screenplay before they will buy your work, but, by all means, glean whatever input you can on the treatment before launching into the screenplay. It is certainly easier to adjust a story based on reaction to a treatment, than to bluster ahead and write the script and then have to rewrite massive chunks of it because you didn't bother to listen. Film making is a collaborative art and the collaboration starts early, even taking the form of pointed criticism at the idea stage.

Once you have polished a draft of the screenplay, fit it with a script cover before sending it out. Avoid the fancy ones with plastic windows or the expensive ones that look like book bindings. Cardboard covers held in place with brass fasteners are the industry standard. Include with the script a one-page synopsis of the story.

Finally, be patient. A treatment may get a response in as little as a couple of weeks; a full screenplay will probably take longer.

THE THIRD CRY (a case study)

The Third Cry is a prime time movie for television starring Richard Hatch, Laurie Walters, and Mel Ferrer. Produced in 1981 by Transda Productions for the Adventist Church, it represents one of the most ambitious attempts to bridge the gap between commercial television and religious film producers. It is an "inspirational" story that fought its way into the marketplace, and it serves as an interesting model of how ideas can evolve into sellable screenplays.

The story came from a business associate who had had a Protestant minister as a classmate. The minister and his wife had two children born with cystic fibrosis, a fatal genetic disease. It was the story of how this family survived the ordeal through faith.

At the time, both the religious and the secular markets were glutted with "dying kids" shows, as one network official put it. But there were elements in the story line that suggested it might be unique.

First, cystic fibrosis is a relatively "new" disease, having been discovered in 1955, and it had not been the subject of a major dramatic project. Furthermore, there are peculiarities of the disease that have great dramatic potential. For example, the disease is genetically inherited from *both* parents, the majority of marriages with cystic children don't survive, and the recommended treatment is daily "pounding" of the children to loosen up the mucous in the lungs ("How am I supposed to tell my three-year-old daughter that I'm 'beating' her because I love her?").

Moreover, the irony of the story happening to "righteous" people added a certain Jobian twist. The question "Why suffering?" is universally pondered, but the fact that the story ended in triumph for the family gave it a strong, upbeat ending. All of these considerations were very important in terms of "story."

The author wrote the script in about four months and submitted it as a personal favor to a network reader, who said the story was too "soft" (a network euphemism for a glaring absence of sex and violence). A rewrite produced more tension between the characters, showing them closer to the breaking point. The network passed on the project.

What followed was a furious campaign to generate grass roots support for the script. Copies were sent to local and national cystic fibrosis foundations for their endorsements and moral support. Letters from other parents of cystic fibrosis children began arriving, the parents wanting to know what they could do to help.

The major breakthrough came when a high ranking executive of another network was given a script as he boarded a flight bound for the East Coast. He read *The Third Cry* on the plane and later remarked that he put on his dark glasses so no one would see that he was crying. On his approval, production finally began—almost two years after the script was written.

The lessons learned from *The Third Cry* experience are vital. Find a story with universal appeal. Capitalize on the ironies, the uniqueness of the story. Document that the audience exists. Get your treatment read by important (yet sympathetic) people in the Christian media, and possibly the commercial media as well. Be patient. Write lots of letters. Strive to be happy.

A Partial List of
Christian Film Producers
and Distributors

Gateway Films
Box A-CT9
Lansdale, PA 19446
(215)368-8430

World Wide Pictures
2520 W. Olive
Burbank, CA 91505

Cathedral Films
P.O. Box 4029
2282 Townsgate Rd.
Westlake Village, CA 91359
(805)497-6870

Ken Anderson Films
P.O. Box 618
Winona Lake, IN 46590
(219)267-5774

Outreach Films
P.O. Box 4029
Westlake Village, CA 91359

Faith Films Limited
P.O. Box 1096
Coquitlam, B.C. Canada V3J 624

Family Films
14622 Lanark
Panorama City, CA 91402
(213)997-7500

Gospel Films
Box 455
Muskegon, MI 49443

Quadras Communications
128 Kishwaukee
Rockford, MD 61101

Part Five

CHAPTER EIGHTEEN

GETTING HELP AND TRAINING

by Norman B. Rohrer

Norman B. Rohrer of La Canada, California, founder and director of the Christian Writers Guild, is probably helping more writers improve their skills than anyone else currently in the field. He himself began writing and selling when he entered college more than thirty years ago. After graduation from seminary, he served as publications director for International Students in Washington, D.C., and later as managing editor of The King's Business *magazine and editor of* World Vision *magazine. He also was executive secretary of the Evangelical Press Association for fourteen years and wrote the weekly* EP News Service *during that time. He is the author or ghost writer of twelve books. Besides teaching students in his guild's home-study course, he directs the "Write to Be Read" workshops in twenty cities each year and is an instructor at several other Christian writers' conferences.*

your spiritual insights. "You should be published!" they exclaim.

An idea for an article on a religious theme begins to formulate. You rush to your desk and start to write. Several paragraphs into your project you halt at frustration's gate. The writing seems to be flat. You need accurate statistics to prove the point you are making, illustrations to give it color, anecdotes to *show* the reader instead of merely *telling,* and you need supportive quotations by people who are knowledgeable about your subject. And since you haven't formally studied grammar, syntax, and composition since school days you could use some guidance in that area for completing your article. Is there anyplace you can turn for help?

Indeed there is help and training for the writer aiming at the religious and inspirational market. Editors want to help writers not only because they share like interests but also because the editors need material to feed their hungry presses deadline after relentless deadline.

Editors produce guidelines for writers, turn out newsletters, manufacture cassettes, and publish books and magazines—in short, they do everything but look over your shoulder with helpful direction (and they even do that at writers' conferences, seminars, and workshops across the land).

Following are tips on how you can get the most help for the least amount of money and time expended. Lay aside reluctance, bury reserve, do not be ashamed of ignorance, seize every opportunity to learn. Let it be said that you gave it your best.

In addition to the assistance to be found in workshops, conferences, correspondence courses, formal classes in adult education sponsored by colleges and universities, the Y and community centers, and informal writers' clubs in living rooms, there is also a less obvious technique for self-instruction. With that time-honored do-it-yourself method we begin.

IMITATION

Probably the best way to improve your writing is to read authors of enduring literature and imitate their style. No matter what you may eventually create, you learn first by observing and imitating.

Benjamin Franklin is remembered for this practice. He wrote a couple of centuries ago:

About this time I met with an odd volume of the *Spectator*. It was the third. I had never before seen any of them. I bought it, read it over and over, and was much delighted with it. I thought the writing excellent, and wished, if possible, to imitate it. With that view I took some of the papers, and making short hints of the sentiment in each sentence, laid them by a few days and then without looking at the book, tried to complete the papers again, by expressing each hinted sentiment at length and as fully as it had been expressed before, in any suitable words that should come to hand. Then I compared my *Spectator* with the original, discovered some of my faults and corrected them.

Naturally, you could imitate slavishly and learn only a bag of tricks. Worse, you could become only an imitation of someone else's opinions and writing style. But if you observe well and use your observation to advantage, imitation can give your writing loftier sentiment and a "take away" ingredient by which the reader can enrich his own life.

You can imitate in two ways. The first is to study the outline and structure of a piece and apply the principles of composition to an entirely new subject; the second is to take a passage and write about the same thing, supplying different modifiers that give it your own slant and color. For example, you could read a jungle scene and afterward modify the general outline to describe a football game. Or you might take a favorite passage from literature or the Bible and supply an entirely new set of adjectives and adverbs.

Whatever method you select, imitation can be a first step toward editorial skill.

WORKSHOPS

While you read and imitate the writers you admire, good solid instruction in basic writing technique is available in area workshops, seminars, and conferences. These programs are designed to inspire and encourage, but there are other things to be learned at these editorial gatherings.

Composition. A writer without a knowledge of proper syntax, grammar, spelling, punctuation, diction, and paragraphing cannot hope to achieve good writing skills. Usually, a writers' conference will schedule at least one session offering help in this area.

Research. Helpful leads on where to find information are an enormous aid to beginning writers. Workshops offer tips on how successful writers tackle an assignment. Students can observe how professionals follow leads, prepare for interviews, mine the libraries, and garner facts that make a piece salable.

Marketing. What good is a manuscript if it is never published? At workshops, the writer learns how to approach an editor, what periodicals are buying what kind of material, how much is being paid, how to prepare a query letter to sell the idea first and develop it later, when an agent is needed, and how to spot a trend in publishing.

Record keeping. Every writer is also a business person. The work produced is a literary property. It can be lost, stolen, forgotten, or destroyed. Good records are required so a writer knows where material has been sent, who might have rejected it, who has accepted it, what rights were offered, whether assignments have been fulfilled, and how much has been paid (for income tax purposes if for nothing else).

Friendships. Editorial assignments are often given by editors to writers whom they know and trust. Writers tend to send their material to editors they know through previous contacts. The friendships made at conferences and workshops often flower into profitable leads. Be aggressive in reaching out. If you don't, friendships might not happen.

CORRESPONDENCE COURSES

Writing is probably the easiest art (some prefer to call it a craft) to teach by mail. A correspondence course requires putting something down on paper and completing an editorial assignment. These manuscripts can then be read and critiqued by an instructor.

Several home-study courses for the religious writer are available. How can you select the right one? First, ask specific questions of the school and see how you are treated. Are your questions answered personally or are you given a computerized letter? Is the school interested in developing your talent as a writer or only in selling courses?

Second, inquire about the person doing the teaching. Has he or she had experience not only in writing but also in marketing a manuscript successfully? Those who can, write. Those who can't, sometimes limit themselves to teaching. Degrees won't tell you much. Experience talks in writing.

Correspondence courses should offer a careful reading of your lesson material by your instructor and reveal both your strengths and weaknesses. Your editorial handiwork should have more than brief notations in the margin reading "good" or "nice touch" or "weak." Your instructor should indicate that your writing is good *because* . . . or it's bad *because*. . . . Each critique is but one person's opinion. That is what your are paying for. Not all writers, editors, and publishers agree about the worth of a manuscript. Some bestselling books were first rejected many times by editors who did not suspect that the material would be so well received by readers.

Stick with your instructor. Accept the guidance you are paying for. Don't try to pit one viewpoint against another while you are in the learning process. If your instructor is a successful writer, listen to him. Later you will be in a better position to be objective and make up your own mind about variables.

Editors won't lecture you on developing good work habits, but your correspondence course teacher will. Your teacher is your first editor. Listen carefully and complete your piece as directed. The famed writing teacher William Strunk, author of *The Elements of Style*, is remembered for his admonition that he thundered at his students: "Completion! Completion! Completion!" Finish what you start. It will teach you more than project hopping and dabbling.

The two best-known correspondence courses for religious writers are those offered by the Christian Writers Institute, 396 E. St. Charles Rd., Wheaton, IL 60187, and by the Christian Writers Guild, 5306 Stardust Rd., La Canada, CA 91011. A third is offered by the Christian Writers Fellowship, 3037 Woodland Hills Dr., Apt. 24, Ann Arbor, MI 48104. There are also individual instructors who advertise their personal counsel as teachers of writing.

The Christian Writers Institute of Wheaton offers three divisions of specialization with five courses of study. The divisions are the Professional Writing Division, the Specialized Writing Division, and the Advanced Writing Division. Subjects include writing techniques, magazine writing, fiction writing, juvenile writing, and writing the novel.

The course offered by the Christian Writers Guild is entitled "Discover Your Possibilities in Writing" and introduces the student to forty-eight lesson topics. The guild has a single instructor, whereas the institute employs many writers. There is a cassette approach to instruction by a third organization which will be discussed later.

To get the most from your investment in a correspondence course, fulfill each assignment completely. Question editing marks that you do not understand. Ask if your instructor will read and respond to extracurricular writing. Some charge an additional fee for such services, others do not.

Make time each day for your course, be it only fifteen minutes. The steady attention to the reading of the lessons and preparation of assignments will earn you the certificate of completion.

Any correspondence course worth its paper and ink will offer guidance in marketing the completed manuscript. It is not enough merely to perfect the piece. The writer must sell it. But how? Where? To what type of periodical? A teacher can advise, but it eventually becomes the writer's responsibility to study markets—to pick up new periodicals and to investigate current needs of book publishing firms.

The stimulus of face-to-face encounter in a classroom cannot be discounted. But if you live too far from such an opportunity, or if you are restricted by job obligations or other handicaps, by all means investigate the correspondence courses.

COMMUNITY EDUCATION

If you live close enough to a metropolitan center you will undoubtedly find courses available at a college or university, at the Y, in a church, or at a community center. Before you enroll, investigate. Don't succumb to the spell of a catalog advertisement alone. Find out who the instructors are. Check biographical and other reference works. Learn whether your instructor is a published author and what his or her specialties are. If you are interested in fiction and your instructor has published only nonfiction, better try to find an instructor who has had success in marketing the type of writing you wish to produce.

Talk with campus bookstore clerks. Search for a student publication that evaluates teachers. Look for a professional active writer, editor, or agent. Such a person can guide you as you write and also help you to eventually be published. Many writing courses offered by educational institutions do not include this most important step—the marketing of a manuscript.

Avoid nonsense courses with titles like "Stratification Grammar," "Sexual Awareness through Literature," "Literature of Evil," and "Futuristic Literature" taught by intellectuals who shun simple, basic instruction. One professor in a well-known state university talked about "semantic structuration of discourse," "composing behaviors," and "intra-sentential deployment of syntactical structures." He advised pupils to pay attention to these things and ignore the advice of E. B. White, Edwin Newman, and others who talk about clarity and simplicity in writing. Is it any wonder we have raised a generation of people who can't communicate in writing?

As you take direction from a teacher, remember that writing is an art. Therefore, tastes may differ. No teacher has the final word on writing. Ask questions; don't sit there nodding your head if you don't understand or if you disagree. Challenge your teacher's opinions. Don't be intimidated by classmates' statements about your views or about your writing.

Write as you learn. No teacher can guide you if you aren't making an effort to get something down on paper. Submit your assigned work early in the term so that your problems will surface in time for your instructor to correct them.

Don't look to your teacher as a collaborator by continually asking for progress reports on bits and pieces of writing. Submit only completed manuscripts.

Finish each assigned or suggested reading. Most teachers build their courses around extensive collateral reading. In class they may pass over this material, but it is vitally important to have it in your mind.

While you are enrolled in the course do not show your work to friends, pitting their views against those of the teacher. Confusion will overwhelm you. And never take two writing courses simultaneously. The load of responsibility will dilute the effectiveness of each course and leave you fragmented and discouraged.

You are entitled to full criticism of material assigned. If you receive pats on the back or quickly scrawled commentary on a manuscript, go back for a better analysis. Teachers enjoy instructing pupils who don't wilt under criticism. The way to become a professional writer is to decide not to become emotionally involved in the commentary on your handiwork. Accept criticism gratefully. Consider your manuscript a literary property that is marketable, given the proper polish and rewriting.

Don't wait for back-to-school September. The doors of the classroom are probably open to you right now. But don't expect a course in writing to transform you magically into a professional writer. You would not expect a violinist to be accomplished after a semester or two of lessons. Learning to write also takes time. Build a good base for later proficiency.

PUBLISHED HELPS

Books

For writers aiming at the religious market there are not only dozens of workshops, several correspondence courses, and four cassette tape learning programs, there are also shelves of books on how to develop material for the religious press. The titles that follow are among the most popular (see also the titles listed by chapter in the Bibliography).

The Christian Writers Handbook, by Margaret J. Anderson, Harper & Row, 1974, 270 pp. $8.95, $5.95 paper. The author, a seasoned writer for the religious press, offers pointers on preparing brief forms, feature-length nonfiction, fiction, and the business end of writing.

Writing Award-Winning Articles, by Glenn Arnold. Thomas Nelson, 1979. 247 pp. $7.95. This anthology by a college professor offers award-winning articles gleaned from member periodicals of the Evangelical Press Association to help journalism students in Christian schools to improve their writing.

The Christian As Journalist, by Richard T. Baker. Association Press, 1961. 121 pp. Considered a classic in its field, it sets forth the journalist's motivation.

Dimensions of Christian Writing, by A. Donald Bell and John C. Merrill. Zondervan, 1970. 96 pp., paper. This volume is a study of the qualities of effective Christian writing, covering semantics, credibility, and other characteristics.

Pathways for the Poet, by Viola Berg. Mott Media, 1978. 234 pp. $9.95. The author has written more than 1,600 published poems and here presents a resource tool of definitions, forms, and illustrations valuable to any serious poet.

Techniques of Christian Writing, by Benjamin P. Browne. Judson Press, 1960. Other books by Browne include *The Christian Writers Conference Comes to You,* 1956, 423 pp.; *Christian Journalism for Today,* Judson Press, 1952, revised 1954.

Handbook for Christian Writers, offered by the Christian Writers Institute (Creation House), Carol Stream, IL, 1974. 155 pp. $3.95, paper. This is a gathering of helpful articles by editors and publishers—many of the editors have changed houses since 1974, but much of the counsel and many informative hints remain timeless.

Contemporary Christian Communications: Its Theory and Practice, by James F. Engel. Thomas Nelson, 1979. 344 pp. $12.95. Professor Engel sets forth the principles for Christian communicators, including journalists, "to present the gospel more effectively with professional communication techniques."

Write the Word, by William Folprecht. Mott Media, 1976. 212 pp. $4.95, paper. This book is an inspirational presentation combining practical suggestions, anecdotes, and personal examples to get budding authors started and keep them writing.

How I Write: A Manual for Beginning Writers, by Robert J. Hastings. Broadman, 1973. 157 pp. $3.95. Hastings provides an informative and inspiring account filled with personal experiences, quotations from experts, and established rules of writing.

Writing the Creative Article, by Marjorie Holmes. The Writer, Inc., 1976. 143 pp. $7.95. Three basic patterns of structure are presented for writing articles of advice, humor, nostalgia, essays, inspiration, and self-help.

Creative Christian Communication, by Gomer R. Lesch. Broadman, 1965. 128 pp. $3.50. How to transmit the Christian message is broadly explained by a member of the Southern Baptist Convention.

Your Church Is News, by Raymond G. Mecca. Judson Press, 1975. 94 pp. $3.50, paper. A veteran Philadelphia news reporter offers publicity officers advice and examples to be used in local churches.

How to Write Articles, by Berniece Roer Neal. Bethany Press, 1963. 64 pp. $1.95, paper. Ideas, formats, composing, details, types, interviews, rewriting, and marketing are discussed to provide you with the techniques of becoming a selling writer.

Writing for Christian Publications, by Edith Filler Osteyee. Greenwood Press, 1953; rev. ed., 1969. 206 pp. $10.50. One of the early guides to writing for the Protestant church press, often used as a text for journalism classes and denominational writing courses.

Wanted: Writers for the Christian Market, by Mildred Schell. Judson Press, 1975. 160 pp. $4.95, paper. The author, director for ten years of the St. Davids Christian Writers Conference, offers tips, guidelines, illustrations, and checklists useful to the aspiring writer.

Write on Target, by Sue Nichols Spencer. Word Books, 1976. 126 pp. $3.50, paper. In a sprightly style, the author presents tips on gathering ideas, handling vocabulary and grammar, and captivating an audience.

Words on Target: For Better Christian Communication. John Knox Press, 1964. 90 pp. $2.95, paper. This book calls writers to clarity, simplicity, and strength in their style.

Write to Discover Yourself, by Ruth Vaughn. Doubleday-Galilee, 1980. $6.95. This thorough guide deals with self-expression in writing through poetry, journals, prayer poems, greeting card verse, and other formats.

The Successful Writers and Editors Guidebook, edited by Robert Walker. Creation House, 1977. 506 pp. $9.95. Walker shows how manuscripts should be prepared, offers market exposure, and a variety of other information useful especially to beginners.

You Can Tell the World, by Sherwood Eliot Wirt. Augsburg, 1975. 128 pp. $3.50. Editor emeritus of *Decision* magazine and a well-known leader among Christian writers, the author wrote this book to "find the trained professional writers, encourage them, and set them to work effectively in the spreading of God's Word through literature."

Getting into Print, by Sherwood Eliot Wirt. Thomas Nelson, 1977. 132 pp. $2.95. The book is the product of the author's fifteen years of teaching at schools of Christian writing around the world.

Writing for the Religious Market, by Roland E. Wolseley. Association Press, 1956. 304 pp. $4. A collection of practical advice presented by eighteen craftsmen in the religious writing field. The material helps the writer to determine the type of writing he wants to do and to distinguish between the secular and the religious media.

Careers in Religious Communications, by Roland E. Wolseley. Herald Press, 1977. 243 pp. $4.95, paper. The author, professor emeritus of journalism, School of Public Communications, Syracuse University, presents case histories and information on what the religious writer can expect to face in a career in religious communications.

Periodicals

Books offer a more permanent literary format but magazines are read by far more people: a good sale of a book is 20,000 copies; several religious periodicals can boast of more than half a million readers issue after issue. Weekly, fortnightly, monthly, and quarterly they hit the news stalls, catching trends, offering millions of words on current issues.

The Evangelical Press Association has approximately 275 member periodicals. These are added to the 135 member magazines of the Associated Church Press, the 400 periodicals in the Catholic Press Association, and the 55 member periodicals in the Canadian Church Press. Denominations such as the Southern Baptist Convention, which sponsors hundreds of state and national journals, often have their own press associations.

Each religious magazine has its own special slant. *The Reformed Journal*, for example, would differ in its editorial position from, say, *The Pentecostal Evangel*. People who read these magazines do so because they look to each for certain theological biases and would be surprised not to find them.

Most magazines publish a set of guidelines that are offered free to prospective contributors of editorial material. These leaflets state word length desired, taboos, doctrinal preference, type of story, article, and filler used, and whether poetry is accepted. They often explain about standing features needing regular contributions written to a precise format. The names and addresses of these periodicals are listed in *Writer's Market*, available in most public libraries or from Writer's Digest Books, 9933 Alliance Road, Cincinnati, OH 45242.

Here are the addresses for the press associations:

The Evangelical Press Association,
Box 4550, Overland Park, KS 66204.

Associated Church Press,
127 Ford, Geneva, IL 60134.

Catholic Press Association,
119 N. Park Ave., Rockville Centre, NY 11570.

280 *Canadian Church Press, United Church House,*
85 St. Clair Avenue East, Toronto, Ontario M4T 1MB.

Newsletters

The newsletter, with its simple, inexpensive format, is increasingly popular with professionals nationwide. Monthly, quarterly, and annual newsletters for writers are also proliferating. They are filled with information about legal matters, book contracts, marketing, and new periodicals, and offer how-to tips on everything from feature writing to photography. Every writer should subscribe to at least one.

There is a newsletter for writers of every persuasion:

Charismatic Writers Association Bulletin,
National Communications Office, 237 N. Michigan, South Bend, IN 46601. A bi-monthly publication for writers interested in or involved in the charismatic movement.

Christian Author Newsletter,
396 E. St. Charles Rd., Wheaton, IL 60187. A publication of the oldest training school for Christian writers.

Christian Writers' Newsletter,
300 E. 34th St. (9c), New York, NY 10016, a bimonthly publication offering inspiration and market tips, along with guidelines for writers in all stages of accomplishment.

Cross & Quill,
c/o Diane Lopez, 3037 Woodland Hills Dr., Apt. 24, Ann Arbor, MI 48104. The official bi-monthly publication of the Christian Writers Fellowship.

Currents,
1604 East Taylor Ave., Harlingen, TX 78550.
The quarterly newsletter of the Christian Writers League of America.

Quill-o'-the Wisp Quarterly,
> Box 707, La Canada, CA 91011, a news sheet primarily for members of the Christian Writers Guild but available to others as well.

Sight Lines,
> One Groveland Terrace, Minneapolis, MN 55403. A periodical of the Christian Theatre Arts Guild with helps and guidelines for writers interested in the theater and other art forms in relation to the Christian faith.

THE LIBRARY

Local libraries have more information than most writers realize or have utilized. It's all public property, and it's all sitting there waiting to be used. Writers can mine these resources created by tax revenue and generate income for themselves.

Most library users gravitate toward the card catalog, but there is much more to explore. Magazines, leaflets, pamphlets, files of newspaper clippings, and microfilm/microfiche collections are but a few of the resources available. Libraries also lend films, filmstrips, photographs, illustrations, phonographs, and tape recorders.

Libraries also offer the services of a trained librarian who is usually eager to help a researcher uncover facts. Many churches have libraries too. There are also specialized libraries scattered across the land with specific information for special projects.

To make the most of this resource, first get a layout of the library. For facts on a topic, check the card catalog and find out what books are available on the subject. For short briefings, check the encyclopedias. For updates on current developments, look into the *Readers' Guide to Periodical Literature.* This will tell you what magazine writers have been saying on the subject.

Only a few religious periodicals, such as *Christianity Today* and *Christian Century* enjoy listings of their articles in this weekly service. Religious colleges, theological seminaries, or other nonprofit agencies often display inspirational literature which can be borrowed or read on the premises.

Other reference works your library might offer include *Applied Science & Technology, Biological & Agricultural Index, Facts on File, Finding Facts Fast,* and the *Writer's Research Handbook.* Check other reference works, such as almanacs, yearbooks, and topical information in books of quotations. *The Writer's Resource Guide,* edited by William Brohaugh and published by Writer's Digest Books, will assist you in finding the facts you need.

Many public libraries have seminar rooms available to researchers. Reserve them for special projects. Take in your typewriter and spread out your work. The convenience of uninterrupted time will hasten the completion of your editorial project.

You can conduct interviews in person, by mail, and by telephone to augment basic research gleaned from a library. People who have the facts you want are usually willing to share their knowledge.

Stock your home shelf with inexpensive books of your own for quick reference. Buy books about your denomination, your community, county, state, and nation. For only a few dollars you can buy *The World Almanac, The U.S. Fact Book,* and *Information Please Almanac.* In addition there are statistics and theological information furnished inexpensively by every church denomination and religious agency about itself.

Mountains of free information are available. Much of it is not copyrighted and can be worked freely into articles and books. The first office to contact is the Public Documents Distribution Center, Pueblo, CO 81009. Another is the Superintendent of Documents, U.S. Government Printing Office, Washington, D.C. 20402. Material issued by the government is not copyrighted, generally, and therefore can probably be used by writers to bolster their themes. Some government publications have been known to include copyrighted material without indicating this. Therefore, if there is any doubt, one ought to check this with the source.

Public relations offices are eager to give away photographs, charts, maps, and leaflets about their clients. All you have to do is ask.

CASSETTES

The standard cassette tape player-recorder was invented in the early sixties. Since then it has given learning and entertainment a new dimension.

Writers can buy cassettes containing varieties of information and special training techniques. One agency, The Christian Writers' Seminar, Box 8682, Waco TX 76710, has built an entire writing course around ten cassettes, plus workbook.

When gathering information, use your handy cassette recorder but do not rely on it alone. Always take a pad and pencil for two reasons. The first is that anything mechanical can fail, leaving you with nothing but embarrassment; the second is that you have to listen to the entire cassette(s) if you have no notes or put the message into a typescript before you can do anything with it. That is expensive and time-consuming.

With a note pad you can turn immediately to the place where you wish to start and can develop your article quickly. Schedule an interview or research-gathering expedition just ahead of some free time so you can get your first draft down on paper (a kind of "free writing" in which you move forward rapidly, not paying attention particularly to punctuation, grammar, spelling, and transitions). The sooner you read your henscratchings on your note pad the easier they will be to decipher.

Cassettes can serve well in conducting research by mail. For interviews, send the person several of the little tapes with a sheet of numbered questions. Ask the interviewee to use the questions as a guide in telling his story on tape. The typescript of those cassettes sent from the interviewee will be an excellent help in rounding out a biography or a personality article.

Use cassettes to record radio speakers who offer bits of useful information; use them in your automobile when you get ideas while driving; buy study tapes that will teach and thus sharpen your writing skills; use cassettes also to correspond with friends and thus save time by lessening your typing load.

JOURNALS

Every writer should have notebooks to record fleeting ideas, picturesque speech, leads, and reflections and thoughts gathered from experience. Journal writing has become a subject of interest to people in all walks of life, but it is especially valuable for a writer to keep a record of daily thoughts that can be the source of further ideas and also give practice in putting words on paper.

THE LOCAL CRITIQUE GROUP

Meeting regularly in your community with other writers is taking a shortcut to authorship. These informal groups can give you helpful criticism on what you write. Take the lead in your area and follow these guidelines for a successful critique group:

1. Prepare a news item for your local newspaper announcing the formation of your club for the purpose of reading and critiquing manuscripts.
2. Write an informal letter to aspiring Christian writers interested in meeting regularly.
3. Limit your group to six or eight. Larger memberships won't allow all writers to participate regularly and read their stories, articles, or poetry.
4. Write to editors of periodicals for samples and editorial guidelines and introduce new markets to the group as you learn of them.
5. Sit in a circle in a living room, den, or prearranged meeting hall. Give each club member approximately thirty minutes for reading his material at each meeting.
6. Occasionally invite a special speaker from the community who is a professional writer or who teaches writing.

7. Order cassette tapes offered by writers' magazines, conferences, special speakers, and famous authors. These are available from publishing houses, correspondence courses, and service agencies. Play them during a coffee break, if you elect to serve light refreshments. Many clubs do not.

8. Agree to accept criticism, recognizing that no matter what professional judgment is offered, the writer has the final word. Read at the opening meeting I Peter 3:8, (KJV) "Finally, be ye all of one mind, having compassion one of another, love as brethren . . . be courteous."

INSPIRED WRITERS/INSPIRED READERS

Your readers will be looking for hope and inspiration in everything you write. They will be searching for solutions to depression, illness, loneliness, and despair. Will they find it? The religious market offers you an opportunity to share good news, personal experiences, and messages of hope. If *you* don't write it, who will? If you don't write it *now*, when will it be written?

Get help and training for the most fulfilling of all writing careers.

❧ *CHAPTER NINETEEN*

CAREERS IN CHRISTIAN WRITING

by Roland Wolseley

Roland E. Wolseley of Syracuse, New York, has been a freelance writer since his early college days and has published more than 600 articles and a score of books including Careers in Religious Communications. *He has led editorial workshops for several denominations and has taught at Christian writers' conferences for the past twenty years. He is a professor emeritus of the Journalism School of Public Communications of Syracuse University and was for several years the director of their Department of Religious Journalism.*

CAN WRITING RELIGIOUS material be

a career? And if there is a career in such work, what kind is it? Can I make enough to live? Raise a family? Be happy?

These are some of the questions raised in letters I've received over the years from seminary students, lay people beginning to write, secular journalists in mid-career and high school and college students seeking to establish vocational goals.

To answer these questions you might query someone already working in the field. But journalists are usually reluctant to toot their own horns, and if you asked them this question you might well get the answer, "I wouldn't plan on it if I were you." Five minutes later, however, the same newswriter, book author, or magazine scribe will say he or she would do it all over again. And in another ten minutes they will mention with pride that a son or daughter holds an important position with some religious periodical or is writing for religious television. An earnest questioner encountering such inconsistent pessimists may well wonder.

Another way to answer the question is to look at what is being written. Almost one thousand religious newspapers and magazines are published in the United States alone. In addition, the number of religious books published is growing daily, and religious radio and television stations are springing up all over the country. Someone has to be supplying all those words.

Without question, there *are* careers for religious writers. This chapter will describe what they are and what they entail.

THE PROSPECTS

The prospect in the 1980s for a career in religious writing cannot be stated succinctly in a single sentence—"There never was a better time" or "This is no time to embark on such a career." Conditions within the media vary greatly. An aspirant's talents may not equip him or her for the occupations available. There may be other factors as well, such as the general condition of the economy, job competition, mergers of denominations, etc.

The more varied the religious scene the greater the need for religious writing. In countries with one "official" religion there will be fewer publications and less communications activity than in a multireligion nation. The United States, being religiously pluralistic and geographically large, is one of the more promising areas for religious writers.

Places where social and political changes have led to active local religious work offer more careers than areas whose religious life is static. Although evangelist missionaries are no longer as welcome in many Third World countries as they once were, if they have secular skills to impart the missionaries are appreciated.

What is ahead for religious writers is also influenced by cycles of change in the world at large, which deeply affect the church and all who embrace the religious life. There are times of upheaval and conflict as well as times of progress and peaceful solutions. Writers are always needed to meet the needs of the day for the faithful as well as those outside the faith.

Religious writing careers are varied. They include staff writers of news, features, editorials, and specialized columns; of curriculum materials such as Bible lessons and literacy programs used in religious education; of scripts for radio, TV, and film. Writers who cover religious topics in the secular media produce news, features, reviews, and so forth. All of these jobs may be filled by full- or part-time staffers or freelancers.

In the early stages of a religious writing career sometimes only part-time opportunities are available. Part-time work permits you to explore possibilities and gain experience. It may also enable you to contribute while doing unrelated but financially more rewarding work. However you approach it, it is an excellent preliminary to a lifetime activity.

Writers who aspire to a career in telecommunications are in a better position than ever because more and more outlets for their work are being established every year. Everett G. Parker, director of the Office of Communication for the United Church of Christ, wrote in 1981: ". . . the field of religious communications has burgeoned. Major denominations have greatly increased their communications programs, and there has been a parallel increase in staffing." The reasons? Dr. Parker notes that the commercial religious programs "conducted mostly by clergy have taken over 90 percent of the time on television . . . formerly devoted to all forms of public interest programming." Also, many denominations buy commercial time on the networks or rent satellite time to distribute their programs to cable systems.

On the other hand, writers for religious journals have fewer outlets than they did a decade ago because of mergers or closings of papers and magazines owing to the steadily rising costs of printing and mailing. Opportunities in print areas do exist; they're just not increasing as rapidly as those in the electronic media field.

THE OPPORTUNITIES

Careers in religious writing are offered by denominations, interdenominational associations, and nondenominational religious agencies, such as The

Billy Graham Association, Youth for Christ, and World Vision.

In the religious field, of course, your own commitment to the Christian cause and your preferred style of religious expression are important and should be in harmony with your employer's. Carefully analyze your religious interests as well as those of the publisher or publication you may work for, to assure a good working relationship.

Most denominations have divisions concerned with public relations and publishing, and more and more are using telecommunications. Although the designations may differ (as in public relations, called variously publicity offices, public communications departments, and editorial operations divisions), the duties are more or less standard.

A large denomination, such as the United Methodist Church, employs writers not only in its central offices but also in regional bureaus in major cities. The Southern Baptist Convention's publishing operations produce approximately 100 magazines and as many book titles in any one year, with related departments doing design, editing, advertising, and promotion. (These two denominations even have their own bookstores.)

In addition, the Southern Baptists publish a score of weekly or monthly newspapers and magazines through their autonomous state conventions. Such communications-conscious denominations as the Seventh-Day Adventists and the Mennonites, though small, spend large sums on religious writing for various media.

Similarly the Roman Catholics have scores of diocesan newspapers, dozens of magazines—both official and independent—and a number of long established and influential book publishing firms, with their own stores as outlets.

Smaller denominations may not have as many independent regional papers with full-time staffs, but most of them have some area publications. Often these are supplements of the larger national publications. These publications offer at least part-time opportunities. Information on regional publications can be obtained from denominational headquarters or from offices of the Associated Church Press, the Evangelical Press Association, or the Catholic Press Association.

To these opportunities, add the hundreds of church-supported colleges and universities, each with publicity offices and some with publishing enterprises.

The secular world also employs religious writers. About 100 dailies hire full-time reporters whose beat is religion. The major news agencies have full-time religion writers and syndicates distribute religious columns and other features. There are also freelancers who syndicate their own devotionals, columns on religion, special news stories, and features to papers that don't have regular religious writers.

THE QUALIFICATIONS

Church publishing houses and public relations offices receive many applications from persons who lack experience or training in religious writing. Sometimes these applicants have no church affiliation. Watching a television show, listening to a public speaker or radio program, or just reading a church-sponsored publication may have aroused their interest.

Employers occasionally take such a person, especially a young one without too many financial obligations, and put him or her through an apprenticeship as an editorial assistant.

Beyond a religious background, the writer should possess certain personal characteristics to be successful either as staffer or freelancer. Among these are personal integrity, reliability, cooperativeness, and responsiveness to direction.

The writer aspiring to religious publishing work must know (or soon learn) how to write clearly and accurately, spell correctly, type, operate electronic equipment, and use cameras and recorders. Writing today, even for many a fiction storyteller, no longer means sitting at a table with a pencil and paper or a typewriter, but involves travel, interviewing, and knowing how to use the library and other storehouses of knowledge. Nonfiction writers must be able to take photographs to illustrate their text. More and more writers are producing manuscripts on computer terminals rather than typing paper.

It's also increasingly important to specialize. A writer who has studied church history and theology is more valuable than one who has not. A person with experience in the missions field as doctor, nurse, or educator, for instance, who can also write competently is an asset to many a religious publication and publicity office.

THE TRAINING

The differences between secular and religious communications justify some special training in addition to the basic preparation of standard journalism studies. The best secular university communications programs, even those leading to the Ph.D., ordinarily do not face those differences; in fact, some religious writers found their teachers unaware of the differences. The religious-supported and -managed institutions offering communications training and church-sponsored short courses and workshops in religious communications are staffed by knowledgeable educators.

But such enlightened preparation is not common. Some seminaries offer a course or two, perhaps in publicity or writing, mainly with homiletics in mind, as if sermons were all a preacher would need to write. Lack of time in the curriculum also explains the absence of seminary training of this sort.

About 100 colleges or universities offer majors or minors in communications or journalism at the undergraduate level. Religious writing usually has a share, but much of the offering is little different from the secular except in motivation.

Where, then, shall the aspiring religious writer go for preparation? Writing requires the best training possible; therefore, the would-be religious writer should select the best place he can afford. A religion major in college or a year in a seminary should accompany such preparation, if possible. Experience in the pastorate or in some other religious connection is a desirable supplement to training.

As with other specialties, educational programs for religious writers vary in quality. New scholars need to match their own theologies with those they'll be exposed to in any particular educational program. Denominational connections are also a consideration when applying for scholarships or grants.

Formal training is not always required. But the time when one could easily dispense with it is waning quickly with the growing use of highly technical innovations—video display terminals (VDTs), computerized typesetting, etc.—to lower the costs of operation.

SEEKING THE OPPORTUNITY

One goes about finding a job in religious writing much as one would for any other type of writing: preparing a résumé, developing a list of places to send it, placing situation-wanted advertisements, watching help-wanted ads, seeking help from your college placement office and employment agencies, turning to friends and relatives associated with the religious or secular media.

There are dozens of denominational houses and many non-church-related religious publishing houses who employ book editors, magazine editorial workers, and other wordsmiths in their operations. Some also have writers in residence who work on curriculum materials and other publications. Others do editing and rewriting of material received from freelance authors.

SALARIES AND WORKING CONDITIONS

Writers on religion share the motives of secular writers: the need for money, the hope of self-expression, the yearning for public recognition. Religious writers, however, usually have additional reasons for writing. They write to advance their religious views, to support the work of their local churches or denominations, to help solve social problems about which the church is deeply concerned.

Traditionally, salaries in all religious work, communications included, have been lower than comparable secular occupations. Religious workers have been expected to make sacrifices. Much religious activity would fail otherwise. But the policy has been open to criticism and is changing.

Most religious organizations expect their employees to function in a secular society, and survival in that society becomes more and more costly.

These organizations have been forced to meet the secular competition.

Religious writers, especially those attached to media staffs, can expect pay at the beginner and mid-career levels roughly commensurate with that of other professionals. Relatively high salaries, running into five figures a year, are now common for staff writers on the larger publications. But for the religious professional, the astronomical earnings of the entertainment and sports worlds are confined mainly to the realm of successful television evangelists.

The salaries range from $10,000 to $50,000. A few top writers earn the higher figure but most do well to reach $25,000. Raw numbers of this sort tend to be misleading, for the writer must consider not only base salary but also health insurance, pensions, and other fringe benefits. Independent writers have a more difficult time; they are the piece-workers of the profession. Practically speaking, freelance writers cannot make a living writing for the religious media unless they are highly successful popular novelists or industrious authors of other kinds of religious books for which there is a great demand.

THE FUTURE

What is ahead for religious writers is closely bound up with what is happening to the communications media in general. So long as there are readers there will be a need for experts with words. Some futurists predict that telecommunications will ultimately overwhelm print media. Their evidence for this forecast is the trend toward public reliance on television and radio for news, opinion, and entertainment. People already watch TV more than they read; the cost of producing books, newspapers, and magazines rises steadily as do publishers' charges for subscriptions and single copies of periodicals.

The mass communications media have never been so important and so powerful as they are now. Christians must employ them intelligently and effectively; religious writers will be wise to seek training in radio, film, television (and other media). But don't forget, what we see and hear through the media usually began as words on paper, so strive to improve your craft. There will always be a need for good writers!

CHAPTER TWENTY

THE REWARDS OF CHRISTIAN WRITING

by Charlie W. Shedd

Charlie Shedd, who lives on Fripp Island, Frogmore, South Carolina, is the author of twenty-five best-selling books about family life and the counseling of children. Some of his best-known titles are Letters to Karen, Letters to Philip, The Stork Is Dead, You Can Be a Great Parent, How to Stay in Love, *and* Then God Created Grandparents. *He has been a pastor of churches in Colorado, Nebraska, Oklahoma, Texas, and Georgia. He and his wife Martha are the leaders of the* "Fun in Marriage" *workshop, which has been filmed by Cinema Associates. They also write a syndicated newspaper column,* "How to Stay in Love."

THEY WAITED UNTIL everyone had left the

hall. It had been a Valentine banquet, full house. This had been one of those nights when everything clicked, but I was frazzled. The adrenalin was running low.

Over at the side a young couple waited. I must admit that as I shook hands with the long line, my guard was up. Counseling now? Lord, help me find some hidden reserves, or maybe a side door.

But they weren't there for counseling. Reaching to take both my hands in theirs, they said, "We simply had to tell you what you've done for us. We were married six years—six awful years. Three children, and that was awful, too. So finally we called it quits, got a divorce.

"Then someone gave us two of your marriage books and we could never tell you the difference they made, how they opened our eyes. Suddenly we could see things we'd never seen before—mistakes we could correct and new possibilities. So we decided to start over.

"So here we are married again, and most of the time it isn't half bad, really. We thought you'd like to know about us. We also thought you might like to know that every night before we go to sleep we read a chapter of one of your books together. Then we talk and share our feelings.

"We both agree now that the trouble before was not communicating. One reason was that we needed something to get started. That's probably the main thing your books have done for us. We just wanted to say thanks."

Then they turned and went off, hand in hand. *Reward number one of Christian writing*.

Thank you, Lord, that you can use my humble efforts to turn people down new roads; to return them to each other; to you; to give them more character; make them more open; better able to live with dignity.

Anyone who has written inspirational material for thirty years could go on indefinitely with accounts like this; here's one more of my favorites.

After one of my first books, I had an invitation to write a question-and-answer column for *Teen* magazine in Hollywood. The title assigned me was "Sex and Dating"—straight stuff right out of the back seats of cars. The writer for teens had better be unflappable—and 100 percent honest: no themes excluded, no talking in riddles. Thousands of letters came pouring in and from them I wrote *The Stork Is Dead*.

It was written for young people in junior high, high school, college, and post-college. Parents read these materials too, and they should. But their reading is for a different reason. They read as detectives, protectors, guardians. So anything on sex for the young will addle some father's mind, blow some mother's hair back, and here come the negative letters. But the writer for teens will also receive mail which more than makes up for the negatives.

She was a college sophomore. Her fiance was playing football at the state university. They had dated all through high school and now he was applying the pressure. Here are a few paragraphs from her letter:

> I love him so much, and I don't want to lose him. Because we have gone together so long, we have been very close, but I haven't given in, if you know what I mean. Just this Thanksgiving we had a long talk—he explained how he felt and since we knew we were the ones for each other, why wouldn't it be all right? So I promised him that at Christmas we would.
>
> Then our Sunday school class began studying *The Stork Is Dead* and I realized what a mistake I would be making. I guess I just needed someone like you to tell me what God expects. What got to me was your statement that great sex is not a happening, but a creation. I had never thought about it like that before. But it does make sense, when you say that sex at its best takes years to develop. I'm old enough to know that most of the best things are worth waiting for. Anyway, Dr. Shedd, I want you to know I wrote him a letter and told him what you said. I quoted some of my favorite things from your book, and told him I was taking my promise back. I knew it might mean the end—but you could never guess what happened. He wrote and thanked me for being the kind of person I am. Then he told me he wanted to marry me more than ever.
>
> I thought you'd like to know about this, and I also wanted to say thank you.

Sound that high note again. For the Christian, one sure reward of writing will always be *influence*.

The second reward comes double. I call it *the amazing mix of ego trip and humility factor*.

Every honest writer thrills to praise. "You're my favorite author." "I just love your last book." "I think you're the greatest." This is all heady stuff. Psychologists say we come this way in the original, no exceptions—we all enjoy the strokes coming from folks who like us.

Certainly praise can be overdone, and there are many things more important than public accolades. Yet the writer of Proverbs describes it well: "A word in due season, how good it is."

Side thought for pensive pondering: The more famous we become, the more we fall into the trap of believing everyone around us wants to know how we do it. "Tell us your secrets." That's what they say, but that's not their real interest. We soon learn that even our most enthusiastic fans want us first to know about *them*, what *they're* into, *their* dreams, how can *they* become a bestselling author?

Authors whose books sell well receive countless manuscripts from aspiring writers. Their cover letters begin: "Will you please read this and tell me what you think?"

That's not what they mean. What they mean is, "Please write and tell me this is the great American novel, the next million-seller, the best you ever saw from a beginner."

Most of those who cadge this free advice don't really want advice. So much is this true that I have come to this point: I mark two or three pages with comments and criticisms. Then I return these and suggest the hopeful phone for further analysis. How many phone? Zero.

What's the moral? Everyone loves accolades, deserving or not.

But the veteran author knows there is no such thing as 100 percent approval. Along with the fan mail comes some bitter reaction.

Here is a letter from an irate mother who had just finished reading *The Stork Is Dead.*

> Sir:
>
> I hate to think what is going to happen to you in the last days which are coming soon when we are all going to be judged at the judgment seat like the Scripture says. The government ought to protect us from people like you. But there is so much evil in Washington I don't suppose they will do anything. I don't want my daughter to know the awful things that go on today between all those juvenile delinquents. Don't worry about my Elizabeth. When she gets married, I will tell her about her organs and what she is in for, and that will be soon enough.

Some of these "You cur, sir" classics are simply ludicrous. But others we should take seriously because they point to real faults in our writing. Intelligent readers who call attention to our inconsistencies, to our outright mistakes, can be a real blessing. I have made it a policy to write every one of my critics a thank you. The ridiculous, the angry, the picayunish, all deserve our attention and our gratitude.

Next comes what I believe is one major difference between the successful writer and the unsuccessful. This one we can call, "What do we do when the editor says 'No'?" Before I wrote books, I sold some fifty magazine articles. Those articles averaged *eleven* rejections each. And would you believe the most successful article (both in payment and in reprints) was rejected twenty-nine times before that last brilliant editor said "yes"? (How brilliant? My records show that this article was purchased by the same man who said the thirteenth "no.") So what's the message? The message is, *"Hang in there."* "He that endures to the end shall be saved."

Advice to the young writer: Save your rejection slips. They may be exactly what you'll need down the road. When the day comes that you're overimpressed with yourself, these reminders of previous rejections will have their special ministry to your inflated ego.

Reward three is *the personal satisfaction of honing our skills*—creating our style, learning the craft, improving on strong points, correcting weaknesses, discovering technique.

My own method is to write by rules. I have more than a hundred rules, developed by me for me. I'm constantly checking my writing against my rules. And without exception, the more I check and recheck, the better I write.

Here are eighteen of my rules—six major ones, six miscellaneous, and six I label "The Little Stinkers." Simple plain vanilla, but oh so complicated. Yet exciting, too, when they've done their job.

SIX CARDINAL RULES FOR WRITING

There may be some natural writers whose words flow without effort. Not I. Before my reader hears any flowing from me, I must hear some grinding. This is largely a matter of checking and rechecking against my rules. And each writer must make his own depending on his particular needs. Here are six of my big ones:

1. **Limit: Fifteen words per sentence!** This is tough, but today's markets demand brevity.
2. **Limit: Don't use the same word twice in one sentence.** Exception: Words of three letters or less, but the real pro seldom repeats even these. Be especially wary of "that."
3. **Limit: One adjective at a time.** Whenever I use two or more I should discard one (or both) and find something stronger. Piling up description is one sure mark of the amateur.
4. **Limit: Two commas per sentence.** This keeps me from saying more than one thing at a time. It may also prevent the overuse of adjectives.
5. **I must write like I talk.** Formality is a sure sign of uncertainty. This rule eliminates many pulpit terms, such as "shall we not?"

6. **I must not insult my reader's intelligence.** Example: "The great gray girder fell to the earth below!" So? Where else could it fall? "They took a trip to the Sierras out West." Where else?

Important note: In addition to mastering his rules, the skilled writer learns that every rule is made to be broken. At the right time, in the right way, for the right effect, he says, "Rules, take a hike! Right now I couldn't care less about number of words, number of repetitions, number of adjectives. What I want here is feel!" But he only breaks rules wisely who knows them.

SIX MORE RULES FOR WRITING

7. **Use only "grab me quick" beginnings.** The pro seeks a powerful start, then makes it more powerful. Ponder: It takes several seconds to turn off the television; one second to close a book.
8. **Keep it moving.** This means skillful use of verbs. Here's where the action is; verbs provide energy. They propel; they pace. They transfer feeling. Good writing feels strong; verbs give it vigor.
9. **Aim to become an expert in transition.** The amateur jerks. He hops the clods. He wearies me. Transitions take my reader from sentence to sentence, paragraph to paragraph, section to section. I must become a master builder of bridges.
10. **Make the negatives positive.** Today's reader wants to know where it's at, not where it isn't! The Lord for whom I write changed all law from "thou shalt not" to "this do and thou shalt live!"
11. **Avoid Protestant Latin.** This is particularly important for the preacher in me. I must purge my writing of theological gobbledygook! Reconciliation, transcendence, covenant, incarnation—these may turn me on, but they turn off too many.
12. **Say it differently.** I must develop the art of writing in happy surprises. The pro touches his prose with poetry. He paints pictures; he sings songs. By long self-training he has mastered the science of picturesque speech.

Important Note: Observe how many of these rules deal with the economy of words! The skillful writer knows what to leave out. Generally, when something is not quite right, it can best be improved by cutting.

13. Subsidiary on repetitions (See Rule # 2): **The longer I can go before repeating words, the better my writing will sound.** Rugged discipline: Aim not to use the same word twice in succeeding sentences. Watch for overuse of the uncommon, the unusual.

14. Subsidiary rule on beginnings (See Rule # 7): **Withhold the most important item long enough to build up anticipation.** Don't give away the key word or idea too soon. At the same time I am accomplishing this, I must do almost the opposite. My reader must be told soon enough what this is about. Neat trick. Tough challenge.

15. **So far as possible, keep moving toward the main thought.** The experienced writer is a skillful roamer—he strays far enough to make it interesting, but never loses his landmark.

16. **Check for identical word beginnings and word endings in the same sentence.** Examples of the not-so-good: "He was considering resigning." "Whenever he was exasperated, he always exaggerated." The good writer avoids "similars" as well as "identicals." Of course, there will always be exceptions for rhythm and swing.

17. **Avoid threadbare word combinations**—two-worders, or three: *there is, there was, it is, it was, he said, they had, who is, which was, have got, one who, a little, and finally, so good* (or *so anything*), *of course*, and, of course, a bunch of others.

18. **Watch for unnecessary prepositions.** These are the buggers—*of, for, about, to, into, in, unto, upon, with, by, before.* Prepositions at the end of sentences usually mean one thing: This could be written better some other way.

Say it again: In skillful writing there will be exceptions to every rule. Rules should be personalized, adapted to individual needs. True, some rules do apply to all, but each of us must write by those we need; those we follow on our own.

So this is reward three: the satisfaction of honing our skills.

If we are faithful, we finally arrive at that great day when the hard work is plain fun. We have the compounded personal satisfaction of knowing we're improving. I wrote and rewrote the final chapter of *The Stork Is Dead* more than one hundred times. Looking back I can honestly say that agonizing process was *exciting*.

Words from an ancient mystic, "Commit thyself to labor: The roots may be bitter, but the fruit will be sweet."

Reward four is *Money*.

Thousands of aspiring writers hope to reach the promised land where they write for a living. No interference now; nothing but writing; 100 percent of our income will be earned by the pen. How many reach this astral region? Very few.

Although we may not see it, at the outset most of us will write better if we have a regular income. Until the great day comes, a steady paycheck is one sure assist to sanity.

Comes now the single most important economic fact, the secret of secrets for financial success with typewriter and pen: *A sacred covenant with the Lord, to whom it all belongs!*

Early in our career Martha and I pledged 50 percent of our royalties for charitable purposes. With legal help we established our Abundance Foundation.

Advised by the Internal Revenue Service that we must specify, we designated the money for hunger relief, agricultural missions. When they insisted we be even more specific, we designated the funds for livestock: dairy herds in Africa to provide milk for starving babies; horses, cows, hogs, laying hens, and bees for retarded high schoolers in Virginia; sheep, chickens, swine, milk cattle, beef cattle, goats, new strains of water buffalo (heavy milkers) for the Philippines. Around the world, dollars from our writing feed and bless his people.

Most of us know personally how tricky the human mind can be. We may be tempted to do good for wrong reasons, but giving in order to get is never the answer. Happy is the author who gives first out of love, for such an author is sure to experience these two things:

1. The self-satisfaction of helping others help themselves.
2. The quiet thrill of becoming a channel for blessing. And here we are again, when the motive is right, blessings invariably return to the blesser.

This is why in our books *Letters to Karen* and *Letters to Philip,* as well as books on the church, we have recommended this formula:

Give 10 percent

Save 10 percent

Spend the rest with thanksgiving and praise. Then go from that joy to the greater joy of more giving.

Often we hear it said, "When I start to sell, I will make a commitment." Will you? Probably not. Why? Because it doesn't work that way. The deeper joys of giving are reserved for those who launch out in faith. And the great giver seems to work most through those who begin where they are rather than where they would like to be.

The last reward and most important is *knowing that we are pleasing the Lord, serving him, building his kingdom with our pen, our efforts, our hard-earned success.*

Is there any sure way to tell whether we are honoring the Lord or merely serving our own selfish ends? Every honest writer has the experience of putting the words together and then suddenly realizing, "This is beautiful, clever, super, real artistry." Yet down deep inside the Spirit asks, "Is this for his glory, or something out of the id?"

So we need testing places. For me this means praying often, praying much, praying specifically for guidance. Without help I find it easy to wobble and scatter in prayer. For that reason I have developed what I call "My Little Prayers for Writing." Here too each writer must individualize. My rules are for my needs, and I offer my prayers here in this spirit: These are one writer's attempts to keep his writing tuned to the higher wavelengths.

MY LITTLE PRAYERS FOR BETTER WRITING

1. **Prayer for Right Purpose**
   "Lord, write through me!"
   Matthew 6:33 "But seek first his kingdom and his righteousness, and all these things shall be yours as well."

2. **Prayer for Inner Cleansing**
   "Teach me to be honest."
   Psalm 139:23-24 "Search me, O God, and know my heart! Try me and know my thoughts! And see if there be any wicked way in me, and lead me in the way everlasting."

3. **Prayer for Discipline**
   "Help me to love work."
   Luke 9:23 "If any man would come after me, let him deny himself and take up his cross daily and follow me."

4. **Prayer for Skill**
   "Hone my talents to their maximum."
   I Corinthians 12:31 "Covet earnestly the best gifts."

5. **Prayer for Ending When I Should**
   "Stop me when I'm finished."
   Psalm 141:3 "Set a watch O Lord before my mouth, keep the door of my lips."

6. **Prayer of Release**
   "Here, Lord, I give it to you."
   Psalm 37:5 "Commit your way to the Lord; trust in him, and he will act."

7. **Prayer of Gratitude**
   "Thank you! Thank you! Thank You!"
   Colossians 4:2 "Continue in prayer, and watch in the same with thanksgiving."

So here we are back where we started. We write for:

INFLUENCE

EGO AND HUMILITY

THE FUN OF HONING OUR SKILLS

MONEY

But more than any of these the Christian writer knows that all we have said, all we could ever say, comes down to: *Who's writing this? Am I or am I not an instrument in his hand?*

BIBLIOGRAPHY

Note: An annotated bibliography of books about Christian writing in particular is included in Chapter 18, "Getting Help and Training," by Norman Rohrer. In several chapters you will also find individual recommendations of books on the subject at hand. The following books are additional reading suggested by the authors of this book to be of help in the areas covered by their chapters.

CHAPTER 4: HOW TO GET STARTED, by Cecil Murphey

Nichols, Sue. *Words on Target*. Atlanta: John Knox Press, 1967.
Subtitled "For Better Christian Communication," this paperback hits the danger spots for would-be religious writers.

Provost, Gary. *Make Every Word Count*. Cincinnati: Writer's Digest Books, 1980.
This guide to the basic techniques of good writing (for both fiction and nonfiction) shows you how to make every paragraph, every sentence, every word, do what you intended it to do.

Shedd, Charlie, and Floyd Thatcher. *Christian Writers' Seminar*. Waco: Creative Resources, 1976.
This "seminar" includes tapes and a workbook. Helpful step-by-step lessons for those who want to get started. Highly motivational.

Shimberg, Elaine Fantle. *How to Be a Successful Housewife/Writer*. Cincinnati: Writer's Digest Books, 1979.
For anyone trying to write at home, this book covers how to save time and cope with distractions; where to write; how to interview, research, and act like a pro in your dealings with editors.

Spencer, Sue. *Write on Target*. Waco: Word Books, 1967.
A sequel to *Words on Target* designed for those who have mastered the basics of that work. Both of her books embody the message they teach.

Wirt, Sherwood Eliot with Ruth McKinney. *You Can Tell the World*. Minneapolis: Augsburg, 1975.

Toward the end of improving the quality of Christian writing, Wirt offers insights and tips on writing for the religious market.

CHAPTER 7: HOW TO GET INTO PRINT, by Sally Stuart

306

Appelbaum, Judith, and Nancy Evans. *How to Get Happily Published: A Complete and Candid Guide.* New York: Harper and Row, 1978.
A good overview of the world of book publishing including specific information on how to write queries and proposals as well as when to contact editors by phone or personal visit.

Cassill, Kay. *The Complete Handbook for Freelance Writers.* Cincinnati: Writer's Digest Books, 1981.
Contains a good chapter on agents and gives helpful guidance on when and how to use one. Also includes information on bookkeeping, sales, and the whole range of business concerns of the working writer.

Duncan, Lois. *How to Write and Sell Your Personal Experiences.* Cincinnati: Writer's Digest Books, 1979.
Includes informative chapters on both mechanics and the query letter; covers the basics of writing to sell.

Olsen, Udia. *Preparing the Manuscript.* Boston: The Writer, Inc., 1978.
A good all-around handbook on the mechanics of the writing profession.

Weisbord, Marvin, ed. *A Treasury of Tips for Writers.* Cincinnati: Writer's Digest Books, first paperback edition 1981. Professional tips and shortcuts on all the basics of the (nonficton) writer's trade, from the American Society of Journalists and Authors.

WRITING FOR AND ABOUT YOUR LOCAL CHURCH (in Chapter 8), by Sue Spencer

Nichols, Sue. *Words on Target.* Atlanta: John Knox Press, 1963.
A basic guide for the beginner, especially in making words say what they are meant to say.

Sumrall, Velma, and Lucille Germany. *Telling the Story of Your Local Church.* New York: The Seabury Press, 1979.
A complete handbook for the amateur writing for the local church—

for newspapers, radio, TV, as well as the church's own publications.

Wilson, Raymond H. *Words Ring Louder Than Bells*. Evanston, Illinois: United Methodist Communications, 1976.
Prepared for the specific purpose of helping the reader produce better parish newsletters. Guidance on the philosophy and purpose as well as the mechanics of writing and producing the best.

WRITING BOOK REVIEWS (in Chapter 8), by Connie Soth

Kammerman, Sylvia. *Book Reviewing*. Boston: The Writer, Inc., 1978.
Tips and ideas from a wide variety of specialized critics, reviewers, and book editors. Also contains essential guidelines for neophytes, especially Chapter 4: "Do's and Don't's of Book Reviewing," and Chapter 16: "Structure of a Book Review."

Hunt, Todd. *Reviewing for the Mass Media*. Radnor, Pennsylvania: Chilton Book Co.
Discusses "obligations of a reviewer" to his audience and defines differences between a notice, a review, and a critical essay. Discusses books, plays, movie and TV reviewing as well as the philosophy of the craft of reviewing.

WRITING INSPIRATIONAL FILLERS (in Chapter 8), by Shirley Pope Waite

Boggess, Louise. *How to Write Fillers and Short Features That Sell*. New York: Harper and Row, second edition, 1981.
Includes a markets listing and excellent chapters on tips and shortcuts, anecdotes, personal experience and personality fillers, as well as other filler categories.

Burack, A.A., ed. *How to Write and Sell Fillers, Light Verse and Short Humor*. Boston: The Writer, Inc., 1977.
Experienced authors and editors give practical instruction on writing and selling such short items as anecdotes, light verse, quips, epigrams, how-to hints, proverbs, quotes, unusual facts, contest entries, cartoon captions.

Teeters, Peggy. *How to Get Started in Writing*. Cincinnati: Writer's Digest Books, 1981.
A basic beginner's handbook covering everything from querying to

mechanics, from finding ideas to slanting for specific markets, as well as how to write stories, columns, and fillers.

CHAPTER 9: WRITING THE INSPIRATIONAL ARTICLE, by Georgiana Walker

Duncan, Lois. *How to Write and Sell Your Personal Experiences.* Cincinnati: Writer's Digest Books, 1979.
Comprehensive and interesting instructions for turning everyday experiences into marketable articles and books. Includes good ideas on how and where to sell what you write.

Emerson, Connie. *Write on Target.* Cincinnati: Writer's Digest Books, 1981.
Shows how to dramatically increase your sales by analyzing your target markets. Also examines the six most popular article types and tells how to write them to order for a given magazine.

Gunther, Max. *Writing the Modern Magazine Article.* Boston: The Writer, Inc., 1976.
Specific, practical guidelines for writing salable articles for general and specialized magazines.

Holmes, Marjorie. *Writing the Creative Article.* Boston: The Writer, Inc., 1976.
A bestselling author tells how to write up your experiences, ideas, and opinions such that readers (and editors) will be interested.

Hull, Raymond. *How to Write "How-To" Books and Articles.* Cincinnati: Writer's Digest Books, 1981.
A lively, informative guide that takes the writer step-by-step from idea to finished work.

Jacobs, Hayes B. *Writing and Selling Nonfiction.* Cincinnati: Writer's Digest Books, sixth printing, 1978.
Covers all aspects of the nonfiction writing business, from developing ideas through preparing outlines and query letters, all the way to final copy and submission. Also includes information on magazine and book opportunities, organization and research, finding new markets, interviewing, correct form and style, humor, agents, and more.

Rockwell, F.A. *How to Write Non-Fiction That Sells*. Chicago: Contemporary Books, 1975.
Solid information on writing articles in a variety of genres: interview, survey, travel, how-to, etc.

CHAPTER 10: WRITING INSPIRATIONAL FICTION, by Lee Roddy

Block, Lawrence. *Writing The Novel: From Plot to Print*. Cincinnati: Writer's Digest Books, 1979.
Covers all the tricks of the trade—developing plot ideas; using backgrounds that are familiar and researching what's not; facing the blank sheet of paper and getting started; developing characters and theme; how, and to whom, to sell your novel.

Boggess, Louise. *How to Write Short Stories That Sell*. Cincinnati: Writer's Digest Books, 1980.
Shows how to firm up an idea, develop plot structure, create the essential characters, block out the scenes, and tie them all together to complete the story.

Brady, John and Jean M. Fredette, editors. *Fiction Writer's Market*. Cincinnati: Writer's Digest Books (annual).
Lists editors' names, addresses, editorial needs for more than 1,000 publishers of fiction. Also includes 40 chapters of writing instruction, with tips from such masters as John D. MacDonald, Eudora Welty, Lois Gould, and Louis L'Amour.

Knight, Damon. *Creating Short Fiction*. Cincinnati: Writer's Digest Books, 1981.
Explains how to begin a story, how to keep it under control, how to develop ideas, how to wrap up the story, plus some valuable advice on developing your talent and growing as an author.

Peck, Robert Newton. *Secrets of Successful Fiction*. Cincinnati: Writer's Digest Books, 1980.
Offers concrete tips and formulas for creating convincing plot and characters, handling viewpoint, the place and use of humor, finding a title, dealing with editors, and why a successful author must in fact be a salesman.

WRITING BIOGRAPHY FOR THE CHRISTIAN MARKET (in chapter 11), by Dorothy Nafus Morrison

Bowen, Catherine. *Biography: The Craft and the Calling*. Westport, Connecticut: Greenwood, 1978.
A reprint of the 1969 classic in the field of biography writing.

Clifford, James L. *From Puzzles to Portraits: Problems of a Literary Biographer*. Chapel Hill: University of North Carolina Press, 1970.

Edel, Leon, et. al. *Telling Lives. The Biographer's Art*. Marc Prachter, editor. New Republic, 1979.
The collective experience of several writers of biography, full of tips and anecdotes.

CHAPTER 12: WRITING INSPIRATIONAL POETRY, by Viola Jacobson Berg

Berg, Viola. *Pathways for the Poet*. Milford, Michigan: Mott Media, 1977.
A resource book for the aspiring poet, teachers of creative writing, and poetry lovers. Illustrated by examples of more than 200 patterns, poetic tools, and terms.

Hamilton, Anne. *How to Revise Your Own Poems*. Boston: The Writer, Inc., 1958.
Gives the reader a solid foundation of poetry writing.

Untermeyer, Louis. *The Pursuit of Poetry*. New York: Simon and Schuster, 1969.
A guide to the understanding and appreciation of poetry with an explanation of its forms and a dictionary of poetic terms.

Wood, Clement. *The Complete Rhyming Dictionary and Poet's Craft Book*. New York: Doubleday and Co., 1936.
An indispensable tool for the poet who uses rhyme.

Jerome, Judson. *The Poet's Handbook*. Cincinnati: Writer's Digest Books, 1980.
Detailed but unmysterious instruction in the mechanics and the art of poetry writing. Answers the questions most often asked by beginning poets.

CHAPTER 13: WRITING FOR CHILDREN AND YOUTH, by Patricia McKissack

Boyle, Deirdre, and Stephen Calvert. *Children's Media Marketplace.* Syracuse, New York: Gaylord Professional Publications, 1978.
A comprehensive listing of publishers of children's materials of all kinds, as well as bookstores, libraries, TV and radio outlets, etc.

Schreivogel, Paul A. *The World of Art and the World of Youth.* Minneapolis: Augsburg, 1968.
A review of children's story book art and how it relates to child psychology.

Wyndham, Lee, revised by Arnold Madison. *Writing for Children and Teenagers.* Cincinnati: Writer's Digest Books, 1980.
A classic of concrete instruction in the field of writing for youth, revised several times by the original author previous to the present edition.

Yeager, Allen. *Using Picture Books with Children.* New York: Holt, Rinehart and Winston, 1973.
Teachers' aid book designed to accompany ten "owlet books" used in the classroom.

WRITING FOR WOMEN (in Chapter 14), by Lois N. Erickson

Holmes, Marjorie. *Writing the Creative Article.* Boston: The Writer, Inc., 1969, 1973.
This readable book by a writer of much material aimed at women shows how to use subjects of lasting and universal interest with which the reader can identify.

WRITING NEWS OF RELIGION (in Chapter 16), by Gary Warner

Angione, Howard, ed. *Associated Press Style Book and Libel Manual.* New York: Associated Press.
This is considered the "bible" for all news writers.

Baker, Bob. *Newsthinking: The Secret of Great Newswriting.* Cincinnati: Writer's Digest Books, 1981.

Shows how to set up a system of mental organization that will make the facts fall into place.

Brady, John. *The Craft of Interviewing*. Cincinnati: Writer's Digest Books, second printing, 1977.
A down-to-earth guide on all aspects of the interview—from getting it to researching, from taking notes and taping to writing it up.

Strunk, William Jr. revised by E.B. White. *Elements of Style*. New York: Macmillan and Co.
First published in 1935 but revised many times, this is a concise, snappy guide to clear, factual writing.

INSPIRATIONAL GREETING CARDS (in Chapter 16), by John McCollister

Sandman, Larry, ed. *Guide to Greeting Card Writing*. Cincinnati: Writer's Digest Books, 1980.
Successful greeting card writers and editors give practical advice on every type of greeting card writing. Includes a glossary.

GAMES AND PUZZLES (in Chapter 16), by Carol Schmelzel

Schmelzel, Carol. *Teacher's Guide for Making Classroom Games and Puzzles*. Atkinson, Wisconsin: Nasco Publishers.
Guidelines for developing and constructing card games, board games, crossword and word search puzzles. Shows how these games teach and how to incorporate subject matter into them.

WRITING SONGS AND HYMNS (in Chapter 16), by Jaroslav Vajda

Jerome, Judson. *The Poet and the Poem*. Cincinnati: Writer's Digest Books, 1974.
An excellent introduction to English poetry, its principles and practices. Necessary for any writer of hymns and songs. A shorter but excellent concise guide is the same author's *Poet's Handbook* (Writer's Digest, 1980).

The Hymn, Quarterly publication of the Hymn Society of America, Wittenberg University, Springfield, OH 45501.

Membership in the society brings you information about the literature, workshops, contests, and books relevant to Christian hymnody. Memberships start at $18 per year.

CHAPTER 17: WRITING FOR CHRISTIAN TELEVISION AND FILM, by Donald Davenport

Brenner, Alfred. *The TV Scriptwriter's Handbook*. Cincinnati: Writer's Digest Books, 1980.
A thorough and thoughtful guide to dramatic writing, with detailed how-to instruction for the most popular—and easiest to break into forms of television drama.

Ellens, J. Harold. *Models of Religious Broadcasting*. Grand Rapids, Michigan: Wm. B. Eerdmans Publishing Co., 1974.
An overview of the religious television market, past and future.

Geduld, Harry M., and Ronald Gottesman. *An Illustrated Glossary of Film Terms*. New York: Holt, Rinehart and Winston, 1973.
An excellent primer for terms and techniques.

Hilliard, Robert L. *Writing for Television and Radio*. New York: Hastings House, 3rd edition, 1976.
A standard survey text about various writing formats.

Kuhns, William. *The Electronic Gospel*. New York: Herder and Herder, 1969.
A philosophical treatise on religious media.

Skilbeck, Oswald. *ABC of Film and TV Working Terms*. New York: Hastings House, 1960.
A good lexicon.

Straczynski, J. Michael. *The Complete Book of Scriptwriting*. Cincinnati: Writer's Digest Books, 1982.
A lively unintimidating guide to the major forms of scriptwriting: TV, radio, film, and theater.

Willis, Edgar E. *Writing Television and Radio Programs*. New York: Holt, Rinehart and Winston, 1967.
A dated but durable study, focusing on dramatic writing.

CHAPTER 19: CAREERS IN CHRISTIAN WRITING, by Roland Wolseley

Baker, Richard T. *The Christian as Journalist*. New York: Columbia University Press, 1961.
The basic philosophy of the Christian journalist who sees his vocation as a calling from God.

Gentz, William H. *Career Opportunities in Religion*. New York: Hawthorn/Dutton, 1979.
A guide to all religiously oriented careers. One chapter devoted to journalist and writer occupations.

Polking, Kirk. *Jobs for Writers*. Cincinnati: Writer's Digest Books, 1980.
Describes the range of opportunities found anywhere that will develop writing skills while providing extra income. Forty-one authors contribute chapters.

Rees, Clair. *Profitable Part-time Full-time Freelancing*. Cincinnati: Writer's Digest Books, 1980.
Practical information on how to make freelancing pay and grow into a full-time occupation.

Stein, M.L. *Your Career in Journalism*. New York: Messner, revised edition, 1978.
A widely used career guide to secular journalism emphasizing newswork and dealing realistically with this field.

Wolseley, Roland E. *Careers in Religious Communications*. Scottdale, Pennsylvania: Herald Press, revised third edition, 1977.
Using case histories and the results of surveys, this book depicts vocational opportunities in the specialized field of religious communications.

INDEX

Note: Titles of books included in the text are listed here. For additional titles of books of interest to writers, see the bibliography, which precedes this index.

319